'Rebel Heart'

George Lennon: Flying Column Commander

Terence O'Reilly

Series Editor Willie Whelan

for Waterford County Museum

Cover Design by Martin Whelan

Photo Colourisation by Ian Hannigan

Republished as part of the 2023 Decade of Centenaries
commemorations for County Waterford.

Prologue

Unmarked Dungarvan Grave Pushes Man To Act As His Father's Son

Jim Memmott, Senior Editor, *Rochester Democrat and Chronicle*
New York State, March 11th 2006

Wrapped in sorrow and silence, this pre-Saint Patrick's Day story seems to linger in time, haunting, unresolved. It has a Rochester angle, certainly. But it focuses on a grave in Dungarvan, County Waterford, Ireland.

Ivan Lennon, 62, a retired Rochester schoolteacher who was born in Ireland, would like to put a marker on the grave. In a sense, he is acting as his father's son in desiring to do this. But Lennon's father is not in that grave. Resting there is a man his father had executed 85 years ago.

The details of that execution and its consequence are anchored in the Irish War of Independence, the uprising against the British that lasted from 1919 to 1921. Lennon's father, George, who later became a pacifist, was an officer then in the West Waterford Brigade of the Irish Republican Army, the force committed to disrupting and supplanting British rule.

On March 18, 1921, he led a group that ambushed some Black and Tans, members of the British paramilitary force. Men on both sides died, and the IRA forces captured Sgt Michael Hickey, an Irish police officer who was with the Black and Tans.

Hickey was well-known and well-liked, a respected community police officer. He was Catholic, he was Irish, but, at least technically, he worked for the British. War has its own logic, and the IRA members decided Hickey had to be killed because he knew their identities.

Right before he was shot by a makeshift firing squad, Hickey turned toward George Lennon. 'George, I knew you as a child,' the policeman said, '... You are the only person in the world that can save me.'

'I would give anything in the world to save you,' Lennon replied. 'But I cannot.'

As George Lennon later recalled in a memoir, Trauma in Time, the two men exchanged a 'glance of understanding''

Hickey, who had turned thirty-six the day before and was about to be married, squared his shoulders.

Lennon tied a bandage around Hickey's eyes. Stepping back, he called, 'Fire'.

Shots rang out. Hickey slumped to the ground, dead.

Lennon walked over to his body and fired one shot into Hickey's head, a coup de grace.

His killers put a tag on Hickey's body that said 'Police Spy'.

Gravediggers at first refused to dig a grave for his burial. They relented, but Hickey's fiancée asked that no marker be put on the grave for fear that it would be defaced.

George Lennon laid down his arms in 1922. Eventually, he immigrated to the United States, only to return to Ireland in 1935. Eleven years later, he came back to the United States. His wife, May, and his son joined him a few years later. George Lennon, who never talked to his son about his time in the IRA, became a Quaker, an opponent of the war in Vietnam. He helped found the Rochester Zen Centre. He died in 1991.

But starting with a trip to Waterford in 1987, Ivan began to pick up on clues to his father's past. Eventually, he understood his father's role in Hickey's death. It has proved to be a sensitive issue. A contact at the Waterford Museum in Dungarvan has told Lennon that there is some opposition to any marker, some concern that it could raise old grievances against Hickey.

But Lennon says that he'll persist. 'It's eighty-five years later,' Lennon says. 'The guy (Hickey) wasn't a hero, but he was a victim of circumstance. He was a decent man.'

Reprinted by kind permission of the *Rochester Democrat and Chronicle*, Rochester, New York www.democratandchronicle.com

Contents

Homecoming, 1971

Chapter 1

The year is 1971. Richard Nixon is in the White House and George Bush (senior) is the US ambassador to the United Nations. There are already some indications of the recession that the coming decade will bring. After nearly thirty years of dramatic economic growth, the power of the dollar is stalling and six per cent of the USA's 200 million population are unemployed.

Although the first tentative steps will soon be taken to establish relations with China, the world is still locked in a Cold War between western democracies and the communist bloc. The space race continues apace: in February, Apollo 14 carries out the third successful manned lunar mission. In turn, the Soviet Union launches manned Soyuz missions to the Salyut space station and China launches its second satellite.

America is still embroiled in the increasingly unpopular Vietnam War. The draft is still in force and young Americans not yet old enough to vote are still liable to be conscripted for the ongoing jungle war in Asia.

Nixon's policy of giving South Vietnam with greater responsibility for fighting the war allows him to decrease American troop strength in Vietnam from 543,000 in 1969 to fewer than 160,000 in 1971. However, any hopes for the success of 'Vietnamisation' are dashed in March with the disastrous failure of a major South Vietnamese offensive into Laos in an attempt to cut the Ho-Chi-Minh supply route. Later that month, US army Lieutenant William

Calley is convicted of the murder of twenty-two unarmed civilians in the My Lai massacre. In April, the official US death toll in Vietnam passes 45,000.

Protests against the war build to a crescendo. On 24 April, a mass rally is held in Washington and a crowd of 200,000 gathers in the grounds of the Capitol building. These protestors include a thousand Vietnam veterans, some of whom throw away their medals as a mark of protest. Their spokesman, a young former naval officer, John Kerry, testifies before the Senate Foreign Relations Committee. On 3 May, when another major protest in Washington attempts to disrupt traffic, 7,000 protestors are arrested and detained under circumstances that raise serious civil rights questions.

It is to be expected that a city with such a liberal tradition as Rochester would play its part in the anti-war protests. On the southern shores of Lake Ontario in New York State, this prosperous city was once a terminus for the 'underground railroad' route for escaped slaves, a home to prominent abolitionist and former slave Frederick Douglass and to suffragette Susan B. Anthony. In April, hundreds of Rochester residents travelled to attend the mass protest in Washington. On 5 May, Rochester itself is the scene of protest when over a thousand locals stage a sit-down protest along the city's Main Street during rush hour, provoking a heavy-handed reaction by police.

On 15 May, an elderly couple are travelling from Rochester to New York, specifically to the city's airport, named for the assassinated Irish-American president. George Lennon is almost as old as the century; his wife, May, is a decade younger. A committed pacifist, George has been an active protester against the Vietnam War since before 1968, when the Tet offensive

2

proved to be the turning point for American public opinion. A long-time member of the Society of Friends (Quakers), in more recent years he has also become a practitioner of Zen Buddhism. Of his seventy-one years however, only half were spent in America; the remainder have been spent in the land of his birth, from where he emigrated a quarter century before. Life for George Lennon has been a long journey and now he is returning to where the path began.

At JFK airport, one airliner is distinguished by the large shamrock painted on its tailfin. As the Lennons board the Aer Lingus Boeing 707, they are greeted by smiling stewardesses with Irish accents:

"Now we are ensconced in the belly of the great bird. May is looking exultant. She knows there are other countries in the world but May is quite cool to them. She is going back to Ireland: in fact, she never left it".[1]

"The airliner's doors are closed, and the cabin crew begin a well-practised routine of checks and safety briefings as the four turbines are whining to life. The aircraft proceeds slowly to the runway as the stewardesses complete their tasks and are seated. The cabin lights dim and the engines' whine builds to a roar and the aircraft moves forward, gathering speed as the runway lights flash by. The nose lifts and the passengers are pushed back into their seats while the aircraft soars into the darkening sky. The city lights are briefly visible before the Boeing climbs higher and higher to over five miles high over the Atlantic. The big aircraft levels out and the interior lights brighten: Pleasantly virginal looking Irish hostesses wait upon our needs.

---

[1] George G. Lennon, *Trauma in Time,* extracted from 'Trauma in Time' (1971).

George Lennon is going home."

Two days later, George is exploring Dublin. The first time he flew the Atlantic was in 1946, aboard a Pan Am Lockheed Super Constellation, four powerful propeller engines lifting its graceful frame out of Shannon airport. Much has changed in Dublin since then. The streets are thronged with small cars rather than bicycles. The trams and tramlines are long gone. In O'Connell Street, one of the angels at the foot of the statue of Daniel O'Connell has been blasted from its plinth by a UVF bomb placed on Christmas Day 1969 , an echo of the upsurge of violence in Northern Ireland. The street is no longer dominated by the statue of Admiral Nelson atop its high pillar after a mysterious bombing in 1966. In that same year, a Garden of Remembrance was opened at the top of the street, dedicated to the memory of the Irish rebels killed in the Easter Rising of 1916. Oisín Kelly's striking bronze sculpture of the Children of Lir is yet to be unveiled.

"... A ghost walks down O'Connell Street ('The Moon Shone Down O'Connell Street'). I pass the Rotunda Hospital where my son was born. Almost at a run through Parnell Square I have come looking for Vaughan's Hotel. But Vaughan's Hotel has gone."

Vaughan's Hotel at 29 Parnell Square was an unofficial headquarters of Irish republicans during the rebellion of 1919–1921, where Michael Collins had held court and received young guerrilla leaders travelling from all over the country to report and to seek assistance. But by 1971, although the building still stands, it has ceased to be a hotel and there is not even a plaque to mark its former importance. A fleeting memory:

September 1920. Dublin.

"Pat and I are in quite a gay mood as we hand out valise full of bombs to Christy , who looks at us with dismay.

4

'You know you should not bring that stuff in here.'

Taking the valise to hide he goes off crying, 'Mr Collins would kill me if he knew I was doing this.'

Collins is in one of his boyish moods but listens intently, as he always does, while I explain my latest invention, the mud bomb. Then with a yell he declaims, 'Out from many a mud-bombed barracks peelers were fleeing through the night'. I feel deflated."

When Lennon left Ireland for America in 1946, he was in the vanguard of a massive wave of emigration that saw the departure over the next fifteen years of over half a million Irish people forced to seek a living elsewhere. Éamon de Valera held power along with a group of fellow 1916 veterans and continued to follow a disastrous economic doctrine until his eventual departure from office in 1958. In 1971 de Valera is still fulfilling the largely ceremonial role of president, his age of nearly ninety making him the world's oldest head of state. This long overdue relinquishing of power delayed the reforms of Seán Lemass, who achieved remarkable advances before his retirement in 1966. Realising the value of human resources and utilising the considerable talents of such men as economist T.K. Whitaker and education minister Donagh O'Malley, Lemass sought the development of an educated and skilled workforce. Under de Valera, secondary school, and third level, education had been the strict preserve of the nation's elite. O'Malley brought about free secondary school education and doubled the number of third level students by 1970.

By the time of Lemass' death in May 1971, Ireland had been enjoying a decade of relative prosperity. There was modest economic growth despite the damage done to the important tourist industry by the unrest in Northern Ireland, and by a series of strikes throughout 1970 that placed Ireland third in the world for work days lost due to industrial actions.

Social change was slow to occur, despite such reforms as the relaxation of the draconian censorship of literature. Irishwomen were barred from apprenticeships, all but absent in the professions and female public servants were expected to give up their careers on marriage. Contraception was banned, in strict compliance with the Catholic Church's stance on birth control. In March 1971 the young senator Mary Robinson displayed considerable moral courage by proposing a bill to repeal the relevant section of the 1935 act. This bill was rejected and Robinson subjected to a barrage of hate mail. In May, the Irish Women's Liberation Movement staged a protest by illegally importing contraceptives on the Belfast to Dublin train. This is the Ireland to which George Lennon has returned.

May 23, 1971. Dublin.

"Today, Sunday, I went to Quaker meeting. The atmosphere is always the same; the quietness, the silence and the happiness of being amongst Friends: above all, the motivation of Peace. As I sat I should not have allowed my mind to stray but it has a seemingly incurable habit of wandering off."

May 24, 1971.

"First impressions: The country seems quite foreign to me and all the people look remarkably 'Irish'. The courtesy and the kindness of everybody is disarming. Good manners and politeness ease the way of the pilgrim in his passage through this painful world. The police are not police at all, they are bobbies, that is, they are the Garda Síochána, or guards of the peace. Compared to the storm troopers in the United States the Irish guards look positively angelic. Police usually make me nervous. When the FBI came on their investigations they informed me that my dossier went back to 1927 and when I go on peace marches they take my picture. But this does not seem to apply here, to me at any rate.

"Irish journalism is of a high standard. There are three Dublin daily papers, all good. A very large amount of space is devoted to politics, sport and the heroic dead – the three great national preoccupations."

May 26, 1971. Dublin.

"We have secured quite a tiny flat in Sandymount. Sandymount Strand is almost at our door, where the broody Joyce ambled beside the 'the snotgreen sea'. Mr Smith said he was the happy man to have acquired such nice tenants. He has a prosperous butcher business at the other side of the city and he is bursting with kindly affluence. As to the services to the little flat, he wrote them right off. All the services are electric but Mr Smith said they would go on his personal bill – 'Sure, isn't it the least I might do'.. He charged us an enormous rent and the first month's rent, in advance, made quite a hole in my bank account."

May 28, 1971. Dublin.

"A visit from a neat young man who was representing the Jehovah's Witnesses and who told me that 'the Creator was going to strike very soon'. I told him I was all too well aware of that and I thanked him for his timely reminder. Finished reading Margery Forester's admirable book Michael Collins – The Lost Leader. It brings to mind Joyce's Ivy Day in the Committee Room.

"Back again to the noble house of Hodges Figgis, after a full quarter of a century. Disciples of the great Gurdjieff have described me as a bookworm. How right they are. I got hot on the scent and grabbed a splendid edition of Pacata Hibernia. My mouth was watering for the Journal of the Royal Society of the Antiquaries of Ireland (formerly The Kilkenny Archaeological Journal). According to the catalogue: 'there is no need to mention to the librarian or to the scholar that this most important and profusely illustrated journal is unrivalled as a source for the study of Irish antiquities. The likelihood of again acquiring a set of such beauty is indeed remote.' Price: £1,250. I make a rapid calculation into dollars and regretfully decide that this treasure is quite beyond my means."

June 1, 1971. Armagh.

"A long deferred visit to the home of my ancestors, the Crollys, who were at one time closely associated with the O'Neills. (How strange that I should be seeking the last resting place of Niall O'Neill in the north, not knowing at that time that he lies buried in Waterford.)

"The most attractive secular buildings in Armagh are a row of beautiful old Georgian houses and, strangely enough, the gaol. This is the only attractive looking gaol I have ever viewed, and I have inhabited a few.

"We had time to pay a visit to the Armagh planetarium and were wafted aloft into the stars. A minor interruption was caused by some small boys' whistles and giggles. Our lecturer mildly remarked that some birds must have got into the building and he was turning up the lights. The whistles stopped abruptly and we returned to the Milky Way. A visit to a planetarium is a chastening experience and you get cut down to proper size. Across from the planetarium is the place where the Duke of Wellington is said to have received his early education. It has an iron look."

July 1, 1971. Dublin.

"On the train.

"Who will not feel sad at the passing of the railroads? And the romance that will disappear with them? Trains hooting through the night as they cross the great American Plains. The famous train in Dr Zhivago, puffing and screeching its way as it goes tearing across the vast Russian Steppes. My memory of coming into Savannah with the sun just coming up, dew sparkling on the grass and the dogwood twinkling out from the forest.

"From my corner I keep my face pressed to the glass in case I miss anything. It is years since I have seen the Irish countryside.

"The farmsteads in the midlands look quite prosperous today. Not much more than a century ago the great masses of the rural population were said to have lived worse than kaffirs – their only food the potato, their only beverage water. Driven from their native lands they were compelled to become rack-rented serfs to a propertied class of landlords. Property is original sin and its hand agent is power. The New Testament is quite emphatic on the sinfulness of property. Proudhon said property is theft and Marx declared that money is the alienated ability of mankind.

"You come to Cork suddenly, out of a tunnel, and into the brightness of the lively little city. Many of my memories of Cork are bright ones."

1971. Cork.

"The train arrived in earlier than I had expected and there was ample time to wander through the principal streets. Something directed my steps towards the Grand Parade and I went looking for the house where we held that fatal secret meeting during the

9

Treaty negotiations – Collins seemed resigned and his manner was almost gentle."

1971. Killarney

"Twenty-seven years is quite a lapse in time. My initial desire was to visit Ross Castle, as it was once a project of mine to have it restored and converted into a museum as a resort of local interest for visitors. When I suggested the matter to H.G. Leask he concurred and he indicated that he would find it a fascinating job to undertake but no funds were available for this work at that time. It still may be a feasible project.

"Killarney is described in song and in story as 'a little bit of heaven' which is not altogether an exaggeration as it contains a scene in incomparable and breathtaking beauty. The area is best seen by taking the popular tour through the Gap of Dunloe on pony back and returning by boat to disembark near Ross Castle. The distance covered is thirty miles and takes the greater part of a day, and a day well spent.

"The Gap of Dunloe is described by geologists as a product of the Ice Age but I prefer to think of it as a gift from heaven. We all milled around Kate Kearney's Cottage for an hour until we got sorted out and started off on our trek; eleven mounted riders and three pony carts. It takes about four hours to go clop-clopping along through the great mountain pass. When you finally arrive at the top of the great defile the view is quite awe-inspiring. The boatmen meet you with your lunch and help you into the boats for the long scenic journey through the lakes.

"When passing beneath a high mountain our ferrymen rested on their cars and told us that was where the leprechauns lived. We looked incredulous. The leading boatman said he would count three and would then altogether shout a welcoming 'Hello'. We did so and lo and behold an answering 'Hello' came faintly but distinctly back from the top of the mountain.

"Our ferrymen regaled us with strange and interesting tales of the district. One story was particularly intriguing: A great local matriarch had a set too with the Evil One whom she worsted and from him she exacted a price that no Irish person would ever be taken into his domain. Wishing to test this bargain two Irishmen called at the outer door of Hell but were told that no Irish need apply. Chasing the two away his satanic majesty presented his visitors with a box of matches and a lump of coal and told them to go and establish a private hell of their own. Putting us ashore, the bold boatmen warned us against paying any attention to the tall stories the jarveys might tell us."

1971. Kilmallock.

"Once called the 'Balbec' of Ireland, the early history of Kilmallock is little known. The place derived its name from an abbey founded by St Molach in the early 7th century. Later on in history the town was fortified by walls of great strength.

"[Another fleeting memory of this place from fifty years before, of a barracks blazing in the early morning and a chance bullet that slays a nearby comrade ...]

"The town once contained several castellated mansions and a street of post-medieval houses of which now only one, used as a store, remains.

"Kilmallock had all the appearance of a ruined village at the beginning of the 19th century. The rebuilding into the present shops and residences began about 1830.

"For a person with a feeling for such places, the well-preserved ruins of the Dominican abbey can be breathtaking. Almost as imposing in its own way is a nearby structure, said to be of the thirteenth century, known as the church of SS Peter and Paul. It is most solidly built and at the end of the north aisle has a very peculiar looking tower, evidently an ancient Irish round tower considerably altered.

"Other interesting items, to the antiquarian, are the King's Castle, used at various times for different military purposes, and Blossom's Gate the only survivor of the town's original five gates."

1971. Limerick.

"It was about the year 1905 that my mother and her lady companion, Miss Condon, took me to Limerick to see the exhibition. Exhibitions were all the rage at that time. In a glass case were Sarsfield's sword and his blood-stained great-coat. Mama told us Sarsfield was killed at the battle of Landen and she declaimed his supposedly last sentimental words. This was not quite exact, the great Irish soldier was gravely wounded at Landen and he died from fever in a French town some distance away. My poor dear mother was of an emotional nature and she worried a lot about the tribulations of royalty. Her special concern was for the Russian Czarina and 'the poor dear little Czarevitch' – who was always being threatened by anarchists. She was outraged when 'that brute Edward' was alleged to have pushed his stately queen down the stairs in some palace or another.

"Limerick is a very beautiful city but some people find it hard to establish rapport with it.

"On this, my final visit, I sought some human companionship but the hotel was exclusively occupied by tourists of the American variety known as Yanks. Communication being quite impossible, I wandered down the long Georgian street poking my nose into various pubs seeking a kindred soul. In one near to the railway station was a picture of Ezra Pound and this led to an introduction of two imbibing poets who took me under wing with offers of intellectual nourishment and convivial entertainment. The entertainment was satisfactory but fearfully expensive. I arrived back at the hotel at 2 a.m. and had to have a consultation the day following with a bank manager so as to have sufficient funds to continue on my journey. When I was checking out of the hotel I drew the attention of the lady cashier to my room charge of £3.62 ½. The official Guide to hotels, guesthouses, holiday camps and hostels was explicit the high season charge for this particular hotel room was £2.87. How come this difference? The cashier drew my attention to the figure 64 in the column marked 'with bath'. She explained this did not indicate the number of rooms with baths but meant sixty-four new pennies were to be added to my room rate. All this was very confusing and still left eleven and a half pence to be accounted for but as I have an inferiority complex about figures I gave up and paid over."

1971. Clare.

"Here in Bunratty a castle was erected in 1277 by the de Clares and it was afterwards the residence of the Earls of Thomond. The castle was enlarged, or, more likely, rebuilt by Thomas de Clare at the end of the 16th century. In more recent years it was used as a constabulary barracks. The castle has now been completely restored and reflects great credit on the dedicated people who took the work in hands. A young vivacious and well-informed guide took me around and pointed out the different furnishings. She explained that all the furnishings were replicas or antiques imported from Germany and she related that Irish artifacts were not available as our ancestors in their numerous wars burned each other's furniture with everything else.

"I was hoping to be a guest at one of the widely advertised and popular medieval banquets provided for visitors. Mead, sack and other ancient beverages of the Middle Ages are provided and you dip your fingers into a communal bowl and fish for meaty titbits. My knowledge of ancient Irish banquets is confined to the picture in Pacata Hibernia where a cow is being stewed in its own hide and happy kerns relieve themselves on the castle floor – not that I anticipated anything as exciting as this. The banquet was booked out so I wended my way to Durty Nelly's famous pub hoping for some excitement. Alas, the once dear place was full of tourists sitting glumly about hoping to imbibe some of its bygone atmosphere.

"Corbett's house is now a hotel, and a very pleasant one indeed. One of the family showed me around and I tried to pick out the rooms where we once retired to bed with splitting gelignite headaches. It was booked out so I had to stay in the luxury motel run on American style. The inhabitants were grimly intent on their steaks, salmon and 'Irish' coffee. Public eating is not an uplifting spectacle and sometimes it can be quite revolting so I left quite soon and like my forebears of old, I recrossed the Shannon."

1971. Comeragh Mountains.

"I wore my best tweed jacket as I was going to meet Máire and I wanted to make a favourable impression.

"As we drove in the direction of the mountains Máire pointed out the place at a turn in the road where she saw the apparition one menacing All Soul's Eve night. The man was wearing the peasant costume of one hundred year's back – caubeen hat, knee breeches and tailcoat. A murder had been committed on or near that particular pot during the Land War.

"Our intention was to ride ponies up the Nire Valley but as there were ordinations that day all work had stopped at the pony livery so we drove on to where the winding mountain road ended at a lay-by, where there were some rough seats to rest on facing directly towards the Comeragh range.

"What a scene. I am quite unable to describe it and what the guidebook has to say is quite inadequate. Many years ago we had crossed those mountains from the south side and descended into this most lovely valley of the Nire. Coming over the tops a hare started up and Kirby fired his rifle at it and I had to reprimand him most severely for wasting valuable ammunition.

"After we had been sitting for a short while enjoying the view an elderly man approached us and asked if we had brought the bottle of whiskey. We expressed our regrets and he started a lively and mainly one-sided conversation. Could we guess his age? We undershot the mark and he told us that he was eighty-six. For our edification he recited some long poems he had composed in the days of his dashing youth. The poems were mostly about dances and made flattering references to the athletic achievements of the young men he grew up with. He must have been most athletic himself as he said he once walked sixty-two miles in a day and we believed him. He proffered the information that he owned all the side of the mountains facing us – containing two lakes – and on which he grazed eleven hundred sheep. A German man who wanted to build a modern hotel in that place sought to buy his holdings. 'An do you know how much he offered me?' We didn't.

'Seventeen thousand pounds, now what do you think of that?'

"We were glad he did not sell to the hotel man but a hotel will yet be built there and it is to be hoped the architect will make the building conform to the beautiful landscape.

"On our way back from the hills, we stopped at Ballymacarbry and I went into Melody's cheerful hostelry to buy sandwiches. While I was waiting for the sandwiches the man who was standing next to me let out a cry of joy and gripped me by the shoulders. Taking a pace to the rear he came nobly to attention. 'My commander,' cried he, 'don't you know your old column man, Seamus Phelan?' I lied most manfully as I have an awfully bad memory for names and faces.

'Ah, why did you do it, why did you do it? I'm telling it to 'our face, Jarge, and I'll never forget for you, ever'.

"Ah, why did you do it?'

"What on earth was the man talking about?

'There they were with their field kitchens, and their horses – had you given us the order to advance we could have bet them into the ground with stones – it would have been the greatest battle of the war. Why did you retreat from the battle of Ballinamult?'

"While he was furiously berating me with all this he kept slapping me on the back and pumping my arm up and down.

"Now my memory was coming back ...

"Máire had been waiting patiently in the car wondering what had been delaying me when she saw the two of us coming towards her arm in arm. My old comrade held me in an iron grip and he refused to let me go until he had exacted a solemn promise from me that I would stay with him the next time I came to that part of the country.

"(When, oh when, could that be?)

"In about twenty minutes we were at Sleady Castle.

"The castle, now in ruins, had been one of a number of such structures owned by the MacGraths who were princes of the Decies. They also founded an abbey, the tower of which is in use to this day. Sleady, or Curagh-na- Sledy, was not built until 1628 and it had a curse on it from the first day of its construction. The site was selected by the chieftain's wife in the teeth of his opposition and his vassals were fleeced to pay the wherewithal for the building without one penny of outlay on the part of its owner. During its short history the castle caused unhappiness and misery to a number of people who were unfortunate enough to come under the shadow of its baneful influence. During the involved and complicated wars of the period 1641 to 1652, the MacGraths played both sides of the fence and this did not help them at all in the end. English officers rode to the castle to be entertained and to court the chief's beautiful daughters. They rode out once too often. A servant let in the rapparees through a secret door and the Englishmen were dragged out and put to death down by the Lickey stream. It is said that on some summer nights the ghost of one of the girls had been seen in the castle garden frantically seeking for her vanished lover.

"We had to force our way through waist-high nettles and weeds to get to the crumbling ruin. A new farm building had been erected in that ominous place that was once the garden. A stab of remorse came back and I turned away. What had led me back here?

"This had been quite a day of remembrance. We stopped the car on an elevation and sat silently eating our sandwiches. Gusts of rain hit the windshield, clouds drifted over, then the sun came out and it glistened on the sea far away in the distance. We sat motionless surveying the distant scene. Máire and I went to school together, after which we went steady for a while. That was a long time ago. Máire is seventy, and I am seventy-one."

Opening Shots, 1916-1920

Chapter 2

Ιt was Easter Monday 1916 and George Lennon was not quite sixteen.

Dublin had risen in rebellion and Lennon was one of the few Irish Volunteers in the southern coastal town of Dungarvan:

"Strange as it may seem, P.C. and I captured a post office on Easter Monday night in 1916. It was an easy capture. P.C. was the postal night clerk and he immediately answered my excited knock on the door. A telegraph instrument was clack-clacking and P.C. translated the messages. One telegraph message indicated that a train of munitions for the British troops was passing through our town at 2 a.m. P.C. said it should be wrecked. But how? He could not leave his post and we were the only two Volunteers in the county. He let me out the back door of the post office. Grasping my .32 revolver I rushed off into the night to seek assistance. The rain was coming down in torrents."

Outside, the young Lennon met neighbour and fellow Irish Volunteer Pax Whelan, who later recalled:

"We had word that there was a trainload of war material destined for Cork from Waterford, passing through about midnight. We had a couple of revolvers, and, with George Lennon, I went out and blocked the line. The train was held up. However it was an ordinary goods' train; there was nothing in it. We just disappeared. There was no commotion fortunately."[2]

Following the bloody rebellion of 1798, Britain copper-fastened its hold on Ireland with the 1800 Act of Union, which declared Ireland and Britain to be a United Kingdom. Ireland benefited little from this arrangement and while the causes of the Great Famine of the 1840s are complex, the initial indifference of the British government to the suffering of its Irish subjects was the primary factor in the massive depopulation of the country. The late nineteenth century saw a resurgence of Irish nationalist movements: the Gaelic Athletics Association (GAA) and the Gaelic League promoted Irish sport and language. A political movement to establish a measure of independence (the Irish Parliamentary Party) was led by Charles Stuart Parnell, while more covert but no less significant was the Irish Republican Brotherhood (IRB) that sought full independence. Following a split in 1891 on the death of Parnell, the Parliamentary Party was reunited in 1900, and under the leadership of John Redmond gathered strength until the passing of the Home Rule Act in Westminster in 1914. Unionists, persons who wished to preserve the Act of Union and were naturally hostile to this development, formed a well-armed paramilitary organisation named the Ulster Volunteer Force in north-east Ireland. To counter this, Irish nationalists formed the Irish Volunteers, which the IRB began infiltrating. Civil war seemed imminent until the outbreak of the First World War; the UVF pledged their support for Britain and enlisted en masse in the 36th (Ulster) Division. Redmond also announced his wholehearted support for the British cause, and at his urging the majority of the Irish Volunteers also enlisted in the ranks of the

---

[2] Mac Eoin, Uinseann, *Survivors* (Argenta, Dublin, 1980), p. 136.

British army. The more republican minority of volunteers remained at home.

Seizing on the adage that 'England's difficulty was Ireland's opportunity,' the IRB began a largely fruitless attempt to enlist German support and on Easter Monday 1916, Irish Volunteers occupied strategic buildings in Dublin and declared an Irish Republic. Confused by countermanding orders, few Volunteers outside Dublin reacted. Although significant actions took place at Ashbourne, Enniscorthy and Galway, the attempted action in Dungarvan was more typical of the minor skirmishes that occurred throughout the rest of the country. Heavily outnumbered, the insurgents were overwhelmed and the rebellion was crushed within the week.

1918

The Blackwater River runs all the way across the county of Cork, through Mallow and Fermoy to Cappoquin in Waterford where it turns south and drives wide and deep towards the south coast. Although the river does not quite delineate the border between the counties of Cork and Waterford, it was deemed to form the border of the area of operations of the East Cork brigade of the reconstituted Irish Volunteers. The aftermath of the Easter Rising had seismic repercussions for Irish politics. When the 1916 rebels were released from interment in Wales, they were met by cheering crowds on their return to Dublin. Support for Redmond's Irish Parliamentary Party plummeted while Sinn Féin, originally moderate constitutional nationalists, were re-established as hard-line republicans and began making gains in local elections. In the face of increasingly heavy losses on the western front, conscription to the British army had been introduced in Britain but not yet in Ireland, and the Irish Volunteers were reorganising to counter such a threat.

In each town and village in County Waterford, a Volunteer company was raised along the lines of a parish militia. According to Volunteer organiser Ernie O'Malley, such a company could range in strength from thirty to one hundred and twenty men. Each company elected its own officers (a captain, lieutenant and second lieutenant) who in turn appointed NCOs (section and squad leaders). When more than five companies were raised in a region, they formed a battalion, the company officers meeting to elect a battalion commandant, vice commandant, adjutant and quartermaster. The battalion commandant would then appoint lieutenants responsible for 'special services' i.e. engineering, signals, first aid, etc. These battalions would then be organised into brigades: by January 1919, County Waterford had been allocated two brigades: Waterford No. 1 (East) and Waterford No. 2 (West). Pax Whelan was appointed commandant of the West Waterford brigade with George Lennon as his vice commandant. As yet, the Volunteers in these brigades were untrained and almost unarmed.[3]

In 1918 there were two main bridges over the Blackwater river between Cappoquin and the sea; a graceful railway bridge at the former and a wide road bridge to the east of Youghal, serving the main road between Cork and Waterford. Today this wide roadway is thronged with commercial and private vehicles; in 1918 the road was narrow and unsurfaced and what sparse traffic there was was largely of the horse drawn variety. Motor vehicles were rare. Having crossed the Youghal Bridge, the road travels fifteen miles north-east to Dungarvan. The rugged land around this road and the coast, known locally as the Drum Hills, featured

---

[3] O'Malley, Ernie, *On Another Man's Wound* (Anvil, Dublin, 1997), pp. 112–3; *With the IRA in the Fight for Freedom* (The Kerryman, Tralee, 1952), p. 18.

rough terrain, narrow isolated roads and small forests, greatly advantageous to any rebels with local knowledge. West Waterford's 3rd Battalion was being organised in the coastal villages of Ring, Helvic and Ardmore. The latter was the area's largest village and featured a well-preserved round tower, built in the Middle Ages to protect Christian monks from marauding Vikings. With over four hundred men organised into eight companies, James Mansfield of Old Parish commanded this battalion; his brother Mick (22) was his deputy (he later became brigade engineer).

There is a wonderful view to be had of the town of Dungarvan from Windgap, that point where the road twists sharply from the Drum Hills down to the harbour. The countryside is lush and verdant and on a fine day, the sea shimmers in the sunshine. The town of Dungarvan, framed against the backdrop of the looming Monavullagh and Comeragh Mountains, is today a pretty and prosperous coastal town at the centre of a wide and sandy harbour. In 1918, Dungarvan was a somewhat smaller, dingier fishing port. In the north-west of the town, a distinctive building marked the location of the town's gas works, where in pre-electricity days coal was processed to produce tar and methane gas which was fed through an elaborate piping system to provide Dungarvan's 5,000 inhabitants with light and heat. The Volunteer movement was active in the town, designated the base of West Waterford's 1st Battalion. Although headquartered in Dungarvan, this battalion covered the county as far north as the river Suir, eventually numbering eleven companies.

From Windgap, at certain times of the day, an observer might notice a plume of smoke moving through the countryside north-west of the town, revealing the presence of the railway between Fermoy and Waterford city. This single track line was completed in 1878 and five times daily a train travelled across the county and back again. Fifteen miles after leaving Fermoy, the train followed the Blackwater eastward and crossed into County Waterford with its first halt at the charming town of Lismore (headquarters of the emergent 2nd Battalion). Three miles on and a river crossing over an elegant bridge was another stop at Cappoquin, with its thriving bacon and salmon industry, four miles after that there was a stop at the rural station of Cappagh, and then the six remaining miles to Dungarvan. The train pulled into Dungarvan railway station, situated a short distance outside the town. Passengers alighted, others boarded, and with the usual noises of stationmaster's whistle, slamming of doors and hiss of steam, the train pulled out to begin the thirty-mile journey to Waterford. Although certainly scenic, this stretch of line was regarded as difficult (necessitating an average speed of only 30 mph) and featured a tunnel, three viaducts and no fewer than fifty-three level crossings. Gatekeepers resident in small lodges, several of which are still extant and inhabited, serviced the latter. Leaving Dungarvan, this line went east for four miles, closely following the long beach of Clonea before abruptly tuning north into a deep grassy passage cut through the rock. The train then travelled over the graceful Ballyvoyle viaduct that soared a hundred feet over the trees in the Dalligan valley, giving passengers their last glimpse of the sea before heading inland. Moving slowly, the train then travelled over an embankment and, passing through the high green walls of another cutting, entered the darkness of a 418 foot long tunnel. On emerging, the train made its first stop at Durrow station, five miles from Dungarvan. Today this station has almost been reclaimed by nature, ivy covering the crumbling signal tower and the roofless waiting-rooms now occupied only by briars. In 1918, it was a busy station, largely due to the adjoining farm co-operative building, which served the picturesque seaside village of Stradbally and the farmers of the locality. Leaving Durrow station, the train crossed the Kilminnin viaduct over the Tay river and then struggled northwards with an uphill gradient for the next ten miles, passing to the east of the Monavullaghs, a southern extension of the main mountain range.

Not long afterwards, the passengers were presented with an increasingly spectacular view of the Comeragh Mountains. Dominating central Waterford, the central part of this sandstone massif covers nearly eighty square miles and is characterised by steep-sided coums, glacial valleys carved out in the ice age. The train windows offered a view of the huge natural amphitheatre of the Tay valley, ruggedly beautiful and bordered by high cliffs to the north. Uphill to the west, and not visible from the train, was the tiny village of Lemybrien. Further west was the tinier village of Kilrossanty consisting, then as now, of little more than a church, graveyard and a few houses. There was no obvious reason why Kilrossanty was the heart of West Waterford's emergent 4th Battalion, which had companies in surrounding villages including Stradbally. There is an old local legend that a scouting party of Roman soldiers were defeated in battle here; there is certainly evidence here of ancient settlement and an ogham stone, carved with runic markings, stands on the hill above the village. The Kilrossanty company, led by a young athlete named Pat Keating, captain of the village GAA team, was being trained at Whyte's farm. Later on, this valley became the main sanctuary of West Waterford's flying column, and from here they ambushed crown forces in the local countryside.

Passing the Ballylinch level crossing, the train passengers were able to view the rugged Mahon valley with its distant waterfall indicating the source of the Mahon River. While the Tay valley was fertile farmland, this narrow valley was rocky and barren. The Comeraghs were receding by the time the train approached McGrath's Cross over the main Cork–Waterford road, but the passengers would be able to glimpse the high cliffs of the eastern edge of the central plateau. One feature, Crotty's Rock, is named for an eighteenth century highwayman.

From McGrath's Cross onward, trees obscured the view through the train windows. The gradient now tended to favour the railway with the last few miles to Kilmacthomas downhill. This sleepy little village, the half-way point between Dungarvan and Waterford, was dominated by the huge stone railway viaduct over the Mahon river and featured a well-appointed railway station possessing two platforms, waiting-rooms and a goods' shed. The signal box remained intact until recent years.

Only a few locals were involved in the Irish Volunteers, but the Cullinanes in the village were enthusiastic supporters and provided a safe house; the four daughters of the family were members of Cumann na mBan, the Volunteers' unarmed female auxiliary group, and one (Katie) was a trained nurse. Although the few Volunteers in Kilmacthomas were deemed to be an outpost of the Kilrossanty company, east of the Mahon River was the territory of the East Waterford brigade, where three battalions were being organised, centred on Waterford city, Dunhill and Passage East. Leaving Kilmacthomas, the train passed the old workhouse, built in 1854. Symbolic of the Victorian era's concept of social welfare conditions in these grim stone buildings, where the poor were fed and clothed during the latter half of the nineteenth century, were kept deliberately harsh to discourage all but the most desperate. 1918 was thankfully this workhouse's final year of operation, although a small hospital continued to operate there.

After a few more miles, the line descended slightly to Carroll's Cross, more a halt than an actual station. There was another short journey to the small station at the village of Kilmeaden, five miles from Waterford city.

At a time when roads were bad and motor vehicles rare, the importance of the railway to the county's economy cannot be overstated. The IRA never attempted to sabotage the line during the War of Independence; in the later stages of the conflict it was usual for incognito IRA men to travel in the same carriages as armed British soldiers. Most of the railway workers on this line were sympathetic to the republican cause; some were even members of the IRA, for example train fireman Jack Edwards who came from Belfast in 1918 and enlisted in the Waterford City battalion. Another 'foreigner' who joined the Irish Volunteers in Waterford city in 1918 was Corkman Jerry Cronin.

For the last few miles of its journey, the railway line followed the Suir River before crossing the river over a bridge completed in 1908 and pulling into Waterford's main railway station on the north bank. Passengers with business in the city were obliged to travel back across the Suir over the Redmond Bridge; completed in 1912 and named for the leader of the Irish Nationalist Party; this designation gave some indication of the political allegiances of Waterford city. While Sinn Féin and the republican movement continued to gain overwhelming support, Waterford remained the last stronghold of the Irish Parliamentary Party. Then a rather grim city populated by 24,000 persons, Waterford was a railway terminus and a base for cross-channel ferries, both of declining importance.

It is recorded in the 'General Register of Prisoners' of Waterford prison that George Lennon and Pax Whelan were committed there by Dungarvan Court in January 1918 for the offence: 'Enter a house disguised and carry away a gun'. George (described by the

26

prison register as 5'8 ½", 112 pounds with brown hair and eyes) recalled in later years:[4]

"On the first night of my incarceration there the kindly night warder let himself into my cell with the excellent intention of trying to cheer me up. The good man explained that I did not have to wear prison clothes, that I could procure books from the library, that I could have meals sent in, that I would exercise in the yard for an hour every day, and so forth. The poor man finally ran out of goodies and with a deep sigh he said 'But this place was not built for anyone's pleasure. With this wise Buddhist remark he left me for the night."[5]

The Waterford County and City Jail, also known as Ballybricken prison, was a fortress-like complex of buildings, surrounded by a high wall. Towering over its surroundings, the prison commanded the quays of Waterford and of the Redmond Bridge, knowledge which George made use of in 1922.

Although remanded for trial at the Waterford Assizes, evidence was lacking and George was bailed on 11 February. The cause for this brief incarceration was the Waterford Volunteers quest to gather weapons for the impending guerrilla war. Whelan and Lennon had entered the house of a man on leave from the British army and taken his Lee-Enfield rifle, which he had been allowed to take home. For a force struggling to obtain shotguns as weapons, this acquisition was most welcome. The Lee-Enfield was probably the best military rifle in the world at that time; firing a powerful .303 inch bullet, its ten round magazine had twice the capacity of other comparable rifles and its specially

---

[4] INA MFGS 51/ 118 (PRIS 1/39/23).

[5] George G. Lennon, *Trauma in Time*, extracted from 'Trauma in Time' (1971).

designed bolt action allowed a trained rifleman to fire over twenty aimed shots per minute. It is little wonder that the first German troops to encounter British infantry in 1914 believed themselves to be under machine-gun fire. Throughout the First World War, the Lee-Enfield consistently proved itself a reliable and extremely accurate weapon, and remained in military service worldwide for several decades.

Apart from a small military garrison in Waterford city, the Royal Irish Constabulary (RIC) represented the security forces of the British government in Waterford. Originally founded in 1822, the Irish Constabulary was the only armed police force in the UK and was instrumental in suppressing the Irish rebellions of 1845 and 1867. Queen Victoria honoured the force by granting the 'Royal' prefix after the latter rebellion. Wearing a dark green (almost black) uniform modelled on the British Army's Regiment of Rifles, recruited largely from Irish Catholics and armed with pistols, rifles and even grenades, the RIC in Waterford then comprised one hundred and sixty-three policemen based in twenty eight barracks across the county, many of which were fortified posts featuring steel shutters on the windows with loopholes for firing through. Local republicans considered the location of the RIC barracks in Dungarvan to be most fitting; this former military barracks was situated within the crumbling walls of the town's twelfth century Norman castle, originally constructed by the pathfinders of the British colonisation of Ireland.

There were also a number of coastguard stations in the coastal villages of Ardmore, Helvic, Ballinacourty, Bunmahon and Tramore, mostly built in the 1870s. As part of their duties were to intercept smugglers, the coastguards were lightly armed.

In March 1918, parties of Irish Volunteers from across County Waterford travelled to Waterford city to assist in a local election where Dr Vincent White of Sinn Féin was standing against Captain Willie Redmond, son of the Parliamentary Party leader. This election was viciously contested in every sense of the word. Redmond's supporters carried out a series of violent attacks, against the Sinn Féin election workers led by Nicholas Whittle. Éamon de Valera was saved from serious injury only by the swift intervention of a party of Volunteers while Dr White was hospitalised with head injuries after a brutal assault. According to Paddy Ormonde, who travelled to Waterford as part of a group of twenty Dungarvan Volunteers: 'Pax Whelan and George Lennon were in charge of the party, of which I was one. These two men were, to the best of my recollection, armed with revolvers. The remainder of us carried hurleys'. Headquartered in the Volunteer Hall in Thomas Street, these men were subjected to constant attacks from Redmondite supporters: 'These attacks were so menacing that I remember George Lennon from Dungarvan firing his revolver over the heads of the mob to frighten them off. This, I remember, had the desired effect'.[6] Sinn Féin lost the election, one of the few setbacks for the republican political party during that year.

Sinn Féin won a landslide victory in the general election of December 1918, winning 73 out of 105 total seats. The thirty-two remaining seats were won mostly by the Irish Parliamentary Party and unionist parties in north-east Ulster. Waterford city elected John Redmond's son, representing the Parliamentary Party. Rather than taking their seats in Westminster however, the Sinn Féin MPs assembled in Dublin's Mansion House on the 21 January 1919, declaring the first Dáil Éireann and adopting a Declaration of Independence. On the same day, on their own

---

[6] IMA BMH WS Patrick Ormonde.

initiative, Irish Volunteers in Tipperary shot and killed two members of the RIC guarding a consignment of gelignite near Soloheadbeg. In the same month, the West Waterford Volunteer 'battalions were put on a war footing at a meeting of the brigade staff in January, 1919, when it was decided to intensify pressure on the RIC'.

The first death in Waterford as a result of the War of Independence occurred that April in the village of Ballinagoul near Helvic Head. A local man who had joined the Royal Navy brought some fellow sailors to a local public house. Drink was consumed and trouble ensued. Although that month a boycott of the RIC had been ordered by Dáil Éireann, local Volunteer Michael Walsh (24) ran to the nearby police barracks to report the trouble. Knocking on the locked door, he shouted 'Police, Police, there is a row on the bridge.' At that time, there was only one occupant, the nervous Constable Michael McCarthy (20) who drew his revolver and fired through a window. A bullet struck Walsh in the throat and carried down into his lung. He staggered back to the pub and collapsed on the floor. Doctors M.F. Moloney and J.C. Hackett were sent for while RIC Sergeant John Kelly returned to the barracks and placed McCarthy under arrest. The constable was released on bail about a fortnight later, but was re-arrested shortly afterward when Walsh died from his wound. A huge crowd turned out for Walsh's funeral including contingents of uniformed Volunteers from all over the county. His coffin was covered in the tricolour and carried by uniformed Volunteers; three volleys were fired over his grave.

McCarthy ultimately did not face trial; he resigned from the RIC and emigrated to the US in mid-1920.[7]

With the end of the First World War in November 1918 came the end of the threat of conscription and several units of the Irish Volunteers found themselves without those who had volunteered to avoid this threat. An unexpected bonus from the end of the First World War was the demobilisation from the British army of Irish combat veterans, men who now offered their services to the Irish Volunteers. By 1920, two of East Waterford's three battalions were led by Great War veterans, while the Kilrossanty men training on Whyte's farm now had the services of combat veteran Mike Daly of Cutteen. In mid-1919, Dungarvan man John Riordan was appointed as West Waterford brigade's training officer. A pre-war British army regular, one of the generation of professional soldiers that were nearly wiped out in 1914, John Riordan had fought at Mons and Ypres with the Royal Irish Regiment before being wounded at La Bassee, and was later posted to Egypt where ironically he 'was engaged in putting down a rebellion in that country'. By his account:

During the remainder of the year 1919 and the greater part of 1920, all my time was taken up in training work with the various companies in the brigade. I helped in drilling, field manoeuvres, and taught methods of attack and defence. The men were instructed in the use and care of revolvers and rifles and fighting tactics in general.[8]

---

[7] Murphy, Seán and Síle, *The Comeraghs: Refuge of Rebels* (Kennedy Print, Clonmel, 1980), pp. 9–10; research by Waterford County Museum.

[8] IMA BMH WS John Riordan; UKNA WO/372/17 Medal Card 5762 Private John Riordan.

One local war veteran who did not involve himself in the nationalist movement was traumatised former Connaught Ranger Jim Fitzgerald who had fought in France and Mesopotamia. Shortly after being demobilised, 'Lackendarra Jim' as he was later known, withdrew from society into the Comeragh mountains where he lived in a dugout until his death in 1959, a pattern of behaviour closely associated with some Vietnam War veterans in later years.[9]

In April 1919, George Lennon's revolutionary activities resulted in him being imprisoned in the Cork male prison:

"When we arrived at the gaol our handcuffs were removed and we were taken to the part of the prison where the regular prisoners were incarcerated. Some of the political prisoners had been discriminated against and almost all the other politicals had gone on strike in sympathy with them. All had been bodily removed to a disused part of the old gaol known as Wing No. 10. We soon made our intentions known and the police were brought in to deal with us. On being asked if we would walk peacefully to No. 10, or if we wanted to be dragged, we quite sensibly decided to walk.

"My cell in No. 10 was anything but luxurious. After they had taken my shoes away and locked me in, I had ample time to survey my new home for the next three months to come.

"The bed was something that looked like the lid of a coffin, covered by a hard mattress and pillow, a sheet and two army blankets. Nothing else but a sanitary utensil and a wooden salt cellar. We had to eat our meals on the floor. My predecessor had

---

[9] Murphy Seán and Síle, *Comeraghs – Fact and Fancy* (*Dungarvan Observer*, 1974).

vented his wrath on the window, bursting out every last vestige of glass, he had also gouged out some minor holes in the wall. Needless to say, there was not heat of any kind, and the weather was cold.

"A strange silence reigned. The policy, as I was soon to discover, was to break every prison regulation, non-cooperation in short, so we all stayed in bed most of the day and stayed up most of the night yelling out through the cell windows.

"It could hardly be described as 'solitary' confinement as all the cell windows were on one side of the building and quite close together. Sitting on the window ledges and pushing our faces against the bars we carried on a garrulous and active communication. It was confinement in as much as I never saw the outside of my cell door for three months to come.

"Activities began about 9 p.m. when our master of ceremonies introduced us new arrivals (by voice) to the rest of our comrades, about fifty in all. Then the nightly concert began and it was, and I mean it, really entertaining. It was mostly songs, ballads and recitations; speeches were definitely out.

"After a number of the contributions our MC would sadly complain that the applause was not as appreciative as he would have wished and threatened to stop the concert whereupon the yelling would be redoubled and distracted parents living in the vicinity would start calling up the prison governor complaining that they could not get their children to sleep. A favourite song was:

> See who comes over the red-blossomed heather
> Their green banners kissing the clear mountain air
> Heads erect, eyes to front, stepping proudly together
> Freedom sits bright on each proud spirit there

"Then we would all join in:

> *Down the hills climbing, their blessed steel shining*
> *The fire that illumines dark Aherlow's glen*
> *And all who love English law, native or Sassenach, Out and*
> *make way for the bold Fenian men.*

"Many of the ballads were the most beautiful and moving I had ever listened to.

"The recitations were usually quite funny and to annoy the British Tommies on guard outside on the walls we sang the 'Watch on the Rhine' but this dreary anthem passed over the poor fellows heads – they had never heard it before.

"We also sang satirical songs of the revolution such as:

> *When Adam and Eve were courting down in Eden*
> *And Eve she ate an apple just for fun*
> *The serpent said to himself when homeward speeding 'The*
> *constitutional movement's just begun'.*

"The last line was intended as a sneer at the contemptible constitutional activities of the Irish Parliamentary Party which was belittling our physical force movement.

"There were times during our incarceration when we grew deathly serious and then we sang our battle hymn:

> *Armed for the battle*
> *Kneel we before Thee, Bless thou our banners God of the*
> *brave. Who dies for Ireland God give him peace.*
> *Knowing our cause just*
> *March we victorious Giving our heart's blood Ireland to*
> *free...*

"The Irish prison warders were an admirable lot of men and they handled our under-ground mail. They delivered our letters from home at breakfast and took away our replies, to be posted outside. The governor of the prison, Captain King, made his regular inspections. The warder would fling open the cell door announcing 'the Governor' and you were supposed to stand to attention. We just lay in bed and grinned at him. On one occasion he told me I was a foolish boy not to take my exercise and that I would make myself sick, he then slipped me a pack of Capstan cigarettes and a box of matches.

"Reference must be made to poor old Dr Foley, the prison doctor. We played endless tricks on him. He had a different coloured pill for every disease so we thought up a new ailment every day to add to our collection. I kept my collection of pills in a hole in the window ledge.

"There were, of course, many unpleasant things such as the food. The meat was of a most suspicious colour and was said to be once part of a horse. 'Plumduff' was a kind of suet pudding that felt like grape shot in your stomach. The stew, known as 'tyres in paraffin oil' consisted of stripes of stringy mutton floating in a horrible liquid. The bread is not even worthy of mention.

"After some months, Dr Foley began to sound me all over and to shake his head. Five of us, including two other beardless infants, young Barlow and young Phillips from Tipperary, were removed to the prison hospital. After being administered Parish's syrup and other nourishments to build us up we were released. Our friends drove us to a nice lady's house on the Grand Parade from where we were taken to tea with Seán and Mrs Hegarty on the Western Road.

"I came home and I lay on a sunny strand. Or I took my bike and with keen anticipation went to visit my dearest friends the Whelans whose comfortable farm was within easy riding distance. Ballyduff, my home from home. Here lived Mr and Mrs Whelan, Elanna, Mollie, Ned and Aunt B. Aunt B. would feel me all over exclaiming the while 'you poor anishore, when are you going to get some flesh on your poor bones'. At the back of the house was a lovely old world garden, nestling by the orchard, with such flowers as mignonette, flox, boy's love and girl's fancy. The girls made a delicious apple cake for me and we all sat happily down to tea with the perfumes from the garden drifting in the open window. (Dear, kind people when I think of you I know there must be such a place as Heaven.) My poor mother fed me numerous egg flips to speed my recovery."[10]

Released from prison in June 1919, Lennon had recovered enough by September to participate in an attack being organised in Fermoy by Liam Lynch. According to Mick Mansfield:

"It was in the month of September 1919, when George Lennon, vice OC of West Waterford brigade, and I went to Fermoy to take part in an engagement against the British, the OC IRA being the late Liam Lynch. It was observed that a party of armed military, about twenty strong, used parade from Fermoy barracks to the Wesleyan church, Fermoy, to attend services in the church at 8 a.m. on a Sunday and plans were made to ambush this party and capture the rifles. The idea was to have our men in twos at intervals along the road where the military used to halt before entering the church. Another party of our men were out of sight in a public convenience near the church. When the signal was given, the Tommies were to be rushed and disarmed. Everything

---

[10] George G. Lennon, *Trauma in Time,* extracted from 'Trauma in Time' (1971).

came off according to plan. The soldiers arrived as expected. We were in position and rushed them with revolvers pointed, ordering them to surrender. Most of them did so, but there were, I remember, some shots fired which resulted in ... one Tommy being killed. Liam Lynch was wounded in the shooting. However, the badly needed rifles and equipment were captured from the soldiers and taken quickly away by the Cork Volunteers to a place of safety.

"Meanwhile, George Lennon and I were in a rather precarious position. The motor in which we travelled from Dungarvan, and which was to bring us back, was taken to remove Liam Lynch and we were left stranded in a locality more or less strange to us. We made our way on foot quickly out of Fermoy, bearing in a south-westerly direction, whilst the countryside was alive with military in lorries and on horseback, searching for the raiders. Planes were also up 'looking out' for us. We were very fortunate to be able to cross the Blackwater river by a boat which was waiting to take over some men from Araglen, Cork, who were on the job in Fermoy.

"Later in the day we found ourselves surrounded by searching troops, so we hastily took off our coats, got into a cornfield and proceeded to make up stooks of corn. We were seen by the military, who took us to be men engaged in harvesting work; they passed on without suspecting a thing. Eventually we reached Lismore about twelve miles south at about 8 p.m. where we were welcomed in the house of Seán Goulding (afterwards a senator). We remained in his house overnight and returned to Dungarvan safely the following morning."[11]

---

[11] IMA BMH WS James Mansfield.

Eighteen troops of the Royal Shropshire Light Infantry were ambushed outside the Wesleyan church in Fermoy on 7 September, one was killed and three wounded. The Irish Volunteers involved had acted on the natural assumption that the British rifles were loaded; the British later claimed that this was not the case. Two hundred troops of the Shropshire regiment subsequently went on a rampage in Fermoy, looting over fifty shops and causing thousands of pounds worth of damage.

The wounded Liam Lynch was brought to West Waterford to recover.

On the night of 1 January 1920, as part of an ongoing effort to hamper the British civil administration of Ireland, Lennon led a small raid on the office of the petty sessions clerk in Dungarvan. Legal documentation and RIC correspondence was carried to the town square and burned.

It was decided during a brigade council meeting held in Dungarvan Town Hall in January 1920 to carry out an attack on Ardmore RIC barracks, the main responsibility lying with James Mansfield's 3rd Battalion. Mansfield later related:

"This barracks had a garrison of twelve men, some of whom had been transferred from vacated barracks in the neighbourhood. The building was a two-storeyed stone and slated one. It was loopholed for firing and was in the main street of the village. The intention was that a landmine be exploded against the gable end of the building and the barracks then rushed and captured. At about 12 o'clock (midnight) on January 17th 1920, approximately thirty men, practically all of whom were from my own battalion, were in position at the front and rear of the barracks.

"Upwards of forty others were on outpost duty on the roads leading from the village, having erected obstructions to prevent the approach of enemy troops by road, principally from Youghal five miles to the east, or from Dungarvan twelve miles to the west. As the party who were detailed to place the mine in position were about to do so, a shot rang out, fired accidentally by one of our men. Immediately the RIC in the barracks were alerted and the garrison opened heavy fire with rifles and bombs. It was impossible for us to place the landmine in the place originally intended and to put it elsewhere near the barracks would result in the neighbouring houses being blown up."[12]

James Fraher recalled:

"We replied to the fire as best as we could, with what effect I cannot say. After about half an hour of this, we were ordered by George Lennon, brigade vice OC, to break off the action and get away."[13]

With the element of surprise lost and ammunition limited, the attacking party withdrew. It was only the first attack on Ardmore barracks.

The senior RIC officer in Dungarvan at this time was District Inspector King, regarded as a 'particularly zealous officer in hunting down IRA men ... his methods were, to say the least, particularly ungentlemanly'. He eventually over-stepped the mark when he threatened to shoot James Mansfield's mother if she did not reveal her sons' whereabouts, and on the night of 2 February, Pax Whelan, along with George Lennon and three others, set fire to his car outside his residence in Church Street.

---

[12] IMA BMH WS James Mansfield.

[13] IMA BMH WS James Fraher.

King heeded the warning and transferred to Mallow.[14] His replacement was Great War veteran District Inspector Sheehan and the change was fortuitous for the people of Dungarvan. By April, the RIC men in Waterford were seen in the company of armed men wearing a curious mixture of RIC dark green and British army khaki. The infamous 'Black and Tans' had arrived. There had been many resignations from the RIC and recruitment had slowed to a trickle; the response of the British government was to recruit large numbers of British army veterans to take up the shortfall. It was standard British counterinsurgency doctrine to reinforce the police as much as possible, only bringing in the military as a last resort. These new recruits however proved to be unsuited to police work by their temperament and training. Waterford was at least spared the presence of the even more notorious Auxiliary division, comprising units of former officers. In July, Black and Tans in Tuam burned down the town hall and other buildings as a reprisal for an ambush, a pattern of behaviour of which the worst example was the destruction inflicted on the town of Balbriggan in September. There were few such outrages associated with the Black and Tans in the Dungarvan area, which suggested that DI Sheehan kept a tighter leash on his Black and Tans than was usual. A year later, this leash appeared to have slipped, and the Dungarvan 'Tans' showed what they were capable of.

On a night in April 1920, Lennon led a small party of men in a raid on the income tax office in Dungarvan, destroying documents and ledgers, and then driving to Lismore and raiding the office there at 2 a.m. Here, a retired British officer saw them and fired a pistol

---

[14] IMA BMH WS Patrick Lynch; NLI FOD 31,150 (Activities – Waterford Brigade); Mansfield, James 'The Decies Brigade – 1920', *Capuchin Annual,* 1970.

shot to alert the RIC. Pat Lynch remembered: 'Lennon came into us for a moment to assure us that everything was all right outside but to hurry with the job. We completed the task in quick time and brought the sacks of papers out to the country where we burned them'.[15]

In early May 1920, Pat Keating led a party of thirty men drawn from Kilrossanty, Bunmahon, Kilmacthomas and Stradbally in an attack on the RIC station in Stradbally, manned by six RIC men. George Kiely from Kilmacthomas remembered:

"The attack took place about 10.30 p.m. on a dark night and was opened by a fusillade of rifle and shotgun fire from our party. I was in position about thirty yards from the building. The success of the attack really depended on the effect of our bombs on the roof of the building. These bombs consisted of a short piece of lead piping filled with explosive to which a fuse and detonator were attached and the whole lot encased in mud. When thrown onto the roof of the barracks the mud would stick and the explosion blow a hole in the roof. It was intended to pump petrol into the holes in the roof and set the building alight, forcing the garrison to capitulate. After about half an hour of intermittent firing by us to which the garrison replied with rifle fire (sending up Verey lights to summon assistance) it was discovered that the mud bombs failed to stick on the roof and, as our ammunition was insufficient to carry on the attack much longer, orders were given to us to withdraw. It was explained to me afterwards that the failure of the bombs to stick was probably due to the fact that the roof of Stradbally barracks was a particularly steep one. Shortly after the attack the barracks was evacuated and the garrison sent

---

[15] IMA BMH WS Patrick Lynch.

to other stations. The building was burned by us subsequently to prevent its re-occupation by enemy forces."[16]

The Verey lights referred to were flares fired from a bulky pistol; used mostly for distress signals, they were also useful for illuminating small areas at night.

At the end of May 1920, George Lennon travelled to Limerick to participate in the attack on Kilmallock RIC barracks; this was an unusually heavily fortified building garrisoned by twenty RIC men well equipped with rifles and grenades. Preparations for the attack were meticulous, sixty Volunteers being gathered from five counties for the actual assault while others were assigned to render all roads and railways impassable for fifteen miles around the town:

May 28, 1920. Kilmallock RIC barracks

"The West Limerick men picked me up at Newcastle West where we went to confession to Fr Hayes. I was already well acquainted with the others but the boy sitting next to me in the car, with a Lee-Metford rifle between his knees was new to me. He was whistling quite cheerfully to himself. His nickname was Frost and we took an instant liking to each other.

"It was midnight by the time we were in our positions in some houses directly facing Kilmallock police barracks. The barracks was a long, low building and appeared to be only one storey high from my place of vantage looking down on it. The house adjoining the barracks was about two storeys higher and it was from here that the main attack was directed.

---

[16] IMA BMH WS George C. Kiely.

"There was a most eerie silence before the attack began as if all the people in the town were lying awake waiting for something awful to begin.

"The moment the signal light flashed we put our rifle butts through the window glass, knelt down behind the ledge and opened fire. There was an immediate response from our opponents. After the first volley there was a moment of silence and a frightened wail went up from all the houses around. What a strangely satisfying, almost wild, sensation it was to push forward the bolt, feeling the round slide smoothly out of the magazine and into the breach. You snuggled the butt voluptuously into your shoulder, took careful aim and pulled the trigger. The crash of the rifle was orgiastic.

"The top and unbroken pane of glass was soon peppered with bullet holes. Owing to the angle of fire, bullets were passing through the windows below and were coming up through the floor behind me. Pieces of plaster came tinkling down from the ceiling. When you fired there was a double and instantaneous bang caused by the shot striking against the steel shutters from which answering fire kept spitting.

"The barracks had been unsuccessfully attacked during the Rising of 1867 and at least one Fenian was found lying dead in the street. Now we were going to get our own back with a vengeance.

"Resting for a while you could direct your gaze towards the house that adjoined the beleaguered police building. From here heavy weights had been dropped to smash the roof below and kerosene, by the bucket, was being showered down into the aperture made by the weights. Soon that end of the barracks was ablaze. In the confined space of the street the noise was terrific.

"At about 2 o'clock in the morning our leader ordered a ceasefire and called upon the police garrison to surrender. The answer was a shout of defiance and a renewed outbreak of firing from the building, now quite half consumed by the flames.

"So it went on all night until all but a small part of the barracks was enveloped in fire. It seemed impossible that anybody could remain alive there."[17]

According to another eyewitness:

"The defenders had by this time made a dash to a small building in the yard of the barrack. This building, like the barracks, was fortified. In their flight they abandoned most of their bombs and ammunition and the bursting of these within the burning building added to the din and clamour of the fight. From this small building they put up a stubborn resistance. They fought the fight of heroes and although we were engaged in a life and death struggle with them, we readily acknowledged the magnificent stand they made in the face of an utterly hopeless situation."[18]

Lennon remembered:

"Near daybreak I descended into the street and with a young man named Scully, stood watching the now almost consumed building. Suddenly my companion dropped to the ground, shot through the throat."

---

[17] George G. Lennon, *Trauma in Time,* extracted from 'Trauma in Time' (1971).

[18] Quirke, Michael, 'The Battle of Kilmallock', *An tÓglach,* 18 December 1926.

Liam Scully, a schoolteacher from Kerry and a captain in the local Volunteers was killed by a single shot from the ruins, the final shot of the action in which two RIC men were also killed:

"When day began to break we had to withdraw. Frost and I had been running around looking everywhere for each other. We climbed into the back seat of one of the cars happy to be together again. The dead man was on a stretcher in the other car. Black clouds of smoke were going up over the town as we drove off.

"Liam Scully was laid to rest at Templeglantine at night with full honours. All the available rifles in Limerick had been placed at the disposal of a small force led by Seán Finn and Donnchadh O'Hannigan and after a proposed attack on Newcastle West RIC post failed to materialise, this small unit crossed the Shannon to Co. Clare to participate in an attack on the RIC barracks at Sixmilebridge."[19]

Summer, 1920 Bunratty, Co. Clare

"It was from Pallaskenry that we crossed the Shannon to lend our aid to the Clare and Galway men. The night was brightly moonlit and fishermen pushed our boats over the mudflats and rowed us to the Clare side of the river. Our stay was with Mr Corbett of Bunratty House who was a sympathiser. The house, or rather mansion, was quite large and he catered for the lot of us in a most princely manner. What happened on this particular hosting was not without humour (if working with explosives can be called humorous). I remember we had to thaw out a large quantity of frozen gelignite that we intended to use to demolish a police barracks. The thawing operation took place in a fisherman's hut

---

[19] MacCarthy, J.M., *Limerick's Fighting Story* (Anvil, Tralee, 1949) p. 86.

on the banks of the river. A huge pot full of water simmered on the fire and into this we dipped sweet cans full of the frozen explosives. Under such conditions gelignite gives off sickening fumes and the proposed military operation had to be called off at the last moment.

"The tide was in and it was a bright sunny day when we recrossed the Shannon to the Limerick shore. Frost and I rowed together in the leading boat and all lifted up their voices in song. We were always singing in those days of happy unquestioning youth."

Back in Limerick, the unit carried out a thirty mile march across the country in broad daylight. According to O'Hannigan:

"It occurred to us than since we had successfully done so there was no reason why a larger number of men, organised and equipped as a unit, could not do likewise. Thus was conceived the idea of the Active Service Unit which was the original name of the flying column. The idea was revolutionary in its implications in the circumstances that then prevailed, for in fact implied the maintenance in the field of a standing force for the duration of the struggle. What we had in mind was an efficient, disciplined, compact and swift-moving body of men which would strike at the enemy where and whenever a suitable opportunity arose."[20]

The newly formed East Limerick flying column saw its first action at Ballynahinch on 9 July when an RIC patrol was disarmed without casualties, adding four rifles to the column's complement. Four days later, the slightly reinforced column tackled a detachment of the Lincolnshire regiment, capturing eight rifles after a three-hour fight. By 30 July, Lennon had joined the column

---

[20] Ibid p. 87.

in time to participate in an action at Bruree, on a military cycle patrol of an officer and five men.

"The place he liked most of all was Johnnie Lynch's in Tankardstown. John had two spinster sisters whose names may have been Minnie and Maggie and who made the most tasty sweet scones. An integral part of the Lynch household was Billy Boy. Billy Boy, who was about sixteen, was one of those harmless simpletons farmed out by the poorhouses to the farmers, free gratis and for nothing. Billy most industriously performed all his farm chores and had time left over to gape about at a world full of delight and wonder. Everybody loved Billy Boy. One day when he was sitting in the kitchen with the others codding with Billy Boy, a man rushed in and announced that a cycle patrol of the enemy was coming down the nearby Bruree Road. All rushed to arms and dashed across the intervening fields and there was a sudden and headlong collision. His personal contact was with a tall frightened looking constabulary man; by mutual consent they drew off in opposite directions. This was one of the rare occasions on which he distinguished himself as he captured two military bicycles under fire. Coming back he twice passed a young tin-hatted soldier lying face downwards on the road, an ominous stain was streaming down over the soldiers khaki clad buttocks."

The engagement was of approximately a half-hour duration. One military death was later reported. The military took up position in a cottage and, with the possibility of British reinforcements arriving, the column withdrew:

"After this event is was necessary to move a long ways off. They tramped very many miles climbing the many ditches in their path. Nurse Sullivan came with them and they helped her over ditches and the barbed wire fences."

In early August, the column crossed into Co. Cork, and reinforced by local IRA units prepared to ambush an eight man patrol of Black and Tans near the village of Kildorrery on 7 August:

"Skirting the Ballyhoura hills they passed Kilclooney Wood ('where brave Crowley stood') and they eventually came into the vicinity of Kildorrery. Outside Kildorrery they ambushed a patrol of Tans and Nurse Sullivan attended to the wounded. He supported a very youthful Tan while the nurse slashed off the youth's pants with her surgical scissors and applied a tourniquet. But the boy had lost too much blood and he began to sink. Between sips of water the young Tan told him that he came from Liverpool, where he had a wife and kid – he had been unemployed a long time and then he saw this advertisement for policemen in the newspaper. Noticing his distress and seemingly wishing to console him the young Tan said, 'it's all in the game, chum'. They held clammy hands, the boy gave him a wan smile, and in a moment he was gone."

The dead Black and Tan was later named as Temporary Constable Ernest S. Watkins; all of the others in the patrol were wounded. Later that day British troops from Fermoy and Buttevant carried out reprisals in Kildorrery, searching and looting houses and shops in the village. Later, in the House of Commons, Sir Hamar Greenwood, chief secretary for Ireland, admitted that:

"Some shops in the village of Kildorrery were wrecked on the night of 8 August last following the murder of a policeman (but claimed that) no evidence has been forthcoming which would justify the arrest of any member of the crown forces in connection with the destruction."[21]

Following Kildorrery, Lennon returned to Waterford, where in his short absence, a significant military build-up was under way. On 4 June 1920, the 1st Battalion of the Devonshire Regiment arrived in Waterford city, transported aboard several warships. The HQ company and a rifle company (300 troops in all) remained in the city, billeted in the Infantry and Artillery Barracks, while another company was rapidly deployed to Kilkenny and another to Wexford, with a small detachment in Clonmel. A Devonshire officer later noted:

"The Devons were very soon into a pattern of patrols and guard duties, each man working two nights out of three, and operating up to seven miles out of their base locations, carrying out foot, bicycle and vehicle patrols ... Troops soon became expert in dismounting and carrying out anti-ambush drills.[22]

"This was no idle boast as later events in Kilkenny and Waterford demonstrated. An IRA officer in Kilkenny who had occasion to observe the Devonshires at close quarters observed that:

"Like trained soldiers, they remained always alert ... they were men in the 25 to 35 age group. None of them was a chap (i.e. youngster). They were professional soldiers."[23]

Of particular interest was the low-key approach normally adopted by the Devonshires in Wexford. According to one account

---

[21] Hansard HC, 16 June 1921, vol. 143, cc575–6.

[22] Archives of the Devonshire Regiment, Wyvern barracks, Exeter.

[23] Comerford, James J, *My Kilkenny IRA Days* (Kilkenny People 1978), p. 456.

of this time: 'It has been suggested the relatively less brutal behaviour of crown forces in Co. Wexford may have reflected an official anxiety not to provoke a people with such warrior traditions'. Wexford had been the focus of the 1798 Rebellion and Enniscorthy had been one of the few Irish towns to take part in the 1916 Rising. However, the most convincing reason for the relatively quiet stance taken by Wexford from 1919–21 was the county's unsuitability for guerrilla warfare. There was one serious breach of discipline involving the Devonshires in Wexford. In mid-September 1920, a group of off-duty soldiers ran amok in the town square, breaking windows and assaulting civilians. The RIC restored order and brought the unruly soldiers back to barracks, much to the gratitude of the townspeople.[24]

With the deployment of the Devonshires to Waterford and Wexford, the 1st Battalion Royal East Kent Regiment ('The Buffs'), which had until now been widely deployed in small detachments between Mallow and Rosslare, were concentrated in Fermoy. This battalion's soldiers were predominately young and inexperienced conscripts. By July 1920, a company of 'Buffs' had deployed to Dungarvan where they based themselves in the RIC barracks in Dungarvan Castle.[25] One local observed:

"I went along the quayside walls, heavy with ivy and laurel, indicating that about the time Elizabeth's captains were winning the seas it might have been regarded as a sort of fortalice. But ... once more after all these years the ancient building had a garrison. From the summit of the high loop-holed wall khaki-

---

[24] Roche, Richard, 'Events in Wexford – 1920', *Capuchin Annual,* 1970; *Munster Express,* 'Police Restrain Riotous Soldiers in Wexford', 18 September 1920.

[25] Knight, C.R.B., *Historical Records of the Buffs* (Medici, London, 1951), p. 2.

capped faces looked down upon me with mild interest. At the flagstaff the colours of an English regiment ruffled in the salt breeze. And as I passed, the strident call of a bugle sent a brazen call to the four winds. It was elsewhere noted that 'the speed with which the military vehicles go through the streets is a terror to some people, and many are afraid that a serious accident is bound to occur'."[26]

A platoon was billeted at Cloncoskoran, a few miles to the north-east of Dungarvan, at a house owned by local unionist Charles Nugent Humble. Another detachment was based in Lismore.

The standard mode of transport for the crown forces in Waterford was the Crossley tender; this was a small open-topped truck, noted for its distinctive high-pitched engine noise, which could carry ten men. Apart from their Lee-Enfield rifles, the crown forces in Waterford were also armed with Lewis machine-guns. The Lewis was classed as a 'light' machine-gun despite its weight of thirty pounds, although it should be noted that this was a third of the weight of most other contemporary machine-guns and provided a single soldier with unprecedented firepower.

From Somerset, the senior British officer in Dungarvan was a young man of twenty-seven, although he appeared much older. Recent life had been hard for Captain Donald Victor Thomas. Graduating from Sandhurst in 1912, Captain Thomas had originally been posted to India, but had first seen action in March 1915 when his battalion was deployed to France in the second year of the First World War. By 1918 he had spent nearly two years accumulated service at the front, at one point attaining the rank of major, until in September that year an exploding shell

---

[26] *Munster Express*, 'A Native's Word Picture of the Old Borough', 2 April 1921.

near St. Quentin peppered him with shrapnel, temporarily deafening him and hospitalising him for the rest of the war. Thomas had been afflicted with a serious cough since being caught in a gas attack the previous April, and in December 1918 he was hurriedly admitted to hospital suffering from what proved to be serious tuberculosis. Declared '100% disabled' by a medical board, he was admitted to a sanatorium in Scotland. Although he had improved by July 1919, an onset of pyorrhoea obliged the removal of seventeen of his teeth. By Christmas Eve, his condition had deteriorated. A three-month stay at a sanatorium in Switzerland proved beneficial and in April 1920 he rejoined his battalion in Fermoy where he was hospitalised again with a neck injury following a wild night in the officer's mess. Thomas was given a clean bill of health in July and took command of the company in Dungarvan that month.[27]

Like DI Sheehan, Thomas appears to have maintained discipline over his command. Although there were 'official' reprisals in Dungarvan in March 1921, there were no examples of Thomas' company behaving in the way that off-duty British troops did when they essentially ran riot in Youghal in November 1920 or in Fermoy in September 1919 and June 1920.

Thomas' second in command was Captain F.A.J.E. Marshall, another young veteran who had been awarded both the Distinguished Service Order and the Military Cross during the First World War, no mean achievement. While official British records for this time give Marshall the substantive rank of

---

[27] UKNA WO/372/19 Medal Card Captain D.V. Thomas; UKNA WO339/8667 (Personal file Captain D.V. Thomas).

lieutenant, he held the rank of captain in an 'acting' capacity.[28] Both 'the Buffs' and the Devonshires battalions formed part of the 16th Infantry Brigade which was headquartered in Fermoy.

Also in Fermoy at this time was No. 2 Squadron of the Royal Air Force, which operated 12 Bristol Fighters, a two-seater biplane which had proved to be an effective fighter-bomber during the First World War. Despite the Lord Lieutenant's suggestions to the British prime minister that 'air patrolling with bombs and machine-guns ought to put the fear of God into these playful young Sinn Féiners' such methods were deemed unsuitable in Ireland and for now No. 2 Squadron's Bristol Fighters remained unarmed. Apart from reconnaissance missions, No. 2 Squadron mission was delivering important messages to military posts due to the effectiveness of the IRA's interception of military mail delivered by conventional means:[29]

"During the summer of 1920 it was a daily occurrence for the mails to be brought to the Castle by aeroplane. It was interesting to watch the evolutions of the machine as it descended in a spiral and dropped the mail bag into the Castle yard. On one occasion, the bag dropped into the sea, but after a vigorous search, it was discovered. At about mid-day every day the buzzing of the engine would be heard, and people craned their necks to get a sight of the machine, which would swoop around and around, sometimes coming close to the chimneys of the houses, but invariably circling over the Castle until the bag was dropped. When this was found,

---

[28] Knight, C.R.B., *Historical Records of the Buffs* (Medici, London, 1951), pp. 2–3; *London Gazette,* 18 September 1919.

[29] McCarthy, Patrick, 'The RAF and Ireland 1920-22', *The Irish Sword,* Vol. XVII, Issue 68.

the aeroplane was signalled to and the machine continued its flight in the direction of Waterford."[30]

Such operations were not without hazard: on 21 August a Bristol Fighter developed engine trouble and force landed near Lismore. The local Volunteers reacted quickly, burning out the aircraft and capturing the crew, who were released unharmed shortly afterwards. That November, another aircraft crashed onto the rooftops near the Infantry Barracks in Waterford, seriously injuring both crewmen.[31]

Also that summer, the coastguard stations at Ardmore and Ballinacourty were each occupied and fortified by a platoon of Royal Marines. These elite 'sea soldiers' enjoyed (and still do) a fearsome fighting reputation and were a thorn in the side of the local Irish Republican Army (IRA), as the Irish Volunteers were by then being increasingly referred to.

Apart from the military forces actually based in Waterford, there were two companies (300 men) of the 2nd Battalion Royal Hampshire regiment based in Youghal since the previous November. Their job was to reinforce Ardmore in case of IRA attack. Later, in the summer of 1921, British units from Tipperary and Cork were also deployed in Waterford.

As late as August 1920, the Dungarvan RIC were still making some attempts to use the conventional mail system, and daily provided an armed escort for mail being delivered from the town to the

---

[30] Keohan, Edmond, *Illustrated History of Dungarvan* (*Waterford News*, Waterford, 1924).

[31] McCarthy, Patrick, 'The RAF and Ireland 1920–22', *The Irish Sword*, Vol. XVII, Issue 68; *Munster Express*, 'Aeroplane Destroyed by Fire', 28 Aug 1920.

railway station. On the morning of 8 August, a five man party of policemen led by Sergeant Michael Hickey were approaching the station, having been preceded by a single RIC man who had walked into the station and saluted a man wearing the uniform of a Marconi wireless operator, a position equivalent to a merchant naval officer. He was greatly surprised when this man (Pat Keating in disguise) drew a revolver, disarmed him and locked him away. When Sergeant Hickey's party entered the station, ten local Volunteers armed with pistols confronted them. Hickey 'was slow to surrender and went to draw his revolver. A shot was fired over his head at which he put up his hands and was disarmed like the rest'. The Volunteers made their escape with the captured police rifles which were quickly taken to a safe location.[32]

In August 1920, James Mansfield led another attack on Ardmore RIC barracks. At 8 a.m. the local IRA failed to force entry and after a brief fire fight between the thirty strong IRA party and the better armed RIC and Royal Marines, Mansfield withdrew his unit. Reinforcements soon arrived from the British army garrison in Youghal, while a party of Black and Tans from Dungarvan were attacked while marching cross country.[33]

Later that month, George Lennon and Pat Keating led a party of men to Bunmahon to destroy the coastguard station before it was manned by Royal Marines. While there, they learned of the presence in the town of Liam Walsh and Paddy Paul, commander of the East Waterford brigade and commander of the Waterford

---

[32] IMA BMH WS Michael J. Mansfield; INL FOD 31,150 (Activities – Waterford Brigade).

[33] IMA BMH WS James Mansfield; Murphy, Seán and Síle, *The Comeraghs: Refuge of Rebels* (Kennedy Print, Clonmel, 1980), p. 22.

City battalion respectively, who were on a tour of inspection with a view to organising a local unit. The boundary between the two Waterford brigades had not been fully decided but the pair were amicable enough and agreed to help the West Waterford men with the destruction of the station. Lennon and Keating struck up a strong friendship with Paul in particular; this friendship endured throughout their lifetimes, but some lives are destined to be far shorter than others. Paddy Paul, a short and intense individual, was twenty-four at this time. In 1915 he had volunteered for Royal Irish Regiment saw action in Salonika, Egypt and Palestine, and later in France and Belgium. Demobilised in 1919, he joined the Irish Volunteers and was appointed to his present position the previous May.[34]

The burning of the coastguard station proved straightforward enough. Having removed the families residing there, the IRA men sprinkled petrol around the building, and having ensured that it was well ablaze, made their escape to the Comeraghs in a small lorry 'borrowed' from a local merchant and driven by Paul. Having spent the night at the Keating's house, Paul was taken back to Bunmahon in a pony and trap driven by Tom Keating. It was the first example of co-operation between the two Waterford brigades.[35]

In early September 1920, Lennon and Pat Keating met with Paddy Paul and Jim Power of Dunhill to plan an attack on the RIC barracks in Kill, a village ten miles south-east of Waterford city.

---

[34] IMA BMH WS Patrick Paul; UKNA WO/372/15 Medal Card 7962 Private Patrick Paul.

[35] 35 IMA BMH WS Patrick Paul, Andy Kirwan.

Power[36] had fought with the Royal Scots of the British army from 1916 to 1918 and by 1920 was leading East Waterford's 2nd Battalion. Headquartered in Dunhill this IRA unit comprised six companies in surrounding villages including Dunhill, Fenor, Tramore and Kill, none of which numbered more than twenty men. The raid on Kill involved forty men drawn from Kilrossanty and Kilmacthomas in the west and from Dunhill and Kill in the east; half were to take part in the actual raid while the remainder blocked local roads and cut telephone lines. Paul provided five Lee-Enfield rifles seized from local unionists while the Kilrossanty men brought some of the 'mud bombs' used at Stradbally. Willie Keane of Dunhill, vice commandant of East Waterford, described these weapons as 'composed of a short steel tube about four inches in diameter. The tube was filled with bits of broken metal and gelignite. It was filled with a detonator and fuse and covered with a whitish soft clay called "pudlow". This clay is got mostly in bogland and is not unlike putty in texture. It is generally used for lining the stonework of reservoirs to prevent any seepage of water'. The Waterford men still had high hopes for these 'mud bombs' as evidenced by a journey made by George Lennon and Pat Keating to Dublin to show the bomb to Michael Collins.

The attack went ahead on the night of 18 September without Lennon (who had been called away to a training course in Cork) and started badly when the RIC garrison was alerted by a prematurely fired shot and put up a stiff resistance, firing Verey flares to alert the Devonshires in Waterford. A pump intended to spray petrol failed and Paul called off the attack when warned that British troops were approaching the village. His own men

---

[36] UKNA WO/372/16; Medal Card 39371 Private James Power.

agreed with his decision and a local newspaper claimed that 'after much difficulty a contingent of police and military arrived and the attackers retreated ... police and military pursued the raiders but the latter escaped in the darkness'. However, some Kilmacthomas men later scornfully alleged that they had seen no soldiers in the area and it is possible that this insinuation of faint-heartedness rankled with Paul. Of some small consolation was the RIC's decision to abandon their barracks in Kill shortly afterwards.[37]

On 17 September, as the first step to forming the North Cork flying column, a training camp was organised near Glenville in Cork. The local Sinn Féin council funded this venture by providing £400 for equipment, clothing and rations. Participants included Liam Lynch and George Lennon and the supervising officer was Ernie O'Malley who later recalled: 'I trained the column in field work for over three weeks, as we moved around; at night the men attended lectures that I gave to officers of the local battalion. After two weeks of intensive training, the men involved laid real ambushes for local crown forces but these failed to make contact'.[38]

---

[37] *Munster Express*, 'Waterford Police Barracks Attacked', 25 September 1920.

[38] O'Donoghue, Florence, *No Other Law* (Anvil, Dublin, 1986), pp. 97–98; O'Malley, Ernie, *On Another Man's Wound* (Anvil, Dublin, 1997), pp. 182–183.

Flying Column, 1920-1921

Chapter 3

Lennon returned to west Waterford at the beginning of October. There had been a number of incidents in his absence, the most serious of which was the death of Sergeant Martin Morgan (43), the first RIC man to die at the hands of the West Waterford IRA. On the third of September, Pat Keating and George Kiely prepared to accost and disarm two RIC men who were cycling between Lemybrien and Kilmacthomas. According to Kiely's painful memory of the episode:

"We jumped out onto the road and gave the order 'hands up'. The constable, who was covered by Pat Keating, dismounted and put up his hands. The sergeant, however, continued to approach me on his bicycle. I again shouted to him to surrender but he came on. I then fired at him from close range and he fell wounded on the road. We searched the RIC men for arms but found, to our surprise, that they were unarmed. We took the money they were carrying as police pay and handed it over subsequently to the brigade quartermaster. Meanwhile Sergeant Morgan was lying on the ground obviously in a bad way. I went to him and said an Act of Contrition into his ear. He was quite conscious then. We attended to his wound as best we could and sent the constable on his bicycle into Kilmacthomas for a priest and doctor."[39]

---

[39] IMA BMH WS George C. Kiely.

Morgan later stated that 'when shot, the men rushed over the fence and one of them said that they did not want to shoot him. The constable with him was uninjured and was able to obtain assistance.' With a bullet embedded near his heart, the sergeant was removed to the small hospital in Kilmacthomas Workhouse where his condition was described as 'precarious.' He was later transferred to the Waterford City Infirmary where after several operations, he died on the afternoon of the 27th September. A veteran of the Western Front, Sergeant Morgan left a widow and two children.[40]

In anticipation of reprisals by Crown forces, Paddy Ormonde led an armed party of ten men to guard Kilmacthomas the following night. No reprisal ensued.

Shortly afterwards in Dungarvan, an RIC sergeant accompanying a military foot patrol stopped to remonstrate with two local Volunteers. A scuffle ensued during which the sergeant fired two shots from his revolver before being disarmed. The Volunteers escaped with the pistol, the sergeant with broken ribs.[41]

Also in Dungarvan on the 6 October, Captain Marshall who was going on leave sent his batman (soldier servant) to carry his heavy canvas valise to the railway station. A small group of Volunteers waylaid the batman and absconded with Marshall's luggage, which was eagerly searched in the hope of procuring weapons. They found only personal kit which they later destroyed, possibly because of the sleepless night Marshall had caused Pat Lynch previously when he raided his house three

---

[40] *Cork Examiner,* 'The Kilmacthomas Shooting,' 9 September 1920; RIC Register of Service.

[41] NLI FOD 31,150 (Activities – Waterford brigade).

times in the course of one night. It should be noted that due to the recent assassination elsewhere of two men named Lynch (apparently mistaken for Liam Lynch) Pat was inclined to place a sinister interpretation on the raids.[42]

Following the success of the first flying column in Limerick, the IRA leadership recommended that each brigade form an Active Service Unit (ASU), essentially placing the brigades' available weapons in the hands of its most active members; in September 1920 this became an order. The Cork brigades initially formed ASUs on a temporary basis, gathering officers and training them before returning them to their own units. Others, including West Waterford, made a virtue of necessity by forming an ASU from those whose activities had made them a constant target of crown forces, forcing them to go 'on the run'.

There is no firmly established date for the formation of the West Waterford ASU; most accounts vaguely place this in summer/autumn 1920. However, its first action took place shortly after the return of George Lennon to Waterford in October 1920.

The original members were men who were by now on the run. Although accounts vary slightly, a reliable list of the 'originals' is as follows:

> George Lennon (leader)
> Pat Keating
> Mick Mansfield
> Jim Prendergast
> Pakeen Whelan

---

[42] IMA BMH WS Patrick Lynch; NLI FOD 31,150 (Activities – Waterford brigade).

Paddy Cullinane

'Nipper' McCarthy

Jim Lonergan

Paddy Joe Power

George Kiely

Bill Foley

John Riordan.[43]

According to one of the original members, Paddy Joe Power:

"The column had its base, usually, at Comeragh, which is on the eastern foothills of the Comeragh Mountains. This position was particularly suitable because of the protection afforded by the mountain district into which we could and did retire with safety when hard-pressed by much superior enemy forces. The Comeragh area also had the advantage of enabling us to see the military moving down in the lower ground, especially at night, when the light from their lorries could be easily seen."[44]

Such a sanctuary was badly needed; there were one hundred and fifty British troops based eight miles to the south, with three hundred more based twenty miles to the east. A later member, Andy Kirwan, noted:

"I have mentioned Comeragh frequently because this district, from which the neighbouring range of mountains is named, afforded almost complete immunity from surprise attacks by the enemy. It was possible for us to see from Comeragh, enemy forces moving down in the lowlands and should they show signs of approaching our position in strength, we could cross the

---

[43] Mansfield, James 'The Decies Brigade – 1920', *Capuchin Annual,* 1970.

[44] IMA BMH WS Patrick J. Power.

mountain range by paths known only to ourselves, and shelter in the Nire Valley which lies west of the Comeraghs, near the village of Ballymacarbery."[45]

According to James Mansfield:

"The column was continually on the move through Comeragh, The Nire, Colligan, and the Drum hills. George Lennon led the column, which was under the overall command of Pax Whelan and brigade staff. Lennon spent some time studying tactics with other Munster columns and considered the Decies column to be among the best ... Men on the run slept in the open or stayed at houses such as Walshes of Ballyduff, Walshes of Ballymullagh, Mansfields of Crowbally, Cullinanes of Kilmacthomas, Powers of Glen and Powers of Garryduff. Mansfields put up men in a small loft over the kitchen and a large one in the yard.

"Men also slept in the kitchen settle or on sacks before the glowing embers of the open fire. Farmers such as Mike Mansfield of Crowbally sometimes bought equipment for the column out of their own pockets ... On entering a house the column men often scanned the skyline, i.e., the pieces of bacon hanging from the ceiling hooks, in order to gauge how well equipped a house was to feed them. The table at Powers of Garryduff was of such quality that this house was known as the 'Gresham'."[46]

Despite the long distances that the ASUs covered on foot, few of the column possessed boots, most wearing ordinary civilian shoes that sustained a great deal of punishment. Tom McGrath in Kilmacthomas usually repaired these gratis; quite often Pat

---

[45] IMA BMH WS Andrew Kirwan.

[46] Mansfield, James 'The Decies Brigade – 1920', *Capuchin Annual,* 1970.

Keating's mother would bring six pairs of shoes at a time for repair, while the Keating sisters often did the column's laundry.[47]

On rare occasions, the ASU was able to make use of motor transport. 'Nipper' McCarthy was not only an experienced driver at a time when this was a rare skill, but a mechanic as well. Andy Kirwan became the ASU transport officer, responsible for requisitioning motor vehicles which were not only scarce but also required a permit from the British authorities, naturally only granted to those whom the British deemed 'trustworthy'. By his own account:

"Whenever the old Model T Ford refused to function, I visited the house of one of the gentry who I knew had a car and commandeered it for the job in hand at the time ... it was never necessary to use guns. Indeed, we rarely had even to produce them. We requested use of the cars 'for the IRA' and we got them. In every case, we returned the cars when their purpose was served except where exceptional circumstances prevented us."[48]

The column's armament for now was paltry; it consisted of two Lee-Enfield rifles (one of Boer War vintage), an old German Mauser and a single shot police issue carbine. There were also a few shotguns and revolvers.[49] Andy Kirwan remembered that:

"The arms dump at Comeragh was the one most frequently used by the West Waterford flying column. It comprised a cave in the

---

[47] Keating, Lena, *The Keatings of Comeragh* (undated memoir).

[48] IMA BMH WS Andrew Kirwan.

[49] NLI FOD 31,150 (Activities – Waterford brigade).

mountainside, covered with bushes and well-nigh impossible to find except by those of us who knew its exact location."

Later, the West Waterford ASU acquired its own doctor, when young Dr Joe Walsh of Bunmahon volunteered his services, even sometimes accompanying the column on actions.

The first ambush by Lennon's column took place on 9 October at Brown's Pike, three miles north-west of Dungarvan on the road to Cappoquin. Eight Volunteers were involved, including Mick Mansfield, who later related:

"The position was on high ground affording good cover and overlooked the roadway. A short distance on the Dungarvan side of the position was a railway level crossing. Word was received that a lorry with RIC men and Black and Tans had gone towards Cappoquin on a raid earlier in the day and an attack on the lorry was planned for the return journey. Our men, under George Lennon, vice OC of the brigade, took up positions late in the evening. There were a few rifles in the party and some shotguns, possibly also some revolvers. The time would be approximately 6 p.m. When the approach of the enemy was reported, the level crossing gates were closed to halt the progress of the lorry, and when the latter ran into the ambush position fire was opened by our men. The driver of the lorry (who was not hit) accelerated, crashed his car through the gates of the level crossing and drove on out of high speed out of rifle range. I have a recollection that one of our lads threw a home-made bomb at the lorry, but I cannot say with what effect. I do not know whether the British suffered any casualties. None of our boys was hit in the exchange of shots."[50]

According to a newspaper report:

"The lorry returned to Dungarvan and in a short time two lorries laden with military and police went to the scene of the attack and made a minute search but could find no trace of the attackers. They searched the public house close by and all the people that were there. That night raids and searches were made in several houses in town and the parties all closely questioned, but beyond this nothing of any note took place."[51]

There was no reprisal by crown forces. Following the ambush, the flying column withdrew to the village of Modeligo to avoid being encircled by the crown forces' search operation. Arriving after nightfall and carrying some weapons and ammunition in a pony trap, the small column proceeded to the Catholic curate's house where according to George Kiely, they had a close shave with the British army:

"On peering around the gatepost we saw the lights of a lorry and a British officer taking soldiers in to raid a farmhouse a short distance down the road from us. When we spotted the raiders, we immediately rushed up the avenue and told the rest of the boys. Pat Keating gave instructions to have the guns and ammunition taken out of the pony trap and hidden in the laurels growing along the avenue. George Lennon, the column OC, told the priest of what was happening and then he and the remainder of us ran quickly into a turnip field close to the priest's house. We had no sooner

---

[50] IMA BMH MS Michael J. Mansfield.

[51] *Munster Express*, Ambush Near Dungarvan, 16 October 1920.

thrown ourselves down in the field when we heard the military come up the avenue and we were near enough to see the officer when the priest opened the door. I had my rifle with me and I remember quite well training it on that officer if he made a move in our direction."[52]

The priest assured the British officer that there were no armed men in the area after which the military party moved on. The column spent the night in local farmhouses.

On 1 November 1920, George Lennon led the West Waterford flying column in a spectacular ambush at Piltown Cross.

James Mansfield said:

"Late in October 1920, George Lennon and the nucleus of the flying column were in the Old Parish district when a conference was held as to the best means of enticing the British out of Youghal and ambushing them at Piltown. It was finally decided that a feint attack be made by our lads on Ardmore RIC barracks and on the marine post at Ardmore, but that the attack should be a sustained one on this occasion. This, it was hoped, would draw the military out from Youghal. All Souls night - 1st November – was the date fixed for this occasion."

It was decided to lay the ambush at Piltown Cross, the old name for the village of Kinsalebeg. According to Mansfield: 'Piltown Cross is about two miles north-east of Youghal and three miles from Ardmore, the main Youghal–Dungarvan road being intersected at the point by the road leading from Clashmore to Monatrea'.

---

[52] IMA BMH WS George C. Kiely.

According to John Riordan:

"Before the ambush took place I went with George Lennon, the brigade vice commandant, to the Piltown area to select the most suitable place for the proposed attack. I decided that the ground in the neighbourhood of Piltown Cross was the most likely spot from our point of view. Thick hedges bounded the main road here and the ground inside the hedges was slightly higher than the road. At the cross itself was a field which sloped up from the cross and had cover for a firing party to engage the enemy in the front as he came along the road from Youghal. The placing of our men that night were as follows: about a dozen men with four or five rifles and the rest with shotguns occupied the high ground overlooking Piltown Cross and facing westwards to Youghal. About ten shotguns were inside the hedge of the west side of the road and about twenty to forty yards from the cross on the Youghal side.

"On a bitterly cold night, the preparations for the ambush began. There was little room for error; if the expected British force was not caught properly in the IRA 'killing zone', the ambush party armed almost entirely with shotguns would find themselves in an open battle with British soldiers with Lee-Enfield rifles, with disastrous results inevitable."

Mick Mansfield recounted:

"At about 8 p.m. we took up positions at Piltown Cross with George Lennon in charge and myself second in command. I remember placing the shotgun men in positions behind the hedge at the Cross and on high ground overlooking the Cross. I handed two cartridges to each shotgun man to supplement whatever small supply he already had. I was armed with a Lee-Enfield rifle and a revolver."

Pakeen Whelan remembered:

"Pat Keating, Jim Mansfield ... and I were detailed to carry out the feint attack at Ardmore along with the local company. On the night of November 1st 1920 [about 7 p.m.], the three of us went by bicycle to Ardmore. I carried two grenades with the detonators out of them. When we reached Ardmore and had a chat with the local Company Captain, Jim Mansfield and he proceeded to place men in firing positions near the RIC barracks. When this was done I inserted the detonators into the grenades and handed one grenade to Pat Keating. Pat and I walked up the village street until we were immediately outside the barrack door, when Pat threw his grenade in through the fanlight. I got mine in also. When the grenades exploded we ran to a position with cover nearby. Jim Mansfield joined us. The Ardmore company then opened up on the barracks with shotguns. The RIC replied with rifle and machine-gun fire and sent up Verey lights. A party of British Marines stationed in the coastguard station about half a mile to the south also joined in with rifles and Hotchkiss [machine-gun]. When we saw the Verey lights go up we considered our job in Ardmore done and immediately left for Piltown Cross."

Among the shotgun party, lining the road at the ambush position, were Michael Curran and three other men from Ring village. Curran remembered; 'as we lay in our positions, shivering with cold and excitement, the Verey lights went rocketing into the sky from the besieged position at Ardmore. The suspense was now beginning to get on the nerves of our men'.

Keating, Mansfield and Whelan cycled hard over the rough road and hilly terrain, arriving at the ambush position after 10 p.m. Whelan collected a rifle and joined the main position on the road, Mansfield taking position behind it. While the telephone wires between Ardmore and Dungarvan had been cut, the lines to Youghal had been left intact.

James Mansfield said:

"The scouts on duty had been reporting the movements of the British garrison in Youghal. 'Lights out' had been sounded in the barracks at the usual time. At 11 p.m. or thereabouts, the scouts reported resumed activity within the barracks. Lights, they said, began to show there, to be followed by the sound of the buzzing of motor engines."

In Youghal, the odds were building in favour of the ambushers. Incredibly, the British military garrison had no serviceable vehicles available and were forced to commandeer a civilian lorry, being obliged to break into a garage to do so.

James Mansfield continued:

"A little later – about 11.45 p.m. – further reports from the scouts indicated that the British were leaving Youghal. Ten minutes later, the scouts passed on the message ' Here they come'. One lorry of British military appeared out of the darkness heading for the ambush point and ran right up to the barricade."

Michael Curran recounted:

"As it came nearer, I could hear my heart beating a tattoo against my ribs, as I waited to receive my real baptism of fire. When the lorry was halfway through our lines the order to fire was given."

The shotguns fired first, followed immediately by the rifles and shotguns at the barricade. The opening volley split the quiet of the night so fiercely that it was clearly heard in Youghal across the Blackwater estuary. The lorry driver was first to be hit and his body thrown across the RIC man sitting beside him. The British were quickly overwhelmed; a few managed to fire wildly aimed shots, a few jumped from the vehicle and escaped across the fields.

Michael Curran:

"One Tommy [Private Albert Leigh] made a mad dash along the road, but was soon laid in his tracks by our marksmen. He was found to be mortally wounded and only lived a short time."

The young officer in charge of the British unit leaped from the truck and through the hedge and found himself lying among the IRA shotgun party.

Patrick Lynch remembered:

"Meanwhile, George Lennon, noticing the enemy panic and because their reply to our fire was negligible, ordered us out onto the road to charge the enemy at close quarters. We got on to the road and shouted to the soldiers to surrender. They shouted, 'we surrender', and our group moved closer to the lorry. Suddenly a shot was fired by one of the military – whether in panic or not, I could not say – but a few of us dived for cover in under the lorry and began firing up through the floor. Pandemonium again broke loose amongst the Tommies who ceased firing."

Jim Prendergast told a slightly different version:

"The order was given to us to cease fire. The Tommies were screaming and firing indiscriminately. The night was pitch dark. I shouted out to the military to 'get out and surrender' at the same time jumping out onto the road and again shouting to the soldiers to 'fall in'. While this was happening some of our lads again opened fire and I had to throw myself flat on the road, shouting 'cease fire, cease fire'. The firing stopped. I again ordered the military to 'fall in' which they did."

Pat Lynch said:

"George Lennon was looking for the British officer in charge when he (the officer) suddenly appeared as a prisoner, taken by some of our shotgun men. It happened that the officer got out of the lorry immediately the first volley was fired and scrambled through a hedge for safety, right into a position held by some of our lads. They promptly disarmed him."

John Riordan observed that:

"The officer ... looked so young that he appeared to be only a boy. Two British soldiers were dead, the driver and the man who had attempted to escape by the road. Another six were wounded. An attempt was made to drive the lorry away but it broke down after a short distance and was set on fire."

According to Nipper McCarthy (in an interview recorded by Sean Murphy in 1980): "There were two on the ground, two soldiers. And myself and Pakeen Whelan went over to them. I rose up their heads and he said an Act of Contrition into their ear."

Paddy Joe Power recorded:

"We rendered first aid to their wounded as best as we could and before we left the scene, George Lennon, our OC, got a horse and dray to enable the British to take their dead and wounded back to Youghal."

According to Jim Prendergast:

"The two captured RIC men, O'Neill and Prendiville, were taken a short distance up the Clashmore Road and told they would be shot unless they gave their word to resign from the RIC and were thereupon released."

It is said that when O'Neill resigned as soon as he returned to Youghal. Prendiville however, continued to serve in the RIC, with ultimately fatal consequences. It later transpired that only one British soldier had died that night at Piltown Cross; the driver had evidently survived. Private Albert Leigh (22) of the Hampshire Regiment was later laid to rest in the shadow of a 17th century dovecote in St Mary's Church in Broughton, Hampshire.

Eighteen Lee-Enfield rifles and two police carbines were captured, along with hundreds of rounds of ammunition and a quantity of grenades. The flying column, carrying the captured weapons, began the march back to the sanctuary of the Comeragh Mountains. Andy Kirwan did sterling work with his Model T Ford, making two journeys between Piltown and Comeragh to bring the captured weapons back to the column's base.[53]

The night after the ambush, British military headquarters in Parkgate (Dublin) released an official statement:

"On receipt of information last night that Ardmore police barracks had been attacked and set on fire, a relief party of one officer and ten other ranks left Youghal in a motor lorry for Ardmore. They ran into an ambush where the road had been blocked and fire was opened on them by about 120 civilians. One soldier was killed and two wounded. The rest were disarmed and the lorry captured."[54]

However the *Dungarvan Observer* later noted that:

---

[53] IMA BMH WS Michael J. Mansfield, James Mansfield, John Riordan, Patrick Whelan, Michael Curran, Patrick Lynch, James Prendergast, Patrick J. Power, Andrew Kirwan.

[54] *Munster Express*, 'Soldier Killed and Two Wounded in Co. Waterford', 6 November 1920.

"An official report from Dublin Castle states that firing occurred between military and civilians on Friday night in Youghal, and that a private of the Hampshire regiment was shot dead in a shop. One civilian was wounded. An attack on the barracks was repulsed."[55]

Several off-duty soldiers of the Hampshires ran riot in the town of Youghal four nights after the Piltown ambush, attacking local civilians and business premises. At one stage, armed soldiers even attacked the RIC barracks. The *Munster Express* noted:

There is hardly a town in the country where a better feeling existed between the people and the military, and the occurrences are generally deplored. The commandant, Major Bowen, has always endeavoured to preserve the peace of the town and district, and all classes and shades have expressed appreciation of his efforts.[56]

James Prendergast recounts:

"Following the Piltown ambush, we remained in the Comeragh district for several weeks where we received intensive training in the use of the rifle from John Riordan from Dungarvan, a member of the column and an ex-British soldier. Every man in the column was supplied with a rifle now and each man had about 200 rounds of rifle ammunition."

Fully equipped with Lee-Enfield rifles, the West Waterford column was becoming a force to be reckoned with, and they were in action again a short time later.

---

[55] *Dungarvan Observer*, 13 November 1920.

[56] *Munster Express*, 'Scenes in Youghal', 18 November 1920.

According to Mick Shalloe:

"About a fortnight after the Piltown Cross ambush, George Lennon, Pat Keating, Paddy Reilly, Jim Prendergast, Pakeen Whelan and myself – all from the column – were in the district of Rockfield, between Cappoquin and Dungarvan [near Cappagh]. We were moving across country when, in the distance, we spotted a lorry load of military approaching on the main Cappoquin–Dungarvan road. George Lennon, the column OC, ordered us hurriedly to take up positions to attack. The ground around us offered little cover, but we got down and flaked into the lorry as it went by. One of the lads chucked a home-made bomb at it which exploded, wounding some of the Tommies. The lorry proceeded some distance and the soldiers got out. We engaged them for upwards of half an hour when George Lennon ordered us to retreat, as we were badly outnumbered and were firing from a very disadvantageous position. We suffered no casualties in this scrap but I know the British had several men wounded – what number, I cannot say. The ambush occurred early in the forenoon."

In the autumn of 1920, Mo Roche 'was asked by Eddie Power to go with him to ambush troops expected (from Dungarvan) to raid the house of Ned Power of Glen (Kilmacthomas), a brigade/battalion officer. We reached a spot at Kilminnin Bridge which is about eight miles east of Dungarvan and on the coast road, late at night. When we got there, we met the West Waterford brigade OC, George Lennon, and about fifteen men armed with rifles. 'Nipper' McCarthy was there carrying bombs. Andy Kirwan of Boatstrand, Bunmahon, the column motor driver, together with Ned Power of Glen, the man whose house was to be raided by the British, was also there. I was armed with my own Smith and Wesson revolver and about a dozen rounds of ammunition. Eddie Power and I were placed in position on a height overlooking the bridge on the Dungarvan (west) side. On our left were about five riflemen and others with hand grenades. Andy Kirwan with about six riflemen and shotgun men was in position on a grass covered big rock at the Stradbally (east) side of the bridge. We were all set to give the British a hot reception, but although we waited until after two o'clock in the morning, the enemy didn't turn up and we got orders to disperse ... About the same time, George Lennon, brigade vice OC, Mick Shalloe and Jim P[rendergast], all of Dungarvan, sent for me and said we were going to have a go at a military lorry expected to pass through Kilmacthomas. Lennon and Shalloe had grenades to drop into the lorry, but although we waited more than two hours, on the railway bridge under which the road ran, no lorry came along. According to the account of John Riordan:

"I went by motor one day [21 November 1921] into Cappoquin with Mick Mansfield and Kirby. 'Nipper' McCarthy of Dungarvan drove us. We were all armed with revolvers ... when we arrived in Cappoquin and were driving slowly through it, we spotted two RIC men on the street. It was most likely that they spotted us too and knew we were strangers and up to something. We opened fire on them with revolvers and they replied, also with revolvers. One of the RIC men dropped. We later heard he was killed in the exchange of shots. 'Nipper' McCarthy then put on speed and drove us quickly out of town and towards Dungarvan, where we left the car."

The dead RIC man was later named as Constable Isaac Rea (19) from West Cork, who actually died of his wounds on the 28

December. A young woman had her lower leg shattered by a stray bullet.[57]

At about this time, Andy Kirwan and two other men of the column were driven into Ardmore 'to shoot a particularly obnoxious RIC man who used to act as a spotter for the British military parties in the Ardmore area'. Arriving on a Saturday night, the trio waited outside the Catholic church the following morning to shoot the policeman as he left Sunday mass; although three uniformed RIC men emerged, they and the IRA men exchanged only suspicious stares. Kirwan later claimed that the policeman had not been properly identified; but they may not have wanted to shoot someone outside a Catholic church. Kirwan later recounted:

"When we returned from Ardmore that Sunday night and met George Lennon, the column OC at Ballyduff, he enquired how we had got on. We told him what had happened, and he replied, 'No matter! We got one in Cappoquin today'. That same day [27 November 1920] he and Mick Mansfield had gone by motor, driven by 'Nipper' McCarthy, a Dungarvan IRA man on the column, to Cappoquin to shoot the District Inspector of Police, who was particularly hostile to the IRA in that area. Lennon told me he had information that the District Inspector was in the local hotel. Mick Mansfield and he went into the hotel but failed to find the DI there. Just as they were leaving, an RIC man entered, apparently having seen them leaving the car, and noticing that they were strangers, thought he would investigate. Lennon and Mansfield shot the policeman there and then and made off in their

---

[57] IMA BMH WS James Prendergast, Michael Shalloe, Moses Roche, John Riordan; *Munster Express*, 'Dungarvan Lawlessness', 4 Oct 1921.

car, being chased by Auxiliaries who were in Cappoquin at the time. The RIC man's name, I remember, was Quirke."

Mick Mansfield's own recollection of this incident is as follows:

"With George Lennon, the column OC, and Pat Keating of Comeragh, I went into Cappoquin one evening to shoot an obnoxious Black and Tan. We went by motor, all of us armed with revolvers. When we arrived outside the town, we left our car and came in on foot. There were a group of Tans on the street at the time when we had to pass. We did so and saw that the Tan we wanted was not amongst the group. It was decided to wait a while, so we went into Walshe's Hotel for tea. After tea, we rose to leave the hotel and in the doorway, blocking our entry to the street, was a uniformed RIC man. We immediately concluded that our presence in the town had been noticed and that we were trapped. We drew our revolvers and fired, killing the RIC man. Running out to the roadway, we ran into a party of Tans on whom we opened fire. They replied with revolvers and grenades. We made with all haste to where our car was located and with great good luck managed to evade our pursuers and got back to Comeragh in safety. I cannot remember the name of the RIC man we killed that evening in Cappoquin. I think his name was O'Rourke, or Quirke, but I am not at all certain."[58]

Constable Maurice Quirk (33) was shot twice in the lower abdomen and was left wounded in the street. Two local men quickly came to his aid and carried him into the hotel. One individual unfortunately gave him a glass of whiskey and almost certainly sealed his fate; this is almost the worst possible thing for abdominal wounds. Quirk ('a genial strapping Kerryman')

---

[58] IMA BMH WS Andrew Kirwan, Michael J. Mansfield.

underwent surgery the following afternoon but passed away about 45 hours after being shot. He left a widow and three children.[59]

Although the shootings of these RIC men were not premeditated and Cappoquin was not a soft target (garrisoned by twelve armed RIC men and twenty Black and Tans), local IRA man M.V. O'Donoghue (later President of the GAA) was moved to describe the shootings of Rea and Quirk in scathing terms: 'the brutally callous nature of this shooting did little to exalt the status or raise the credit or the character of Republican military prestige in the district.' Quirk was a popular character locally (his funeral cortege attended by 'a very large number' of local people) and was even regarded as friendly to the Republican cause.[60]

On 2 December 1920, James Mansfield received information that a patrol of six RIC men would be stopping at the bridge over the Blackwater the following night to deliver a pension payment to the ex-policeman in charge of operating the swing bridge. Eight men of the Ardmore battalion armed with rifles took up position on the hill overlooking the bridge, and when the RIC patrol appeared on the bridge, the IRA men opened fire, killing one RIC man and wounding two others. The Hampshires in Youghal quickly sent reinforcements to the scene and Mansfield's men withdrew. It soon transpired that the dead RIC man was Constable Prendiville who had been captured at Piltown Cross a month earlier. After this incident, the British army had the bridge

---

[59] Court of Inquiry into Death of Constable Maurice Quirk 1 Dec 1920; *Cork Examiner*, 'Funeral of Constable Quirke' 2 December 1920.

[60] IMA BMH WS Michael V. O'Donoghue.

locked open until the end of hostilities. This effectively left the Royal Marines at Ardmore without hope of reinforcements and involved them in a battle of attrition with the local IRA.[61]

In December 1920 the first ambush took place in East Waterford. In late November, crown forces had carried out a sweep in Waterford city which resulted in the arrests of the IRA brigade commander and several other officers. Later that month, a brigade council meeting elected Paddy Paul to the post of brigade commander, a post he accepted with understandable reluctance. The East Waterford brigade never comprised more than 400 Volunteers (less than half the strength of an average IRA brigade) with weapons for less than thirty. Although the political climate in Waterford was slowly changing, as evidenced by the election of Dr Vincent White to the post of mayor the previous January, the Redmondite influence was still very strong and hostile to the republican movement.

Paul wasted no time in organising his first action. At the end of November he and a group of five other men, all equipped with Lee-Enfield rifles, took up position in the early hours of the morning near Whitfield on the main road from Waterford to Cork with the intention of having 'a crack at any enemy forces who might pass along the road'. This group included Jim Power and a third Great War veteran: Mick Bishop of Tramore who had served as a lance-corporal in the 1st Battalion of the Irish Guards, a crack unit that had suffered appalling casualties on the western front. Bishop had distinguished himself by winning the Military Medal twice in 1918, and on his discharge had succeeded in bringing his rifle back home with him. On joining the Irish Volunteers, he had been appointed captain of the Tramore Company of East

---

[61] IMA BMH WS James Mansfield; *Munster Express*, 'Police Patrol Attacked in Co. Waterford', 11 December 1920.

Waterford's 2nd Battalion, a unit that comprised only a dozen men. Conspicuous by his absence from the group was Paul's vice commandant Willie Keane, probably the brigade's most active officer; it was largely through Keane's efforts that the group at Whitfield possessed the Lee-Enfield rifles that they were using, but it appeared that some friction existed between Keane and Paul.

At 10 a.m., according to Jim Power, 'three military lorries full of British soldiers came into view. At the very moment the lorries appeared, there happened to be three or four carts with civilians driving to the creamery also on the road. We decided not to open fire as if we did it was almost certain that the civilians would either be caught accidentally in the crossfire, or most likely, they would be shot afterwards by the British military when the return was over. We left the ambush position shortly afterwards'. This concern for local civilians was well placed; a guerrilla movement depends greatly on the support of the local populace for its existence.

On 13 December, a slightly different group that still included the three Great War veterans took up position on the Waterford–Cork road at Ballyduff, near the village of Kilmeaden. It was a good position for a small-scale ambush, offering good cover, fields of fire and lines of retreat. That morning two military lorries appeared on the road from Waterford. By his own account, Paul revealed something of his propensity to make rash decisions:

"I knew from previous talks I had with Power that he was excessively concerned always about the safety of the civilian population. In any talk we had of projected action, Power was always worried about damage to civilian property or injury to civilians. I had observed the fact that there were cars going to the local creamery but I said nothing, knowing Power's feelings on such things, but as the military lorries approached he turned to me and said, 'there is a creamery car on the road, Paddy. What shall we do?' This donkey and cart with some milk churns in it had appeared in the middle of the road between us and the military lorries. Knowing it would be fatal to have any discussion on the matter with Power, I made no reply to his remark but, raising my rifle and taking aim at the driver of the first lorry, I fired and my shot was taken as a signal by the others who also opened fire. In any case, with such a fleeting target, there was no time for a discussion as to what was to be done. We just did it."

One of the trucks swerved to a halt, the officer commanding the convoy having suffered a wound in the back. As the escorting soldiers began returning fire, the ambush party were startled to realise that the trucks were in fact carrying the IRA men recently arrested in Waterford, including Liam Walsh, the former brigade commander. With only ten rounds of ammunition apiece to start with, the ambushers withdrew. Paul acknowledged: 'I was pleased to learn that the officer commanding the convoy was not killed. Liam Walsh told me about this and that the officer's name was McNamara. Also another officer with the convoy acted very roughly towards the prisoners following the ambush. He would have given them a bad time but for the intervention of McNamara who, notwithstanding his wound, would not allow the prisoners to be ill-treated'.[62]

In early December, Paddy Ormonde, sick with influenza, returned to his home in Dungarvan where he was quickly captured by the 'Buffs'. 'I was taken prisoner to Dungarvan barracks where I was

_____

[62] IMA BMH WS Patrick Paul, James Power; *Munster Express*, 'Soldiers Ambushed in Co. Waterford', 18 December 1920; UKNA WO/372/23 Medal Card 11794 Lance-Corporal James Power.

closely questioned by an officer named Captain Thomas ... Needless to say, I gave no information, so I was promptly thrown into a cell, with nothing on which I could lie. The walls were weeping water, which did not tend to improve my very low physical state at the time.'

Ormonde spent three weeks in Dungarvan being used as a hostage by raiding parties, who would bring him handcuffed with them to deter ambush. He was thus present when the 'Buffs' raided the Mansfield house in Old Parish. Three young men tried to escape; a clerical student named Power was wounded but was later released. Charlie Mansfield (brother of James and Mick) and Tommy Mooney of Ardmore were arrested and in late December all three were taken by train to Fermoy and then to Cork prison. They were later transported with fifty or sixty other prisoners by naval destroyer to Belfast, where they were pelted with nuts and bolts by unionist shipyard workers. They were then taken to Ballykinlar Camp where they were interned for the duration of hostilities.[63]

In mid-December, Pat Lynch was sent into Dungarvan to deliver a message to Pax Whelan. He ran into a military patrol led by his old 'friend' Captain Marshall and was arrested. After a week in Dungarvan barracks he was transferred first to Fermoy and then to Cork Prison. Like Ormonde, he endured a fifteen hour sea journey to Belfast, where Belfast shipyard workers also pelted his group, before being transferred to Ballykinlar.

George Kiely was also lost to the column at this time having contracted a serious case of scabies, a skin disease with which members of flying columns were often afflicted and grimly

---

[63] IMA BMH WS Patrick Ormonde.

referred to as 'the republican itch'. He recovered by February and was attached to an ASU in South Tipperary.

Edmond Power of Kilmacthomas joined the column in the Tay Valley at this time; recalling that: 'Intensive training was carried out to enable the men to acquit themselves properly when they went into action. Skirmishing practice was carried out by daytime, and general revolver and rifle exercise took place daily. The men were billeted at night in farmhouses within a mile radius, the local company doing scouting duty'.[64]

On the afternoon of 7 January 1921, Lennon's column gathered near Stradbally where Andy Kirwan had organised vehicles; only three cars were initially available, and carrying fifteen men, the small convoy set out for Bunmahon where a rendezvous had been arranged with an officer of East Waterford's Dunhill battalion. The West Waterford ASU was being brought in at the request of Paddy Paul to augment his own forces in a large scale ambush being planned for that night near Tramore. Jim Power, OC Second (Dunhill) battalion, was gathering his own forces (approx. fourteen men armed with rifles and shotguns) at Reisk, about a mile from Dunhill to commence a cross-county march to Tramore to commence at 5 p.m. It was intended that Martin Cullinane, the man he had sent to Bunmahon would guide Lennon's column to this point, where both groups would march to Tramore together.

In 1921 however, motor vehicles were not always noted for reliability, and despite having the mechanical skills of 'Nipper' McCarthy available, the convoy suffered several mishaps on the road and took several hours to travel the road from Stradbally to Bunmahon. Cullinane waited anxiously until 5.40 p.m. and then

---

[64] IMA BMH WS Patrick Lynch, George C. Kiely, Edmond Power.

returned to the Reisk Road where he met Jim Power and his party, and they set off on a trek of five miles across the dark fields to Tramore.

At this time, Paddy Paul took up position at the site of the intended ambush at Pickardstown, a mile north of Tramore. Apart from the West Waterford ASU and the Dunhill battalion, Paul had arranged for another twenty men from the Waterford City battalion to join him. He had directed that that the entire force should be in position at Pickardstown by 6 p.m., but had not allowed for the length of time that a night march cross country can take.

Willy Keane, Paul's vice commandant, was ordered to gather twenty men from the city battalion and march them cross-country to the metal bridge at Pickardstown. He had not been briefed about the forthcoming ambush even though Paul had notified Jerry Cronin (by now CO of the city battalion's 'A' company) of the forthcoming ambush and had shown him a sketch of the proposed dispositions.

Keane later recalled:

"The men selected by me were paraded in the grounds of the Mental Hospital, Waterford, at about 7 p.m. on January 6th (sic) 1921 and I issued to each man a shotgun and about forty cartridges. I myself was armed with a Webley .45 revolver and about thirty rounds of ammunition. On reconsideration, I now recall handing out about six Lee-Enfield rifles which would make our strength fourteen shotguns and six rifles."

One of this group, Nicky Whittle remembered:

"Willy Keane, the vice brigadier, distributes the ammunition and the guns. I get eleven rounds of buckshot for my shotgun. The vice brigadier in a low voice speaks a few words of guidance to the men: he tells them they have some distance to travel and a tough job to do. He announces that all men will follow the call of a curlew, which will be given at regular intervals by Tom Brennan, who knows the district intimately. We avoid the roads and trudge through the fields, and the whisper goes around that our destination is to be near Tramore."

Willie Keane's account was written in 1954, Whittle's ten years later.

The majority of actions of the Irish War of Independence were not properly recorded for several years after the events, with the result that many details were confused or forgotten. Due to the circumstances of the Tramore ambush however, an internal inquiry was ordered by the IRA which involved the taking of statements from several of the key participants only a few months after the incident. These give an unusually vivid picture of the events of that night.

At 7 p.m., Paddy Paul was still waiting at Pickardstown alone, except for Jim Power's vice commandant. He later recalled that the ambush he was planning:

".. had as its primary objective the securing of much-needed arms and ammunition and secondly, the drawing away of the enemy from more hard-pressed areas ... I wanted to have this action in the heart of an area which was regarded by the enemy as absolutely quiet and safe. The terrain thereabouts was absolutely flat and unsuitable for our operations in daylight and this fact therefore compelled us to adopt a night attack, although I realised that night operations are always dangerous because of the inability to control forces and the likelihood of their becoming scattered and detached. There was also a very good road network in this area which made it an easy matter for the enemy, equipped with motor vehicles, to surround us ... it was these considerations which influenced the carrying out of the Tramore ambush as a night attack."

Paul described the details of the plan:

"The general plan was to get the enemy out of barracks in a position on the road where they could be boxed in and attacked from four sides at close range ... the ambush party were arranged in four separate parties, each occupying one position on one side."

The site of the intended ambush was close to the Waterford–Tramore railway line which ran directly from south to north at this point. Just to the east of this line and running alongside was the 'new' Waterford– Tramore roadway which abruptly turned west and passed through the railway embankment under the well-known 'Metal Bridge' before passing uphill to Tramore Racecourse. Before the road reached the metal bridge, two roads branched away from it, one (the Old Waterford Road) travelling north-east, the other travelling south-east to Ballinattin. Paul had originally planned to deploy his forces as follows: the West Waterford ASU in a position on the 'Glen Road' west of the metal bridge, deployed near a barricade. The ASU were the best armed and most experienced men in the ambush party, and Paul intended that they initiate the ambush. This position did not offer a particularly good field of fire and Lennon later redeploy his men slightly. A shotgun party of ten men from Dunhill battalion were positioned on the railway line overlooking the Waterford–Tramore road. These men had a very limited amount of ammunition; one source suggests no more than two shotgun shells each. In 1921 Paul claimed that 'orders were given to all men [at Pickardstown] not to fire until first lorry had struck barricade'. In 1953 however, he claimed that these ten men, 'were instructed to pour whatever number of shots they could into the lorries as they came near enough to them and then withdraw.

This confusion of orders would have far reaching consequences that night'.

Another group of men from both Dunhill and Waterford City battalions placed along the Ballinattin Road, overlooked the metal bridge, which was separated from the main road by very marshy ground. This group was divided into ten men with shotguns, close to the main road, led by Jerry Cronin, and six riflemen further uphill. Another four riflemen from Waterford city were 'manning the position on the road junction between the old and the new roads. These men would be in a position to bring enfilade fire to bear on the rear of the enemy troops, presuming that these came into the position as we had it arranged they should'.

Paul's preparations for what became known locally as the Pickardstown ambush have been described as 'elaborate'. A modern-day soldier in Ireland's special forces who reviewed the dispositions observed:

"This plan is far too complex – the whole principle of an ambush is Keep It Simple. Command and control, vital in a situation which can go wrong very quickly, is non-existent here. The commander would have had poor contact with even the group on the Ballinattin Road, and none at all with the groups on the railway and beyond it. No plan survives contact with the enemy, and this particular plan practically required the enemy to be co-operative to work. It might be necessary in a large-scale ambush to have the troops dispersed, but here they're spread so thinly that the British would have had no trouble overwhelming two of the three groups – incidentally, the three main groups couldn't even see each other, let alone support each other. Most of all, the commander has missed the best tactical ground here – the railway embankment. An ambush party here would have had good cover and an excellent field of fire. A more experienced leader would have put all the rifles here with the shotguns as flank security, and nearly twenty Lee-Enfield rifles in trained hands were capable of putting down a hail of fire, enough to drive some of the British unit off the road and onto the marshy ground where it would have been difficult to reorganise. Last of all, this ambush took place at night, which unless your men are very well trained, led and deployed, can be a recipe for disaster. But overall, this whole ambush was a disaster waiting to happen."[65]

Later in 1921 Liam Lynch, by then one of the IRA's most proficient guerrilla leaders, reviewed Paul's plans and noted: 'Waterford No. 1 Brigade should not have undertaken such a large operation for the following reasons (a) Operation too big as men had never before fired a shot; (b) Men had neither discipline, morale or arms for such a fight, especially night fighting'. Lynch also commented on Paul's failure to make use of the vital tactical ground offered by the railway embankment: 'Waterford No. 2 men [West Waterford ASU] should have been more at rear of barricade along No. 2 position [railway embankment] – as it was the fighting fell only to the shotgun men who naturally did not fight at all.'

Paddy Paul was a young man with experience of war but little of command. He undoubtedly possessed many leadership qualities that included a drive and determination that was sorely needed in East Waterford at the time. IRA chief of staff Richard Mulcahy later noted of him: 'personally, I could not get any good of any officer in Waterford, or get any scrap of organisation in the brigade as a whole, until the present brigade commandant took

---

[65] Interview with Sergeant 'X', Army Ranger Wing.

command some months ago. He has put the brigade on something like a satisfactory footing, I think'. Paul however, had not been trained in guerrilla warfare by the British army nor had he the benefit of the sort of training course that Liam Lynch had organised in Glenville the previous September. Neither was he a natural tactician.

A party of men from Dunhill reached the Pickardstown area and arrived at Tramore Racecourse after 7 p.m., where another six men from Jim Power's 2nd Battalion were waiting. On arrival, Paul ordered Power 'to take all the men into a field where he divided them into parties and gave them their orders ... We then proceeded towards Metal Bridge where we expected to meet party from [City] battalion. On the way we were told that the B[lack] & T[an]s had returned to barracks. The party from No. 1 Battalion came along and we were put into positions'.

This party arrived after nine o'clock. Three men from this group were deemed to be under the influence of alcohol and were not allowed to participate in the ambush. William Keane and three others went to work preparing a barricade, thirty yards west of the Metal Bridge, using farm carts borrowed locally. Originally, according to Jim Power, 'the idea was to go to the Marine Hotel, Tramore, and fire on the Black and Tans there. The Tans would send word to Waterford of the attack and we would then ambush the enemy force coming out from Waterford to relieve the Tans in the Marine Hotel.' Since the Black and Tans had already returned to barracks for the night, the plan was modified; a small party moved in to Tramore and attack the RIC barracks in the middle of town, in the expectation that reinforcements would be dispatched from Waterford. Soon afterwards, the West Waterford flying column finally arrived, parking the cars on the Glen Road a mile from the ambush site. George Lennon subsequently recounted:

'We had several mishaps on the road and didn't get to place of ambush until near 11 p.m.'.

William Keane recalled that 'Pax Whelan inspected the guns and ammunition of the men from the East Waterford brigade and placed them in position for attack. George Lennon, vice commandant of the West Waterford brigade was also there and I remember him inspecting the guns of the Dunhill company before putting them into position'.

Lennon's 1921 statement (as dictated to Pax Whelan) continues:

"I met commdt of No. 1 [Paul] and went to a position he allotted us on Glen Road. Our position commanded the Railway Bridge and road up from it, a barricade was placed on road about thirty yards from bridge. I placed an outpost of two shotguns and a rifleman down near barricade to protect our right. I was given to understand that first lorries were to be allowed up so far as barricade and we were to be the first to fire. When we had taken up positions a feint attack on barracks was decided, the object being to draw enemy. I gave commdt No. 1 Bde two men to help in attack."

Paddy Paul opted to lead the attack on Tramore RIC barracks personally – why he felt it was necessary to do this when his correct place was at his command post at the Ballinattin Road is not quite clear. Perhaps the insinuations of faint-heartedness on his part after the attack on Kill RIC barracks still rankled. Paul opted not only to lead the attack on Tramore barracks, but also to bring some of his most experienced men with him, including Jim Power, Mick Bishop and Pat Keating. Also in this party (all of whom had volunteered) were Martin Cullinane and Nicky Whittle.

Jim Power struck an ominous note when he related:

"Before I went to [RIC] barracks I went to men in position on railway to get a revolver. I asked the man in charge where his position was and what his orders were; he showed me his position and told me his orders were to fire on first lorry and then get away as best he could. The man in charge of riflemen on Ballinattin Road told me he had no orders at all."

Paddy Paul's account of the feint attack was as follows:

"A few of us went up to Tramore, which was about a mile from the ambush position, and began an attack on the RIC barracks there. This attack was merely a feint to induce the Tans inside to call for reinforcements and for this reason, we did not cut any wires. We left the telephonic communication intact so that they could ring up Waterford. A few men went in rear of the barracks but I don't think they were able to do anything there."

After the departure of Paul's group, the ambush party at Pickardstown settled in to wait. Most accounts describe this night as 'very cold' with a dark and starry sky. Already some men were becoming anxious; O'Neill, the man in charge of the rifle party on the Ballinattin Road later claimed:

"The late VC [Willie Keane] was on my right. I went to him and asked what were the signals for 'Open Fire, Cease Fire and Retreat', he said he didn't know but would find out. After a time I saw him again, but he didn't know signals. The commdt of No. 2 Brigade [Pax Whelan] then came up and I asked him if he knew what the signal to fire was and he told me to wait until the other parties had started and then to open fire. He also told me to be sure and keep any fire 'down' as I might be endangering men on the Railway Line by my fire."

George Lennon had clearly not been entirely happy with the position allocated to him, having moved his position slightly, while Pax Whelan had taken the eminently sensible step of walking the ambush position himself and had observed that there was a strong chance of two of the IRA positions firing on each other. As for the Dunhill men on the railway line, one later stated that 'I was told to fire on the first lorries and then get away'. According to another: 'I was ordered by brigade commandant [Paul] to fire on the first enemy lorry that approached'.

Back in Tramore, the attack on the RIC barracks was beginning. According to Nicky Whittle:

"Suddenly a Mills Bomb exploded in front of the barracks. It was Comdt Pat Keating, who in his socks had dashed across the road in front of the barracks and flung the bomb through the fanlight over the barrack door."

Paddy Paul remembered:

"Myself, Keating and another West Waterford man opened up fire on the front of the barracks. We could not get close to the door of the barracks because of the barbed wire which was in front of it but when our fire opened, the Tans inside returned it and after a while began to throw grenades out at us. The grenades came fairly close to us but in the position we were, we had cover from them. In the dark we could not even see them coming to us. The first intimation we had was when each one exploded ... After some time we concluded that it was time now to return to the ambush position so as to be ready to receive the enemy reinforcements when they arrived. Going down the road we met some of the men from the ambush position coming up to enquire about us."

The feint attack on the RIC barracks had taken about fifteen minutes. During the attack, one Black and Tan sustained a serious stomach wound. Nicky Whittle remembered:

"Our next job was to get back to the ambush centre as fast as possible. We moved at the double. On the way I am joined by a member of the West Waterford column [Pakeen Whelan]. As we run together, I pass him a couple of slices of bread. As he munches them he asks: 'what is the strength of the barrack garrison in Waterford? I reply 'about 300.' He flung away a crust he had been about to eat, and muttered 'Oh Cripes!'"

According to George Lennon's 1921 statement: 'After attack men returned and I put my two men into their positions. The commdt of No. 1 and some officers with him were near to my position at this time.' Pakeen Whelan and Nicky Whittle quickly took up their positions, Whittle and another man joining the shotgun party on the Ballinattin Road. It seems likely that a terse discussion then took place near the metal bridge between Paddy Paul and the others for ten minutes. It was now nearly fifteen minutes to midnight. Suddenly, according to Lennon: 'I saw glare of lights coming on Waterford Road. I told commdt of No. 1 to get back to his position as quick as he could, that military were coming, he ran towards it with the others who were with him'. These were the headlights of one of four Crossley tenders, carrying nearly forty soldiers of the Devonshire regiment, with a few RIC men acting as guides. The British had arrived with speed and in strength. This was twice the size of the force that Lennon had faced at Piltown Cross and Paddy Paul was not even at his post.

Based on the subsequent award of a decoration, the officer in charge of the British party was Lieutenant Frederick Charles Yeo. He was well known to the Waterford IRA, who almost invariably referred to him as a 'notorious blackguard' due to his penchant for beating captured IRA men. 'Notorious blackguard' or not, Yeo was a formidable enemy. As a private soldier, he had gone to war with the Royal Engineers in the second month of the First World War, and over the following three years he had been promoted to sergeant, winning the Military Medal along the way. He had been commissioned as an officer in late 1917.

According to one of the four IRA riflemen posted at the road junction between the old and new roads: 'we noticed glare of lorry lights on our rear coming on Old Tramore Road and a small Crossley tender passed going towards the Metal Bridge; when about twenty yards from Bridge it was fired on'.

One of the Dunhill men on the railway embankment later stated: 'I ordered my party to fire on first lorry and they did so. We then retreated. We fired about two shots per man'.

At the road junction, 'after about three minutes another lorry passed with no lights and stopped just beyond the Ballinattin Cross. I could hear shouting and someone saying "Come on you B-!" "Open Fire!" After a while we fired a few rounds down the road at first lorry'.

On the Ballinattin Road, Jerry Cronin 'waited until the men on flanking position on my right between the new and old Tramore Roads had fired then I opened fire'. The Devonshires were already deploying and returning fire. With the Dunhill men on the railway having already having withdrawn as ordered, the British concentrated their return fire on Cronin's shotgun party. Nicky Whittle recalled that 'a hail of bullets began to spatter all around us. All the guns in our section now opened up on a single lorry. In a matter of seconds gunfire was literally cutting the grass from off the top of the ditch from which we were firing'. By Jim Power's 1954 account:

"Whilst all this was going on, Bishop, Cullinane, Paul and I went across, under fire, to the rifle party engaged on the Ballinattin Road ... with great difficulty and under a cross-fire from our own men and the British we eventually made our way up to our comrades on the Ballinattin Road and took up position with our comrades there."

Positioned as they were Lennon and his column were not able to see the ongoing battle:

"[Paul] was only gone a few minutes when firing broke out from some of the positions opposite, I couldn't say from which one; it was probably directed at first lorry. The first lorry stopped at other side of bridge. The headlights were shining underneath the bridge. The other lorries seemed pretty far back, none of them came into our position at all. There was pretty heavy firing for about ten minutes from the other side of the embankment we threw a Verey light near first lorry on road, it showed a good light around but we couldn't see anything."

Back at the Ballinattin Road, things were going from bad to worse. According to the leader of the four riflemen at the road junction:

"Another lorry had now come behind us and we were in danger of being surrounded, and we took cover. Another lorry was now about one hundred yards further behind us. The enemy left lorries and were marching down the road; some of them stopped near us and we could hear them saying: 'There is an ambush here, we'll make Tramore pay for this!' They went in extended order to Ballinattin Road ... we retreated as our position was untenable."

Seconds later, thirty Devonshires were forming up at the road junction to begin an assault on the Ballinattin Road. Paul and his small group reached the road, between the shotgun party and the riflemen just as the position was becoming desperate. Paddy Paul recalled:

"Making a quick survey of the position I realised then that something had gone wrong because only the men on the Ballinattin Road and the road junction were engaged. The enemy lorries, or some of them, had not come into the ambush position and I could see some of them on the road in rear of our position ... as it was now, we were in serious danger of being surrounded by superior forces, so I passed the word on to withdraw towards the position in which I then was."

Mick Wylie, one of the shotgun party, 'noticed some of the shotgun men passing me up the road; after about six passing I retreated up the road myself. I had gone a short distance when I was hit in both legs'. Willie Keane said:

"A comrade of mine named Mick Wyley (sic) of Waterford city was badly wounded in the legs as he stood beside me against the ditch. He told me he was unable to stand and asked for my help. I got hold of Wyley, slung him over my shoulder and carried him over the ditch on the eastern side of the Ballinattin Road under heavy fire from the British on the opposite side. He tried to crawl up the hill but when I saw he couldn't do it I picked him up again and carried him up over the top of the hill and out of the line of fire."

Nicky Whittle recalled:

"To hold our position was now impossible and we fell back under cover of the ditch towards our riflemen. I was moving in a crouched position when suddenly I heard the sound of the voices of English soldiers at the other side of the ditch. I pulled out involuntarily. It looked that we were being surrounded. The next thing I was aware of was the sharp stab of a bullet in the back of my neck. It was a British officer who fired at me with his revolver. I have a recollection of jumping into the air. As I fell he got me again with another bullet in the small of the back. It was probably a matter of seconds before I came to and regained consciousness ... I clearly recall that I could discern the voices of our own lads at the side of the road ... they were firing from the shelter of the ditch. From the other side of the road I could hear the British officer's voice urging his men, 'Get out lads and get into them!' There was no sign however of his orders being obeyed, the only response from his men being a chorus of shouts of 'Bayonet the B-s'!"

Paddy Paul 'could plainly hear the talk of the enemy soldiers and their officers and from their talk I gathered that the soldiers were very nervous, but they seemed to be well-led by their officers who rallied them and encouraged them to pursue us'. Beside Paul, Martin Cullinane saw 'some of the shotgun men went up the road behind us. I asked "what's up?" and someone said the enemy were coming up the road – we were surrounded. I asked bde commandant [Paul] what would we do. He said nothing.' 'there was a lull in the firing of enemy. I asked the brigadier if they were surrendering. I thought the first lorry was at the time. I ordered my men to cease fire – one of my men continued and the brigadier then gave the order to 'cease fire'. The enemy then started to fire again and we fired some more rounds. As it was then getting hot we shifted position ... twenty-five yards further up. At that time the shotgun men were retiring towards our position. We were again about to open fire; the enemy seemed close now and [Mick Bishop] told us not to fire as it would give away our position. We lay down on the road and the enemy fire came over our heads. Suddenly', according to O'Neill, in charge of the rifle party:

"There was a lull in the firing of enemy. I asked the brigadier if they were surrendering. I thought the first lorry was at the time. I ordered my men to cease fire – one of my men continued and the brigadier then gave the order to 'cease fire'. The enemy then started to fire again and we fired some more rounds. As it was then getting hot we shifted position ... twenty-five yards further up. At that time the shotgun men were retiring towards our position. We were again about to open fire; the enemy seemed close now and [Mick Bishop] told us not to fire as it would give away our position. We lay down on the road and the enemy fire came over our heads."

John Riordan, with the flying column on the far side of the railway embankment, summed up their situation thus: 'We were "in the dark" in every sense of the word. Nobody seemed to know exactly what was happening'. According to Lennon:

"The firing died down on the other side and after a short time it started again. We saw an enemy soldier running across road underneath bridge at this time we fired another Verey light underneath Bridge and ordered my men to fire a volley under bridge. I don't think it had any effect. I had a pretty good idea of what was after happening. I held a consultation with my own officers and we decided to hold our position for some time longer, as we could easily hold them back from coming up from the Bridge. I sent two scouts to our left through a bog towards the railway line, they came back and reported that they heard someone breaking through bushes. [The Dunhill men withdrawing from the railway] The volley we fired under the bridge was the only shots fired by my party during the scrap with the exception of a few shots fired at the lorries away back the Waterford Road."

O'Neill's account recalls: 'Another man [Michael McGrath] and myself advanced down the road about fifteen yards. Then I got over fence in front. As I did so I heard the other man being surrounded and captured'. Both the shotgun and rifle party had abandoned the Ballinattin Road and were escaping across the fields. Willie Keane and Jerry Cronin were carrying Mick Wylie to a safe house where he was given first aid. But there were a few IRA men still left on the Ballinattin Road, including Nicky Whittle and Michael McGrath. George Lennon said:

"The firing died down with the exception of an odd shot on hill over Ballinattin Road. We could hear the enemy (they had English accents) interrogating someone near Ballinattin Road, this was followed by some shots and we could hear someone crying and groaning; a lot of shooting was going on and cries of 'Halt'. This died down after about twenty minutes."

Nicky Whittle, lying wounded on the road, was shot a third time by a Devonshire:

"Pulling up a few yards from where I lay, he fired into me with his rifle. Fortunately for me the previous woundings seem to have left my body numb to any sense of further pain ... the fact that I did not moan apparently gave the British soldier the idea that he had wasted a good bullet on a dead man. I recall feeling in my mind a contempt for the fellow who had fired into a man on the ground ... I heard the sound of running footsteps coming up the road. The English soldier shouted: 'Halt, who goes there?' A voice responded 'Friend'. Then there were two shots in rapid succession and the British soldier dropped to the ground beside me ... it was Connie Dorgan of Waterford who had shot him ... I should point out that a number of the British officers were in mufti [civilian clothing] that night, hence the challenge of the British soldier."

This soldier, badly wounded in the groin, was the only casualty suffered by the Devonshires that night. His agonised cursing and shouting was clearly heard beyond the metal bridge. Other

Devonshires were quickly on the scene, the soldier carried away, and Whittle examined and assumed to be dead:

"The group of British soldiers around me rushed to the other side of the road shouting 'Bayonet the B-, bayonet the B-' as they ran. They had discovered Tom O'Brien of Dunhill, who had fired his last cartridge and was crouching close to a bush. I recall hearing the officer's order: 'Don't kill him, take him prisoner'. I heard Tom O'Brien's voice for a moment, then the sounds of the butts of rifles beating him into insensibility. He never moaned, which suggested that he was knocked unconscious after the first blow. Once again I heard the officer's voice saying; 'Take him down to the lorry.' Then I could clearly discern the skithering sound on the road of Tom O'Brien's boots as they dragged him along the road."

By now, Lennon:

"..knew that the game was up as far as a successful ambush was concerned. I sent men to withdraw the outpost near barricade and told them to fall back on Glen Road. I fell in men and withdrew back towards racecourse. We could have remained longer and put up a good fight but our line of retreat would be cut, they could have come up under bridge to us but could easily surround us. We abandoned the cars and retired across country, west towards Dunhill and Kill. The ambush would probably have been a success if the lorries were allowed to run into barricade."

This was the only sane option to take. There were forty British troops only a short distance away and over 250 more less than ten miles away, most of whom could be expected to be on the scene quickly. Liam Lynch later noted that 'Waterford No. 2 vice OC [Lennon] showed his qualities on this occasion as a leader'.

According to John Riordan: 'The order was given to abandon the cars and move westwards. This was easier said than done, as we were all strangers in the locality and did not know that particular bit of country at all. However, my British army training came in handy here, as I was able to take my bearings from the stars and guide the party safely to the west without contacting any enemy forces'. This involved a hard forced march for fourteen miles across country; by dawn, the party had reached the vicinity of Stradbally where they went into billets for the day. It was here that Andy Kirwan received a strange request from Pat Keating:

"I remember him asking me to have him prayed for (as dead) in Kill chapel the following Sunday. He explained to me that his reason was that word would go around that he was dead (killed at Tramore) and that, when the British got to hear this, it would cause them to ease off in their efforts to track him down. Pat seemed to have a presentiment of either being caught or killed in action in the near future."

This was to have fatal consequences for Jack Fitzgerald of Kilrossanty, then living in England. Hearing a report of the 'death' of his old friend Pat Keating, he immediately returned home where finding the rumour to be untrue, he joined the flying column.

It later transpired that two deaths had taken place at Pickardstown, under decidedly sinister circumstances. According to the *Munster Express* of 15 January 1921:

"After the engagement at Pickardstown three dead bodies of civilians were seen on the road by the military, one of whom was subsequently identified as Michael McGrath, carpenter, Poleberry, Waterford. At least ten of the attackers are also stated to have been wounded. Two of the bodies were taken into a lorry, and on returning for the third it was found that it had been carried away by the attackers."

This was actually Nicky Whittle, who despite having been shot three times, was painfully crawling away from the ambush site. He eventually reached the house of a relative where he was hidden. The following day he received medical treatment from Dr Purcell of Waterford who also treated Mick Wylie.

Subsequently, at a military enquiry held at Waterford military barracks, a British army medical officer stated that in the case of one of the dead IRA men: 'The cause of death in my opinion was due to laceration of the brain, haemorrhage, and shock. The wound could have been caused by a gun shot. Death was instantaneous'.

Michael McGrath's death certificate states that cause of death was due to 'gun shot wound in head'. The cause of death of the other dead man [Tom O'Brien, unidentified at the time] was 'due to a gunshot wound passing through the heart and lungs'. In both cases the court added a strange rider: 'That no blame whatever attaches to the military or any member thereof'.

The IRA later carried out an internal inquiry into the failure of the ambush. Pax Whelan attributed the failure to 'the premature firing in position No. 2 on the railway embankment' although he noted that this group appeared to have received conflicting orders. Liam Lynch's judgement was that 'the failure of ambush and loss of life' rested either with Paddy Paul or the officer in charge of the Dunhill men on the railway. He also noted Paul's absence from his post and Jim Power's failure to warn Paul that some of the ambush party did not understand their orders. It was the final judgement of Richard Mulcahy that 'the matter should be left lie'.

In later years, the opening salvo by the Dunhill men became a thorny issue. In a 1954 account, Jerry Cronin even blamed

Lennon's ASU for firing these shots. Ironically, the outcome of the ambush could have been far worse. Had things gone according to plan and the British trucks advanced to the barricade, no more than one truck of the Devonshires would have been in the flying column's killing zone. The Dunhill men on the railway line would have opened fire on the remaining three trucks and without ammunition would have been quickly overwhelmed, leaving the Devonshires in a position to catch the ASU in a pincer movement. The Ballinattin group would not have been in a position to lend support. It is very likely that the action of the Dunhill men, attempting to obey their conflicting orders, saved several lives that night.[66]

Shortly after the Tramore ambush, martial law was imposed on County Waterford. One of the provisions of martial law allowed the execution of IRA men captured while bearing arms.

Later that month, Lennon's column lost the services of John Riordan and Pakeen Whelan; both had returned to Dungarvan when the Buffs raided the house of Riordan's sister, capturing the pair and bringing them to Dungarvan barracks. Riordan 'showed them my British army papers but they told me that they knew I was an IRA man. Whelan was brought to Dungarvan barracks with Riordan, where I was questioned for a long time about my association with the IRA. I gave no information, of course. I was not ill-treated by the military in Dungarvan'. Both were soon

---

[66] IMA BMH WS Andrew Kirwan, Patrick Power, James Power, William Keane, John Riordan, Jeremiah Cronin; *Munster Express*, 'Tramore Sensation – Police Barrack Attack', 15 January 1921; UCDA MP P7/A /22 (Inquiry into Tramore ambush); *Sunday Press*, 'The Story of Nicholas Whittle', 7–21 April 1963; GRO Death Certificate Michael McGrath; *London Gazette*, 31 May 1921 (award of MBE to Lieut. Frederick Charles Yeo).

transferred to Kilworth Camp near Fermoy (where Whelan was used as a hostage by Black and Tan raiding parties) before being taken to Cork and transported to Belfast aboard Royal Navy destroyers. On arrival, they were subjected to the traditional barrage of rivets and bolts by loyalist shipyard workers, after which they were taken to Ballykinlar internment camp where they stayed until December.[67]

According to a contemporary account:

"During the year 1921 the castle of Dungarvan was the scene of much activity. Prisoners were arrested almost daily and lodged in the barracks. But these were zealously attended to by the lady members of the Cumann na mBan, who carried to them provisions and ministered to their comforts by every means in their power. The lorries of the military would rush incessantly through the streets, carrying with them a machine-gun, the soldiers being armed with rifles pointing in every direction. Having made an incursion into the country, they would return with the same terrific speed, shoot down the Main Street, and lodge themselves in the barrack. Oftentimes rifle shots would be heard at night, and explanations would be sought for in the morning. The military were ever on the watch, for, owing to the guerrilla warfare in vogue, they knew not where or when they would be attacked."[68]

Many IRA activists had been arrested by military patrols, guided by RIC men who provided the British army with valuable local knowledge of individuals and places. By now most of the rural RIC

---

[67] IMA BMH WS John Riordan, Patrick Whelan.

[68] Keohan, Edmond, *Illustrated History of Dungarvan* (*Waterford News*, Waterford, 1924).

barracks in Waterford had been abandoned and destroyed (see Appendix Two), police duties being carried out by the IRA under the jurisdiction of republican courts. Under the martial law provisions, two IRA men had already been executed after capture; twenty-four similar executions followed.

In early February 1921, according to Andy Kirwan:

"The column, under George Lennon (OC) and Pat Keating (vice OC) lay in ambush at Carrickmourn, a district about two miles west of Lemybrien and about eight miles east of Dungarvan, on the main Dungarvan–Waterford road. I remember being sent down to a farmhouse, to take the steel ropes off the drum of a threshing machine which was on the farm. We got the steel rope, brought it onto the road and fixed it to two trees on either side of the road at a sharp bend and at a height of about six feet or so from the ground. Scouts were placed on high ground overlooking the road to Dungarvan, to signal the approach of British lorries. There were about twenty of us all told. We had about fifteen rifles and some shotguns. I myself had one of the Lee-Enfield rifles, captured from the British at Piltown in the previous November. Several false alarms were given but, when darkness came on, we pulled out and moved back to Kilrossanty, about two miles westward. Next day, we again returned to Carrickmourn, took up the same positions and awaited developments. During the day, a message was received from Dungarvan to the effect that the military had been tipped off as to our position and were getting ready with a large body of troops to carry out an encircling movement. We thereupon retired to the Comeragh Mountains and across them into the Nire Valley, between the

Knockmealdown and Comeragh mountains, where we remained until the British had finished their roundup."[69]

On 11 February 1921, an ambush was being prepared near the village of Ring, the Irish-speaking fishing village a few miles south-west of Dungarvan. James Mansfield recalled:

"Sometime early in February 1921, I received word from George Lennon, OC of the column, to contact him immediately. I met him about a mile west of Dungarvan when he told me that it was intended to ambush the British at Killingford Cross about two miles west of Dungarvan on the main Dungarvan–Ring road. Lennon had sent word to Dungarvan barracks that Cathal Brugha had been seen going to Ring Irish College and it was expected that the British would be out hot-foot to capture him. The message of course, was just a trick to entice the British out of Dungarvan."

According to Mick Mansfield:

"The Ring and Old Parish companies were mobilised for this job, together with the column under George Lennon ... the column, of which I was one, was marching in file at either side of the road near Robert's Cross, going to take up position at the Cross, together with some men of the Old Parish company. The night was dark."

James Mansfield said:

"The time was about 9 p.m. when the column was moving into position along the road to Killongford, when quite unexpectedly, a lorry of troops came along from Dungarvan proceeding to Ring. The road in this district has many turns and twists with the result

---

[69] IMA BMH WS Andrew Kirwan.

that the British were almost on top of the column before the latter were aware of the fact. Lennon had just time to get his men over the hedge and under cover when the military passed by."

Michael Curran of the Ring company had been sent a dispatch to gather all available men from the village at Egan's bridge (three miles from Dungarvan) at 8 p.m.; he did not receive this message until that time and had to work quickly. Ring was a tiny fishing village and a pre-arranged signal from Curran brought a dozen men running. Grabbing their weapons, the group set out on foot for Egan's Bridge. Curran later related:

"Just when we reached Robert's Cross, which is three miles or so from Egan's Bridge, a pony and trap with a lantern in front of the trap held by a man, approached us from the Dungarvan direction. There were six men in the trap in civilian clothes. We paid no attention to them, believing them to be farmers coming out of Dungarvan. They passed us and were gone on a few yards when they stopped the pony and peppered our ranks with rifle fire. They were military who had left a lorry further down the road and who had dressed in civilian clothes which they got from farm houses nearby. The military lorry was now approaching from Dungarvan and we found ourselves caught between two fires. I ordered a retreat to the north, as we had a good advantage with the fall of ground and had little difficulty in finding cover. One of our men, Declan Regan, who was alongside of me, was seriously wounded in the left hand, the whole knuckle of which was shattered by a .303 bullet. As he got over the fence he collapsed. Jack Curran, Tom Hayes and myself, who were about forty yards in front of him, heard him shout 'I'm done!' I called the other two and came back to Regan in a crawling position under a hail of lead. One man caught his (Regan's) two legs and one man under each armpit. We finally succeeded in getting him out of the range of fire."

The military party then proceeded to Ring to begin a vain search for Cathal Brugha. James Mansfield remembered:

"Disgusted with this turn of events, George Lennon moved the column to a more favourable position for an attack on the returning British convoy. We waited for an hour or more and then saw the lights of the military cars returning to Dungarvan by another road which was well out of range of our guns. There was nothing we could do but watch the British return in safety to Dungarvan."

The column, according to Andy Kirwan, 'pulled out then and marched across country in the direction of Kinsalebeg which we reached just after daybreak. We billeted in that district, having walked about thirty-six miles with no sleep for a day and a half'.

In the meantime, the men from Ring were still carrying their bleeding comrade to safety across a dangerous marsh. They eventually reached the village of Ballinagoul where Dr Moynihan, who had served as a British army medical officer in the 1914–1918 war, treated Regan.[70]

By March 1921, the republican courts had almost superseded the British system of justice in Ireland. Even in Waterford city, the British had to bring in jurors (usually people with unionist sympathies) from as far afield as Fermoy. According to an official IRA summary:

---

[70] IMA BMH WS Michael J Mansfield, James Mansfield, Michael Curran; NLI FOD 31,150 (Activities – Waterford brigade).

3 March '21; Durrow Engagement

"It was decided to attack the 7.30 a.m. train, containing jurors in order to draw out the [British] into an ambush [position]. Bde ASU and local Vols from Bn 2. The train was held up at Millarstown. The Vols took up [ambush position] near Ballyvoyle."

On 3 March 1921, according to Mick Mansfield:

"Plans were laid to hold up a train proceeding from Cork to Waterford carrying jurors to the courts in Waterford. The idea was to take those jurymen off the train and so prevent the British court from functioning. It was also hoped to draw British forces out into an ambush prepared by us when word of the train reached the military authorities. All the members of the column were engaged, as well as about a dozen men from the local battalion. The venue for this train hold-up was at a place called Millarstown [about a mile to the north of Durrow station]. The ambush position was about a mile or so further along the line at Ballyvoyle where the railway bridge crosses over a steep gorge. The railway then enters a tunnel, the next station being [Durrow] about 1½ miles to the east. About 7 or 7.30 a.m. when the juror's train came on from Dungarvan. It was flagged to a stop at Millarstown, the jurors taken off and left sitting on the railway embankment in charge of a few IRA men. After half an hour or so the train, without the jurors, moved off to Waterford. By this time, about fifteen or eighteen of us, with George Lennon the column OC in charge, took up ambush positions on the railway line at Ballyvoyle and overlooking the coast road from Dungarvan to Waterford. We were all armed with rifles."

It was anticipated that the British garrison in Dungarvan would send troops by road into the Ballyvoyle area. Obstructions had been laid on local roads to divert this force into the ambush position; the column's deployment on the railway track overlooking the road was an excellent position to attack troops on the road, but things did not go according to plan.

The IRA summary noted: 'A train with [military] came at 11.30 a.m. and was attacked by IRA forces – two soldiers being wounded. The train went through to Durrow Stn and it was followed there by the IRA'. A subsequent official British statement claimed that: 'The 10.40 train from Fermoy carrying troops, was fired on near Durrow on Friday at noon. The troops returned the fire, dispersing the rebels.' According to Mick Shalloe:

"We weren't very long in position when our scouts reported another train coming out our way from Dungarvan. We moved off the line and as the train passed, we saw it was full of troops, probably en route from Fermoy. We had a crack at them and they replied. This train kept going and when it was out of sight, George Lennon proposed that we should follow it up to Durrow, a mile to the north, where it was likely that the military would detrain."

Edmond Power said:

"After about two hours waiting, the time would be about 12 noon, a train approached from the west – Dungarvan – towards Durrow. At a signal shot to be fired by George Lennon, general fire was to be opened. When the train was about forty yards from the tunnel at Ballyvoyle Bridge, George Lennon gave the signal and rapid fire was poured into the railway carriages which contained what appeared to be a large number of military. We learned afterwards that a good number of British were at least wounded in this action. This train went on its way and stopped at Durrow station."

Mick Mansfield reported:

"When we reached Durrow ... we found that the military train hadn't stopped there. We also learned from scouts that a party of military had come out the coast road from Dungarvan and had passed through the ambush position at Ballyvoyle, which had recently been vacated by us. The British troops had returned to Dungarvan by the same route having apparently got word that a large number of IRA were in the Ballyvoyle area."

Mick Shalloe recalled:

"In the meantime, we learned from scouts that the military, for whom we had laid the ambush, had in fact come along to the ambush position a short time after we had left it to move on to Durrow. They had released the jurymen and had returned to Dungarvan."

According to Mick Shalloe:

"The time was now about mid-day and Lennon decided to split the column into small parties and go in search of food. With a few of the lads I was fairly close to Durrow when we spotted a large force of military at the railway station. We opened fire and they replied. While this was going on, others of our lads returned and joined in the attack. The troops deployed in the neighbourhood of Durrow station and a long fight ensued."

Mick Mansfield remembered:

"I was having some grub with Pat Keating and two others named Kirby and Lonergan when we heard firing going on in the direction of Durrow, about 1½ miles from where we were having the meal. We ran out onto the roadway and met a fellow with a jennet and dray which we commandeered and drove on towards Durrow. We approached Durrow station from across the fields and as we drew near, came under heavy machine-gun fire from the British military. We got under a hedge to size up the situation. Firing was going on all around us. Eventually we located the machine-gun at the back of the Co-operative Stores which adjoins Durrow Station. We concentrated our rifle fire on the machine-gunner and soon put him out of action. A British officer then ran over to man the machine-gun but we got him too."

Andy Kirwan said:

"I remember being about half a mile from Durrow at the time and with a few others of the column, returned towards the station from which heavy rifle fire was coming. We were crossing a field near the railway when I came under machine-gun fire from a Tommy who had mounted his gun on a little knoll at the edge of the field. He gave me the full pan of bullets and I dived for the nearest ditch, as did the boys with me. One of the latter got his rifle on to the machine-gunner and quickly silenced him ... I discovered my leg all sloppy and wet with blood which was pouring into my boot. I had been badly wounded in the leg by machine-gun fire. First aid was applied and the bleeding stopped.

"Kirwan was treated by Dr Joe Walsh who was at Durrow to treat any of the wounded column. Kirwan's leg wound kept him out of operational duties although he was later able to resume as ASU transport officer. According to the subsequent British statement:

"A military patrol sent from Waterford by special train to clear up the situation, came in contact with the rebels south-west of Durrow, and after a short engagement, dispersed them."

The Durrow railway station, particularly the Co-operative building next door, provided an excellent defensive position for the British troops, providing good cover and fields of fire. Immediately surrounding these buildings was a ring of open ground which provided little cover for an attacking force. Any

British soldier peering into the surrounding fields would have no idea if twenty men or two hundred surrounded him. The British could not break out but neither could the IRA break in. The noise made by dozens of Lee-Enfields firing in close proximity would have been deafening, the acrid smell of cordite hanging in the air and clinging to clothing. Paddy Joe Power said:

"After about two hours of intermittent firing, the British retreated gradually from the vicinity of the railway station in to the Co-operative Stores, which was a good stone building and very suited for defence. We contained the British forces in the Co-operative Stores until late in the evening – somewhere about 4 p.m. – firing at irregular intervals. By this time, our supply of ammunition was beginning to run low. The officers of the column had discussed the possibility of a direct assault on the Co-operative Stores, but it was decided due to the nature of the terrain, which offered little cover and the fact that our ammunition was by now very nearly exhausted, that it wasn't possible to push home the attack. The column therefore, was ordered by George Lennon to break off the engagement and retire north-west to Comeragh. We did this and reached Comeragh without contacting any enemy troops, which was lucky for us, as we had little stuff left after the Durrow affair."

The IRA summary noted that:

"The [British] were unable to withdraw until the IRA retired while the British statement claimed: Two soldiers were wounded, one dangerously, and at least three rebels are believed to have been wounded."[71]

---

[71] NLI FOD 31,150 (Activities – Waterford brigade); Michael J. Mansfield, Michael Shalloe, Edmond Power, Patrick J Power, Andrew Kirwan, *Munster Express*, 'Attacks on a Train in Co. Waterford', 12 March 1921.

The official history of the East Kent regiment notes that at this time: 'In and around Dungarvan the Buffs had several brushes with the rebels and, in the course of a series of patrols, effected a number of important arrests ... a gallant action in this district during one ambush earned for Captain D.V. Thomas the OBE, Lieut. F.A.J.E. Marshall being similarly decorated with the MBE'.[72]

While today the Order of the British Empire is a high civil honour on a par with a knighthood, military personnel and civilians alike originally established it in 1917 to recognise gallantry and distinguished service. In 1918 a separate military division was established to recognise service by members of his majesty's forces in actions 'other than war'. It was decreed by the British army that acts of courage by British soldiers during the Irish War of Independence would be rewarded by the OBE or the MBE (Member of the British Empire) rather than purely military decorations. While no citations for Thomas' and Marshall's decorations are yet available, Captain Thomas' OBE was published in the *London Gazette* of 31 May 1921 (dated 28 April) which indicates that the action for which the award was made took place in March.[73]

On 5 March 1921 the flying column, operating near Kilmacthomas, moved to take over the railway station to ambush British troops known to be travelling on the Rosslare Express. The *Munster Express* perhaps best describes the subsequent occurrences:

"On Saturday night last a party of soldiers were proceeding on leave to England from different parts of Cork by the Rosslare

---

[72] Knight, C.R.B., *Historical Records of the Buffs* (Medici, London, 1951) pp. 2–3.

[73] *London Gazette,* 31 May 1921.

Express. Prior to the time at which the express was due to pass through Kilmacthomas, a large number of men suddenly appeared at the station platform and proceeded to hold up the entire staff, including the station master and the signalman. The latter was ordered at the point of a revolver to put the signals against the oncoming train and had no alternative but to obey. By this time the little station was filled with armed and disguised men. When the express slowed up it was boarded, and passengers, including the military, to the number of fifteen men, were ordered out on the platform. A selection of the military was made, and they were lined up on the platform and closely questioned. Four of their number, one who produced a telegram calling him to the bedside of his dying mother, and three others who were proceeding to visit sick relatives, were allowed back on the train and told they could continue their journey. The remainder, numbering eleven men who were all unarmed, were all formed up on the platform and eventually marched through the village street, headed it is stated, by a fiddler playing amongst other lively tunes 'The Rocky Road to Dublin'. It is also stated that a council of war was subsequently held by the raiders as to what they were to do with the soldiers. Some suggested shooting them but other counsels prevailed, and it was decided to billet the soldiers in various houses in the village. It was suggested that the post office would be a likely place, and accordingly the officials in that building were knocked up and most of the men were accommodated for the night there, the remainder being sent to other establishments in the village. Some of the soldiers kit bags, it is alleged, were taken away, as well as some clothing. The matter was reported to the authorities, and a party of military arrived at Kilmacthomas on Sunday from Waterford, and escorted the stranded soldiers back to the city, where they were billeted in the military barracks. Subsequently a detachment of military to the number of one hundred arrived in Kilmacthomas from it is stated, Fermoy, and took charge of the village. They quartered in the workhouse there."

The fiddler was James Mansfield, now temporarily attached to the column. Ned Kirby took advantage of the situation to requisition a pair of army boots, one soldier fortunately having a spare pair. The British troops based in Kilmacthomas workhouse, according to Ed Power, 'proceeded to search the foothills of the Comeragh mountains for what they were told was a "large body of the IRA". We had knowledge of all this and were waiting for them to move further into the Comeraghs where we were positioned to give them a very warm reception. Some sixth sense must have warned them not to proceed too far because, when less than a mile from where we awaited them, they turned back for Kilmacthomas. A day or so afterwards they returned to Waterford'.[74]

This was the first time that the British army used the Kilmacthomas Workhouse as a barracks. Not only was the building ideal for this purpose, it was also located only five miles from the flying column's base in the Tay Valley.

On the night of 7 March, Paddy Paul launched a 'brigade offensive' in east Waterford. Parties of local IRA men dug trenches across the unsurfaced roads around Waterford city, Dunmore East and the Cork Road receiving particular attention. At about 10 p.m., Jim Power took up position at Carroll's Cross railway station with twenty men armed with shotguns and rifles and closed the level crossing gates, with the intention of ambushing a party of military from Fermoy known to be aboard the Rosslare Express. This train however did not normally halt at Carroll's Cross and due to the

---

[74] *Munster Express, Rosslare Express Held Up at Kilmacthomas,* 12 March 1921; IMA BMH WS Edmond Power.

gradient it was moving too fast to stop immediately, instead crashing through the gates and pulling up some distance away. It then continued to Waterford city where the passengers and military discovered that local Volunteer Dan Ennis had raised the central span on Redmond Bridge (with the willing co-operation of the bridge operator and his assistant). It had been intended that the Ferrybank company would then attack the military party with a few pistols that Paul had brought from Dublin, at great personal risk. The accounts of this incident do not state whether the British party was armed or not; had they been, such an attack would have been suicidal – there were about a hundred British troops aboard the train. In any case, the planned attack from Ferrybank did not occur. At about 11 p.m., a party of six IRA men armed with rifles and led by Jerry Cronin launched an attack on the RIC barracks in Dunmore East, garrisoned by fourteen RIC men. The attack continued for two hours without losses despite a high expenditure of ammunition, and some damage to the building. Two nearby thatched cottages were burned down, almost certainly by Verey flares fired by the RIC.

Paddy Paul later declared himself, 'very disappointed by the failure of this operation. I had intended this to be a test of the brigade training and organisation, and I attributed the failure to a lack of offensive spirit amongst the officers'. Attempting to stop the Rosslare Express at Carroll's Cross or ordering a few armed men to attack a hundred soldiers however, did not indicate skilled planning on Paul's part. Paul however blamed his officers and Willie Keane in particular, replacing him as vice brigadier with Mick Bishop. Liam Lynch later commented: 'I consider it a mistake to have two ex-soldiers be brigade OC and vice OC as there is the danger of developing the area on regular army lines instead of training the men to suit guerrilla warfare'.[75]

From the memoirs of George Lennon

March 1921. Comeragh Mountains.

"Glenanean, the glen of the birds, is a little coum or vale sleeping in the heart of the Comeragh Mountains. A wee burn, or stream, wanders and sings its way down the glen's central depression. It was all too peaceful there and the lads were getting restless from inactivity. Our column consisted of thirty men, some quite hard chaws, the others innocent country lads. Some time back we had pulled off a completely successful affair with a detachment of the Hampshires, all of them taken prisoners, and sometime afterwards we had an almost disastrous affray with a large convoy of the Devons. Since then nothing of any great consequence had happened.

"Our armament was by no means negligible. We had twenty captured Lee-Enfields, five Lee-Metfords, two Krag Jagersons, one service Mauser, one Marlin repeater and one Winchester. In reserve were a Martini Enfield, a Snider carbine somebody had brought back from the Crimea. Total supply of ammunition was 1,600 rounds which could only be replenished by capture. We had a number of side weapons but they were ineffective in a field action."

Yet another Great War veteran joined the column at this time. Jack O'Mara, from Ballinamult, had joined the US Army in 1915 and had fought in France throughout 1918. O'Mara later related: 'The

[75] IMA BMH WS Patrick Paul, James Power, Jeremiah Cronin, Daniel Ennis; *Munster Express, Dunmore Police barracks Attacked,* 12 March 1921; UCDA MP P7/A /22 Lynch to Mulcahy 10/6/21. 35 IMA BMH WS Jack O'Mara.

column invariably travelled at night-time, on foot across country, sending scouts ahead. These scouts, in addition to keeping a lookout for enemy forces, would contact the company captain in the area in which we were to billet. About half a dozen men from the local companies would mount guard at night with a few of the men from the column. The column was paraded twice a day by the OC and field exercises carried out. Each man carried about fifty rounds of rifle ammunition'.[76]

George Lennon said:

"Kirby, Sullivan and Big Patto were passing around sarcastic remarks amongst the others about our inactivity. Kirby was our local poacher and he looked like a brigand. Seán Sullivan was an old British army regular who had served from Mons right up to the end of the World War, a very independent man he had never received a promotion. Big Patto was a sailor who had left ship to take to the hills, a usually gentle man he had occasional wild moments. About a month previous the three of them had taken off without permission and shot up a nearby town: the results were most unpleasant for everybody concerned.

"Pat [Keating] took me off for a walk in the hills as he wanted to unburden himself of his latest plan. He was always enthusiastic about some plan or another and most of his plans sounded crazy. His present plan seemed to make some kind of sense but he wanted to recruit all the inhabitants of the countryside into it. Military raids were a bane to us and we were often caught napping. At the very first sight of the military, he suggested, all the sounds of day-to-day farming activities should be noisily exaggerated. Women would beat on feed pans to call the hens,

---

[76] IMA BMH WS Jack O'Mara.

ploughmen would bellow at their horses and gossoons would wallop the donkeys to make them bray. This general hullabaloo would put us immediately on our guard and save us from surprise. To me it was reminiscent of the famous fairy tale "the ass brayed, the bog barked, the cat meowed, the cock crowed and the robbers ran away".

"On our return we at once sensed the discontent so we decided to come out of the hills and move into the Lickey position right away before the men got out of hand. We would have to devise some clever subterfuge to draw the military out. Clearly something had to be done quickly. Then Stackpoole arrived."

'Stackpoole' was Lennon's pseudonym for George Plunkett, a staff officer from IRA headquarters on a tour of inspection. Pax Whelan ruefully recalled: 'We were hoping Charlie Daly would be on the inspection, as George was very punctilious, always insisting that every rank in the company be filled'. Plunkett was the son of a papal count and the brother of one of the executed 1916 leaders. He himself had fought in the Easter Rising as a Volunteer captain; towards the end of the rebellion he had bravely dashed under fire into Moore Street to rescue a wounded man crying for help. Although this man turned out to be a British soldier, Plunkett carried him to safety while other British soldiers held their fire. A few minutes later, he returned and grabbed the soldier's rifle and dashed back to cover with bullets cracking around him.[77]

"We were all quite overawed as he had some most impressive qualifications. He had fought with distinction during Easter Week,

---

[77] Caulfield Max, *The Easter Rebellion* (Gill and Macmillan, Dublin, 1995), p. 263.

had a public school education and his father was a nobleman. He was also a member of the Third Order of St Francis.

"The Irish equivalent of the bush telegraph got gossipy at once and quite soon the whole countryside knew that 'the Count' had arrived amongst us. We are a people of a kindly and concerned curiosity and everybody was bursting to see him.

"The new arrival carefully explained first of all that his true identity was not to be revealed and that he was to be known as 'Captain Murphy'. On this point he was explicit.

"He was, in fact, a GHQ staff officer sent out on a tour of inspection and he proved to be, if ever I met one, a thoroughly conscientious man.

"From the beginning there was a wearing tension between the two of us and there were times when we circled politely around each other while seething inwardly. Some modern expert on interpersonal psychology will, no doubt, be able to explain this. At the time it greatly bothered us both and proved quite a strain on our relations.

"After the first of many conferences he got down to business straight off and he decided that our brigade was in a really poor state of organisation and our column in it's present condition was not fit to go into action for a long time to come. This decision got everybody sulky.

"Some days later.

"A great cleaning and refurbishing of our arms. [Plunkett] proved to be the personification of military efficiency. Sloppy habits he most disliked. We had a habit of letting our small arms lie about any place; with an almost courtly bow he would confront you with your gun saying urbanely 'I believe you must have mislaid this'. It was one of his most exasperating habits.

"The local company captain had his legs run off putting out scouts day and night. The staff captain informed us that we were no longer a flying column but a commando and that we were not to use the words 'on active service' but the words 'on commando'. So now we were a commando on commando.

"Our man was almost constantly pouring over a military text book by one Captain Kinsman called *The Training of the Infantry Officer*. The book, which he loaned me, was all about sire steps, slit trenches and directions for moving large bodies of men across oceans of mud against coils of barbed wire. It was hard to relate its contents to our little guerrilla war.

"A week later.

"[Plunkett] got a cracked idea – some of his ideas seemed quite dotty. We had dinner with Father Power and our captain decided right away that Father Tom must be appointed official chaplain to the column. (We had already dropped the name commando.) He said he was going to communicate with the bishop about it. Anyway, there was a priest in every parish we moved into and we had such fine friends on call as Father Gleason of Aglish, and Father Sheehy of Kilrossanty. Father Tom fed us, gave us cigarettes, played his Victrola for us and held himself in readiness to perform the last offices for the dying and he considered his religious functions ended right there. He was a holy little man and he did not like receiving religious instruction. The idea was dropped.

"A week following.

"The captain got quite distressed about the lads singing what he called 'music hall ditties'. Their favourite song was 'I'm for Every Blowing Bubbles' and when on the march they sang a song about where the flies went in wintertime. His voice was not one of his many good qualities but he tried us out with such moving native folk songs as –

> One fine morning in spring
> As the birds they did sing
> And the fields were all covered with noneens

"The response was negative. Pat did much better, occasionally he would quite suddenly burst out with –

> Then rally round the banner boys
> That now above us flies
> The die is cast, the night is past
> The dawn is in the skies

"The words, at any rate, were inspiring.

"Then there was the row about the cigarettes. The lads, as their only compensation for their national service, got a packet of ten Players cigarettes each day. English manufacture. The brigade QM was instructed to supply an Irish brand. It was not the fault of the Irish manufacturer that the cigarettes were too long in stock, and consequently mouldy, but it was sufficient to have the native product rejected with scorn.

"A day later.

"We are now ready to move off to a more central point in the brigade area for the purpose of better communication. [Plunkett] has been studying O.S. map Sheet 22 and making frequent reference to Captain Kinsman regarding a correct order of march. The order of the march was to be as follows:

Advance guard: myself and three others
Connecting file: Kirby and Sullivan
Main body under [Plunkett] and Pat
Rear guard
(Total body of troops to be moved, thirty-one men)

"We got off to a poor start. Pegeen's pub at Kilbrien was early on the line of march. Although usually well behaved the two men in the connecting file were sour on the new dispensation and they were acting up. Both emerged from Pegeen' s with bottles of beer just in time to be caught by the main body. Disgraceful business. After we were all got together by whistle the two bottles were immolated against the stones of the ditch and we got a temperance lecture and the march was resumed.

"When we had progressed another mile I was whistled and yelled at for losing distance. The correct procedure was to be rigidly adhered to and was to be as follows: When coming to a road, advance guard to take up a protective or covering a position, then the main body would advance at the double to make the crossing, after which the column would reform and continue the advance.

"While we of the advance guard were covering the first road crossing the main body came charging up. Passing me at full gallop [Plunkett] had just time for an apologetic 'Sorry for yelling at you'. He got a stony response.

"We finished crossing the valley in a series of mad rushes and finally arrived at the foot of the Drum Hills with everybody in a very bad state of humour."

March 1921. Drum Hills.

"On our arrival at Ballymulalla Mrs Welch and Napoleon were waiting to receive us. Mrs Welch was a lady in every sense of the word. She acted as quartermaster to the local company but she really commanded it. Napoleon (his real name, I think, was Foley) was first lieutenant of the company. He did credit to his great namesake as he seemed to be indefatigable. Now he had to quarter thirty-one men on the local farmers as well as providing scouts and having messages properly dispatched.

"Mr. Welch and [Plunkett] took an instant dislike to each other. Behind her back he called her the Duchess quite unaware of the fact that she called him the Count.

"The following morning.

"Mrs Welch whose silvery hair is in a pompadour is sitting behind her massive silver teapot (a relic of better days) and I am sitting happily beside the dear lady. The 'orderly officer for the day' has been marched off by [Plunkett] for what he calls 'inspecting the men's billet'. Mrs Welch is telling me about when she lived in Priory House, Aglish. The great pre-World War manoeuvres are being held in the Drum Hills. General French and his staff are (paid) guests at Priory House. The good lady explains to me that as she was quite at her ease when she presided at the table of General French and his staff she is not going to be overawed by any Count.

"Here we were interrupted in our pleasant conversation by a loud yell outside on the road. 'Are ye there,' Jarge?'

"It was Father Gleason whose voice, it was said, could be heard in the next parish. We both went out to see what he wanted.

'A great day thanks be to God.'

'Yes indeed Father.'

'Jarge would you send around a couple of the lads to plough a bit of land for me?' 'Yes Father.'

'I hear ye have the Count with ye.' he roared.

"We made frantic signs to him to lower his voice but he just whipped up his pony and went spanking gaily down the boreen.

"The inspection did not go off very well and our captain arrived back more sad than angry. He was beginning to become aware of his lack of knowledge of the simple ways of our country people. His first stop had been at Dees. The lads were lounging around the kitchen codding Maggie Dee who was using Elizabethan words the meaning of which she was quite innocent. When he suddenly appeared in Tobin's yard, Mrs Tobin dropped the feed pan and ran into the house crying, 'Mother of God, it's the Count and the family started madly cleaning up for his reception. Luckily at this point, our usually most happy go lucky QM arrived with the typewriter, several reams of paper and an adequate supply of carbon paper. [Plunkett] dictated and we all had a go at two finger typing in carbon triplicate. Now we could get down to work. Instructions to battalion adjutants, instructions to quartermasters (how to care for their few miserable shotguns). It went on for some days and it made only one person happy. [Note: A battalion area covered the area of a barony, the baronies were old tribal lands taken over by the early Anglo Norman conquerors. A brigade area usually comprised four battalion areas and generally fell within the confines of an ancient Irish petty kingdom. The method of living off the rural community (we were welcome quests) was the old Gaelic system of 'coign and livery'. (The reversion to old native ways was remarkable.)]]

"After office hours.

"The staff captain genially suggested a walk up the road. He was in affable mood; said how nice it would be if all farm houses were like Mrs Welch's 'with some decent pictures on the wall'. We talked about soldiers of fortune and agreed that they were undesirable. Byron, we both agreed, was of course an exception. For the first time we seemed to be in total agreement about something. Then he hummed and hawed and said the brigade staff was next to impossible ('What are you going to do about it, Seoirse?'). I said cautiously that this might be true but what was it to be replaced with. We turned around abruptly and he refused to speak to me all the way back to the house.

"Next day.

"At any rate this promised to be one happy day. Napoleon and I were off to select an ambush position on the Ballyduff Road. Even the sun was shining. Outside Aileen, Mrs Welch's daughter, was holding her cob by the head waiting to ride cross-country with his lordship's dispatches. She was a splendid horsewoman. Some of the lads were standing around admiring the horse but paying no attention to the girl. The girls were very useful for carrying dispatches and for scouting purposes.

"We were taking our time as we intended to make a day of it. After a leisurely crossing of the old Mount Odell demesne we came out on the Ballyduff Road but we were quite unable to find a suitable position until we got to Kilbane some miles to the west. Here there was a beetling quarry cliff and lots of natural cover. Napoleon earned his name by picking out an excellent post for the shotgun men. The local company, or companies, usually supplied about eight or ten shotgun men for an ambush. Buckshot set in candle wax was used in the cartridges. Most of the shotguns had choke barrels with the result that the impacted charge blew off about an inch or more of the barrel at the first shot. We always tried to give the shotgun men as wide a berth as possible.

"After selecting the position we directed our gaze to Big Maigue Landy's pub which was close by – altogether too close. We were both thinking the same thing. My companion remarked, in a quite practical tone, that is was too bad the pub had been built in that particular place but the ambush position we had been forced to select was the only suitable one to be found for miles around. He added that we could not pass by without calling to see our old friend.

"Big Maigue was a very fine person but she had an awful tongue and she never spared anybody. She weighed thirteen stone, if she weighed an ounce, and she never had a cigarette out of her mouth.

'Well if it isn't the lads,' said she as we came in, 'having a nice country walk for themselves.'

"We let her think that. In the event of a nearby ambush her house was most likely to be burned to the ground as a minimum reprisal.

"She filled out two half whiskies for us – we dared not ask for lemonade or even sherry. 'I suppose ye been over to Cappagh House having tay with Percy Ussher?' We let this sally pass.

'I hear the Count is with ye?'

'There is a Captain Murphy staying with us.' 'G'wan with you, sure everybody knows who he is'.

"We sipped gingerly at the whiskies.

'I suppose ye don't know that two lorries of Tans passed this way this morning?' This made us prick up our ears.

'Sure 'tis ye have the fine times hiding in the hills, aitin' the poor people out of house and home and letting them divils drive all over our roads.'

"Napoleon got very nettled at this caustic remark and said she was soon going to find out all about that and I had to nudge him to keep his mouth shut.

'And when will you be getting married, Napoleon?' she next queried.

"Napoleon looked vague. Big Maigue was always teasing us about girls whenever we went to see her, in fact, it was her favourite subject. She now got on to this vein and the more embarrassed we got the more vulgar she became.

'What ye lads need is a good hoult,' she said quite coolly. We were getting uneasy and ready to go when she started off 'The night Landy and I was married –' We had heard this before as it was a local legend so we said we had to leave. 'Be careful of yourselves' was her parting sally.

"It was quite late when we got back and I was handed an urgent message from Lynch to the effect that I was to contact him immediately. His headquarters was something over a mile outside the village of Ballyhooly in County Cork and about thirty miles, as the crow flies, from our present location. This posed quite a problem as it might take days to travel such a long distance cross-country, the roads being out of the question owing to their continuous patrol by the police and the military. Lynch, which was typical of him, did not mention such a minor detail but merely gave the address of a contact in the village. After mulling over the matter with the others it was agreed that I might take the risk of going by train after adopting a suitable disguise.

"Aileen Welch harnessed up the pony and drove me to Cappagh station the following morning. As my mind was on serious matters I paid little attention to the conversation she tried to involve me in.

"My dress was an expensive tweed overcoat, a deerstalker hat and my boots were nicely polished. In addition, I carried a copy of the Irish Field in my hand and had a faked letter to the faculty of Cork University in my pocket that would explain my identity in case I was picked up.

"There was only one 1st class carriage in which I took my seat. A number of the other carriages were occupied by Tommies in full field equipment coming from England as replacements. They did not bother me, or anybody else, but spent their time in cursing, sleeping, smoking and wondering what strange part of the world they were in.

"Leaving the train at Ballyhooly I had to bluff my way through a convoy of four Crossley tenders full of Tans on the prowl, so I was still more than a bit rattled when I met Liam. The last time we had been together was five months past when I had helped to train a column for him at Glenville in the Nagle Mountains.

"Now, on this occasion, he pushed me very hard to remain with him and I was quite unable to convince him that I was more needed elsewhere. In any case, I said my underwear was lousy and I had to go home for a change. He offered me half of his if I would stay. This one of my most pleasant memories of Liam, I mean his offering to give me his underwear.

"Lynch was one of the few men I ever met whose authority while under command I accepted without question. He was also my friend, or I liked to think so. How can he be like a military man but have the appearance of a responsible superior of a great religious order. He was by nature most abstemious and he never raised his voice, which was gentle. If he ever smiled I have no recollection of the occasion. Like many people of settled conviction he had his blind spots.

"At the moment of my arrival he came quietly into the farm parlour smelling strongly of a disinfectant ointment we used for scabies, an unpleasant itch we all suffered from due probably to infrequent changes of under-clothing. He had a characteristic habit of fiddling with his eyeglasses when he was tense, which he was now. After gently reproving me for the lack of activities in our area he laid out a map and asked me to study it. Drawing a circle with his pen around Fermoy (a military town) he explained it was the headquarters and the main barracks of the British 16th Infantry Brigade which was causing him constant trouble by raiding all the country isolated, as far as it was possible to do so, by bridge demolitions and road obstructions. Where his area adjoined ours we picked a place for a suitable demolition as well as some road obstructions by tree felling. Not being the kind of person to waste time in idle conversation, he then dismissed me and became immediately immersed in his notebooks. A young lad of about sixteen scouted the road ahead and saw me back to the train for my return journey.

"On the train.

"When the train drew up at Fermoy station he thought that he was taking leave of his senses. A tremendous commotion was going on along the platform. An officer smartly opened the door of his compartment (1st class) and came briskly to attention. A number of English looking ladies were waving regimental colours the three buglers to their front blew a tattoo salute. Then the brigadier general and his two staff officers stepped most importantly in and took their seats.

In a flash his mind cleared and he realised what was afoot. The brigadier's predecessor, one General Lucas, had been taken prisoner and carried off to an unknown destination. Generals are not expendable and they were taking no chances with this one. The train pulled [out] filled with soldiers and a plane was flying around overhead. At the tail end of the platform officers let go a salvo of Verey pistols as a final noisy salute.

'Quite a send-off sir,' said one of the staff officers most respectfully.

"Some of our offensive system going west,' growled the general.

"The General looked like a character out of Punch. He had a walrus moustache, a beefy look and he glared at everything in his immediate vicinity.

"Telephone poles flashed by and the fields with their green ditches seemed to go round in circles. Now what was he to do? When the train got to Tallow Road station Constable Neery, who knew him from childhood, and two other RIC men got into the next compartment. All the other stations appeared to be heavily guarded by RIC men and Tans. He cursed Liam [Lynch] for bringing him all that distance for a fifteen-minute consultation; the whole business could have been dealt with in a dispatch. His one chance was to get off at Cappagh and make a dash for it. The next station beyond that was his own town where every constable knew him and he would be dragged off. At any rate he was unarmed and he would not be tortured. He could imagine the angry plaints of the General, 'Damnable inefficiency, putting me into a carriage with a dangerous Shinner – fellow might have shot me, might have murdered the three of us'.

"Then he realised that he had made a vow not to be taken alive. Nurse Kent [Kathy Cullinane of Kilmacthomas] had given him a slim tube of morphine tablets as the idea of wounds and torture filled him with terror – but he was not going to have recourse to them this time. He had meant to ask Nurse Kent if it was sufficient to swallow the things as she carried around some kind of a syringe and needle. Still, he could not allow himself to be taken; he would have to make a dash for it.

"Coming to Cappagh station he pulled all his mental and physical resources together. One of the officers most politely helped him with the door and quaking inwardly he stepped out. By some miracle the platform appeared to be deserted. Constable Neery in the next carriage appeared astounded for a bare instant and quickly averted his eyes. Oh good and darling man, thought he, may the heavens bless you. The train pulled out of the station carrying the brigadier general to future triumphs. Perhaps to Singapore.

"So I was back safely in Ballymulalla the same day. [Plunkett] , who was a stickler for protocol, did not think it proper to ask me about my recent interview, although he must have been most curious, but sought my views on another matter he had been stewing over during my absence. The local battalion commandant had been complaining for quite a long time about a bridge in his area much used by the military and which he was anxious to have destroyed. Having agreed to the necessity for destroying this particular bridge we all retired to bed.

"Rendezvous.

"We moved off after dark the following evening with the intention of making a wide circuit that would bring us out two miles east of [Dungarvan]. The local company would provide twelve pick and crowbar men and eight shotgun men for its protecting party.

In case of unforeseen trouble the curate's house, two miles back was to be a rendezvous.

"Coming off the hills we passed the Brickey canal and crossed several fields until we came to the Mount Odell demesne, now in the possession of a French community of nuns. After passing through the extensive demesne we made a wide sweep to the east arriving two hours afterwards at the pre-arranged meeting place on time and without incident.

"The bridge proved to be a tougher proposition than we had bargained for and we had no explosives. The working party quite failed to make any appreciable dent in the solid structure which must have been over a hundred years old and very solidly built. The headlights of a night raiding party were now observed coming towards us from the direction of the town and it may have been out of frustration with the bridge and we decided to attack the troops on their return from their marauding expedition.[78]

This party consisted of a car and a Crossley tender carrying troops and under the command of Captain Thomas, returning to Dungarvan from Cloncoskoran via Clonea. They were approaching the Burgery, a suburb of Dungarvan a mile to the north-east of the town: 'a pretty suburb, well sheltered with trees, and along the road there are good fences topped with hawthorn and privet on either side'. George Plunkett later wrote his own account of what was to become known as the Burgery ambush:

---

[78] George G. Lennon, *Trauma in Time,* extracted from 'Trauma in Time' (1971) the unpublished memoirs of George G. Lennon.

"In order to do so, two roads had to be taken into consideration. If, as surmised, the English were to attempt to return to their quarters in Dungarvan.

"Two parties were told off for duty. One was to take up position on the Burgery Road, the other to remain at the crossroad near Mrs Dulea's. The men who had tools and no arms were left with the other latter party.

"As it happened, the former party made contact with the enemy, missing the five seater Ford touring car (commandeered by the English) carrying Captain Thomas, one soldier in uniform, Sgt Hickey RIC, and perhaps two others, but stopping the Crossley tender and setting fire to it. It was impossible to see if there were any English casualties on account of the darkness.

"The firing, including that of the attacking party and that of the enemy covering their retreat, lasted about ten minutes at most.

"The second party of Óglaigh came up at the double to reinforce the attackers, but failed to make contact, even though the distance was short, for the enemy had retired in the darkness.

"Six members of the second party, crossing a field, arrived at the gateway leading to the Burgery Road. They heard a party marching towards them and challenged them. Captain Thomas, CO English troops and irregulars (called Black and Tans) in Dungarvan answered, giving his name, rank and unit. Upon this, the party were called upon to put up their hands. Instead of obeying the command, however, this little party, numbering three or five, who had passed the Crossley when the attack opened, in their Ford car – being, to give them their due, in a tight corner – turned about and ran towards the Burgery and towards Dungarvan.

"The six Volunteers who had been in slight cover, hurried out onto the road and gave chase, calling upon the English to halt. These six soon caught up on Captain Thomas, one soldier and Sgt Hickey, who had run a couple of hundred yards and then gone into the little front garden of a cottage in the Burgery, Seán MacGearailt, of Kilrossanty, was eager to be first in that chase.

"They were taken into custody and disarmed. Captain Thomas had one .455 Colt automatic and some few rounds, and one service pistol; the soldier had a rifle and about fifty rounds of .303 ammunition in a cloth sling; Sgt Hickey had one service rifle and about fifty rounds .303, and one .38 Webley automatic pistol and a few rounds for it.

"Captain Thomas was not in uniform, but was wearing an overcoat with badges and a uniform cap. The one soldier was in uniform, and Sgt Hickey was in the uniform of a sergeant of the RIC. All three were first searched for arms, and afterwards more carefully. Papers were taken from Captain Thomas. He was put into a small house, advised of the danger of coming out before daylight, and afterwards released. The soldier was placed in another house. The Ford car was put out of action by one of 25 hand grenades taken in a box within it."[79]

Back in Dungarvan, the military garrison began firing Verey flares, and were soon joined by the Royal Marines from Ballinacourty. Both groups fired several volleys and many single shots into the darkness throughout the night, to the distress of the town's inhabitants.

---

[79] *Waterford News*, 'The Burgery Ambush', 5 September 1924. Although Plunkett is not expressly listed as the author, certain details (i.e. the shooting of Redman) make it clearly his account.

Lennon's recollection was:

"Impromptu night engagements are likely to have unforeseen results and this one proved to be no exception. The main body of the military lost contact with their officers and retreated in the opposite direction. We destroyed the two enemy vehicles and took some prisoners whom we released. All but one {Sgt Hickey].

'I and Thou'

A Play in One Act by George Lennon (undated)

Persons

A Partisan Officer
A Constabulary Sergeant
A Priest
A Firing Squad

A grey cold morning in Holy Week
Wednesday
Spy Wednesday

The night action has been indecisive on all sides. Both the partisans and the enemy soldiers have got mixed up in the night's darkness and have scattered in all directions.

The partisan officer is walking back and forth outside the priest's house – the agreed re-assembly point. His patience has almost given out when a squad of his men come tiredly up the country road: They surround a prisoner. He restrains his curiosity until they come up.

Subordinate Officer: We ran a bunch of them to ground, we hunted them down and they surrendered. We released the regular soldiers but we had to take him (he inclines his head towards the prisoner, a constabulary sergeant).

Partisan Officer: (He exchanges a glance of recognition with the police sergeant) Ah, it is him.

Subordinate Officer: He is very windy. He knows he is for it.

Partisan Officer (doubtfully): It would be hard for us to release him?

Subordinate Officer (heatedly): Release him. Of course not, it would be the end of us all and our homes.

The police sergeant is a powerfully built man but he seems to have shrunk into his bottle-green uniform. He looks by no means ill-natured but his face now has a sallow, yellow tinge and his lips are white. He has the look of the deepest sadness, if not despair.

Partisan Officer: Call the priest.

One of the men knocks loudly on the door of the priest's house. The priest opens the door with a frightened look and goes back to dress. They all wait in silence. A cold morning mist seeps around and drips from the bare hawthorn branches. The priest comes out into the forbidding morning wearing a stole and carrying a prayer book.

Partisan Officer: Father, get this man a full glass of whiskey and then hear his confession.

The pale young priest re-enters his house and returns after a moment with a tumbler full of whiskey. One of the partisans takes the glass from him and partisans takes it up to the prisoner.

Partisan (not unkindly): Drink this.

The police sergeant takes the glass unsteadily and gets the liquid down in a number or gulps. Then the priest takes him gently by the arm and leads him to his doorstep where they both sit down. The priest places his hand affectionately on the sergeant's arm and hears his confession. When they have finished the others wait uneasily for the moments are pregnant. The officer makes a signal and the priest takes the prisoners arm to assist him up. As they pass the officer the prisoner looks appealingly at him but the officer averts his eyes. They all force themselves into motion. The clergyman is holding the prisoner's arm and he is speaking words of consolation into his ear. They walk back the boreen with the partisan officer bringing up the rear. He is very disturbed but he conceals his unhappiness.

A sharp turn in the by-road. A gateway leading into a field. The partisan officer goes ahead, opens the rusty gate and the all file in. The officer leads the prisoner out in the field and affixes a label on front of his tunic. Written on the label are the words 'Police Spy'. Then the partisan leader whips a handkerchief from his pocket. The file of men slam the bolts of their rifles with an uneven clatter. The partisan officer moves close to the sergeant with the bandage in his hand

Police Sergeant (pleadingly): George, I knew you as a child, you used to play with the head constable's children in the barracks.

Partisan Officer (almost inaudibly): Yes

Police Sergeant (intimately): You are the one person in the world that can save me.

Partisan Officer (pity is choking him): I would give anything... anything in the world to save you ... but I cannot–

They are alone, quite alone, and helpless.... A glance of understanding and deep affection passes between them. The sergeant squares his shoulders and stands straight to attention. The officer quickly ties the bandage over the man's eyes, steps back, drops his arm and calls 'fire'.

The morning silence of the glen is shattered.

The dead man sways on his feet an instant, slowly inclines and falls rigidly on his left side, his head amongst the ferns. The officer draws his Luger, bends down and fires into the man's temple. The priest clasps his hands before his face and runs back towards his house, his shoulders shaken with sobs.

The partisan officer looks down at the erstwhile enemy who is now an enemy no more. His turmoil is calmed. He makes a sign to his men and they go quickly off.

The police sergeant lies peacefully amongst the withered ferns."

Mick Mansfield remembered: "At 7.30 am on 19 March 1921, Plunkett took about six men from the column back to Burgery to have a look around for guns which were discarded by the British in their fight the previous night. Amongst those in the party were Pat Keating, Commandant of the Kilrossanty Battalion and Sean

Fitzgerald, Captain of the Kilrossanty Company. I might mention here that all of the officers were very much against this proposal of Plunketts to return to the scene of the previous night's encounter so soon afterwards. It was argued that the British would be out in strength and that it was simply asking for trouble to approach the Burgery ambush position again. Notwithstanding the representations made to him, Plunkett was determined to go ahead with the idea so, as already stated, he set off with five or six men towards the Burgery, Dungarvan. Crossing a field near the road where most of the fighting had taken place the previous night, Plunkett's party ran into heavy fire from a number of military and Black and Tans."

George Plunkett's account continues:

"Afterwards, the party of Volunteer riflemen made their way towards the scene of the night's encounter in order to find arms or ammunition lost or thrown away by the English in their flight. On crossing the same field ... they perceived a number of men, some in English 'khaki' and others in 'black and tan'.

"These English were passing along the road towards Dungarvan, dragging the burnt-out remains of their Crossley tender of the night before [utilising a commandeered horse]. It was now broad daylight; the Óglaigh had been delayed in finding the priest and by his ministrations to the man about to die.

"The Óglaigh opened fire at from thirty-five to forty yards. Their position was a bad one, in an open field, without any cover except a small earth ditch about twenty inches high, and without shrubs on it, behind them.

"The enemy had the cover of the ditches and hedge on the road. Three or four of the Volunteers, including Pádraig Ceitinn and Seán MacGearailt [Pat Keating and Jack Fitzgerald], were in advance and lay down in the grass to do their work more thoroughly, firing wherever they saw a cap or a sleeve or a puff of smoke. Seán MacGearailt and Pádraig Ceitinn were almost in line three, four or five yards apart. Seán MacGearailt ceased firing and laid his head between his arms. Pádraig Ceitinn, all excitement, said, 'Jack, Jack, are you hurt?' repeating the same question two or three times. He got no reply but a curt 'go on firing' from his neighbour on the right. Seán was on the extreme left. But Pádraig was only concerned for his good friend, and partly rose while repeating his question. Then he shrieked, 'I'm hit, I'm hit!' or something like it, and writhed up in pain. Another bullet had hit him, and he shouted again and again, finally sinking down on the ground moaning with pain. His neighbour on the right had some back cover of a sort in the shape of a hedge running towards a gate, the same gate out of which the Óglaigh had perceived Captain Thomas during the night. This hedge ran downward to the gate from the right hand of Pádraig's neighbour. He now found himself without ammunition, for he had hastily taken one of the captured rifles and only a few rounds of ammunition. He ran over to Pádraig for ammunition, and saw something rise from at the side of the gate-post just as just as he got a round into the breech and the bolt home. He aimed carefully – perhaps a bit high in the rush – and fired. His target dropped. No more bullets were spitting up grass around and in front of him."

George Plunkett had just picked off a Black and Tan named Sidney Redman, who had clambered onto the gatepost to get a clearer shot at the IRA party. Redman was later seen being driven back to Dungarvan, cradled in the arms of a colleague, where he died that evening:

"The only firing now was on the right flank and slightly to the rear. His comrades were covering a retreat from a useless position. Their objective was gone, for the enemy had already covered the ground, and the Óglaigh were tired from marching and counter-marching all night. Seán MacGearailt lay still, even when his comrades attempted to lift him. Pádraig Ceitinn, good, tough, spirited mountainy man, with two bullets right through his body, managed to walk a few paces with help, and lay down behind the little useless twenty inch earth fence. He told his comrade to take his belt and Parabellelum and to get four men as guard and remove him to 'Whytes' [of Monarud], for he was going to die. His comrade tried to lift him again and to encourage him, but he was weak, and all his friend could think of the whole time was the shame it was that the prayers he was trying to say came out in English and not in Gaelic."[80]

According to James Mansfield:

"To me, it was obvious that if we remained as we were we would all be killed, so I passed the word to some men on my left to cease fire and make for a gap in the field which was, incidentally, being swept with bullets by the British. George Lennon, the column OC, then came along and agreed with me that we should chance the gap. We did so, and all of us got through without mishap, except Kelly Donovan who received a bullet wound across his mouth. We now had somewhat more cover, but we still held our fire so as not to betray our position; besides, the Tommies showed no inclination to come out into the open. They continued firing from cover."

George Plunkett continued:

"So this young man left Pat Ceitinn, took his own and another couple of rifles he found lying around and went off to find the

---

[80] *Waterford News*, 'The Burgery Ambush', 5 September 1924.

remainder of his party who were retiring in the direction already determined on. They were not in any condition for further work and continued on their way. They still had a mountain journey before them."

James Mansfield said:

"George Plunkett then made contact with us and agreed that our position was hopeless and that there was nothing for it but to retreat."

Other participants in this action had bitterly opposed the decision to return to the site of the previous night's encounter for very good reason. Lennon himself recalled:

"It was not really a mistake to go back as we badly needed what munitions that might have been left behind by the military when they fled. It was a grave mistake not to have reconnoitred the place in the first instance and the fatal mistake could only have been mine. We walked straight into an ambuscade. I must confess that I did not conduct myself with any great show of bravery. [Plunkett] behaved with amazing coolness and courage. He took over."

It should be noted that much of Lennon's account is unduly modest, written many years later from the viewpoint of a dedicated pacifist.

According to George Plunkett:

"Some friends of Ireland were told of Pádraig Ceitinn's plight, and these went with a pony and trap and brought him to the place he had named. But in the meanwhile the English had removed their own dead and dying and also Seán MacGearailt's body. They had not seen Pádraig's body behind his twenty inch wall."

George Lennon said:

"The remainder of us retreated sadly across the grey fields. I seemed unable to face the fact that Pat was dead. I was weary, unspeakably unhappy and quite dispirited and had fallen a long way behind. The staff captain came back and slipped his arm into mine. 'Come along,' said he, 'there is something you must do for me.'

"Soon afterwards [Plunkett] left us to return to GHQ with his report. As he was fixing his bicycle clips he said coldly that he was recommending that I take responsibility for all activities in the county. As we were still a bit stiff with each other we did not offer to shake hands. He rode away and soon disappeared around a bend in the road."

Local man Mike Heafy helped the badly wounded Keating to a horse and cart where he was covered in hay; despite his agonising pain, he remained conscious and lucid throughout the journey to Whytes', where he was made as comfortable as possible and a local priest and doctor summoned. His wounds however proved too serious and when he realised death was inevitable, Keating asked the Whytes, 'not to let the Black and Tans get his body'. Pat Keating died at 5 p.m. that night, the Keating parents collected their son's body and brought it by horse and cart, accompanied by his siblings, around the back roads to Kilrossanty. In the village school, Dr Joe Walsh and Nurse Kate Cullinane placed the body into a coffin and Keating was secretly buried that night in the Cullinane family plot in Newtown.[81]

---

[81] IMA BMH WS James Mansfield; Waterford News, 'The Burgery Ambush', 5 September 1924; Keating, Lena, *The Keatings of Comeragh*.

A furious Michael Collins subsequently took Pax Whelan to task for releasing Captain Thomas and the other prisoners, but Whelan pointed out that it had been George Plunkett's decision. Otherwise Thomas might have ended his days being held as a hostage and shot in reprisal for an executed IRA man, a fact of which Plunkett was undoubtedly aware. Mick Shalloe later claimed that Thomas had promised not to carry out reprisals for the ambush, although none of the other accounts corroborate this.[82]

An *Irish Times* reporter who visited the scene of the ambush soon afterwards reported:

"About half a mile [from Dungarvan] there is a quantity of blood on the ground outside the gate of a field. This is where the policeman, Redmond [sic], was shot dead. There is also the mark of a bullet on the iron gate ... further on lie what remains of the motor lorry which was destroyed ... All about the road, in the ditches and lanes there have been found considerable quantities of ammunition, and also spent cartridges."[83]

On the evening of 19 Saturday, acting on information received, British troops recovered the body of Sergeant Hickey and brought it back to Dungarvan barracks where it was laid beside Redman's. Medical examination revealed that apart from Lennon's mercy shot, only two bullets from the firing squad had struck home. Initially, newspapers claimed that Redman's body was riddled

---

[82] MacEoin Uinseann, *Survivors* (Argenta, Dublin, 1980), p. 138; IMA BMH WS Michael Shalloe.

[83] *Irish Times*, 'The Shooting of Sergeant Hickey', 22 March 1921.

with bullet holes in the back and chest; the *Dungarvan Observer* subsequently retracted the allegation.

According to the *Munster Express*:

"The interment of Sergeant Hickey took place today [21 March 1921] in the new cemetery of the RC parish church. There was a difficulty about the grave. No one seemed disposed to dig it, and it was only when one of the Catholic curates approached the workmen that the digging was begun. This involved considerable delay, and at about half-past four a company of the RIC led by their officer and carrying rifles, followed by a company of military, also armed, marched through the street to the cemetery. They carried several wreaths for the grave. The interment then took place, scarcely any of the general public participating. A volley was fired over the grave and the Last Post was sounded, after which the military and constables drew away and returned to the barracks."

Shortly before 6 p.m., three local priests went to the barracks and obtained permission to bury the remains of Jack Fitzgerald, with the stipulation that only forty persons take part in the funeral:

"The people were advised to remain in the church and there to await the remains. This advice was followed, and amid a scene of mourning, the funeral passed through the streets. The church was thronged. The remains were carried on the shoulders of young men from the town, who bore it all the way to the church. They were followed by members of Cumann na mBan, who carried several wreaths of natural flowers. No military or police took part in the funeral. On reaching the church there was an immense gathering of persons ... the regulation that only forty persons would be allowed to follow the remains of Fitzgerald to the church was not rigidly enforced."

A curfew was enforced at 7 p.m.

That night, Pat Keating's body was secretly exhumed by his family and the body buried in the rugged Mahon Valley, where it was to remain for the next two months until it was moved to its final resting place. A poem written by Keating before his death proved grimly prophetic:

> *The village church close by the hills*
> *Again I seem to view*
> *It stands as neat and beautiful*
> *As when I bid adieu*
> *The boys with whom I used to play*
> *I seem to see them still*
> *But some are sleeping peacefully*
> *Nigh Comeragh's Rugged Hills*

The following morning, a large crowd gathered at the church in Dungarvan to escort Fitzgerald's remains to the family plot at Kilrossanty. This time, the British army insisted that the public did not join the cortege, and at the request of Fr Egan, the local populace complied. Jack Fitzgerald was laid to rest in the little graveyard in Kilrossanty. He was the first Volunteer to be interred in what was to become West Waterford's Republican Plot.

The *Irish Times* later reported:

"A large number of crown forces left the town on Friday [25 March] and drove into the country to where the ambush occurred recently. An armoured car preceded them. They went to Ballycoe House, the residence of Mrs Dunlea, about one and a half miles from the town and half a mile from the place where the ambush took place. Having driven up the avenue, they halted before the door, and intimation was given to the occupants that the house and its contents were about to be destroyed. The occupants of the house were the two daughters of Mrs Dunlea. The slates were removed and the rafters left bare. The furniture was broken and the building is a complete wreck. The party of crown forces made a detour, and coming home by the Burgery, the scene of the ambush, demolished a farmhouse that lies by the roadside. This is owned by Mrs Morrissey ... On Friday night crown forces demolished the furniture in the licensed premises of Miss English, Sexton Street."[84]

The following day, the Black and Tans and British military thoroughly destroyed the furniture of three more houses in Dungarvan itself. In the following weeks walls were daubed with slogans such as 'Up the Buffs' and 'Remember Hickey and Redmond [sic]'. Such reprisals proved counter-productive; few if any of the parties to suffer were involved with the IRA.

Shortly afterwards, the Dungarvan IRA company shot dead a local man, William Moran, a former British soldier who was accused of passing information to crown forces.[85]

On the 28 March, George Lennon and Paddy Paul attended the second conference of IRA southern brigades at Glenville, Co. Cork, spending the previous night in Cork city before proceeding to the meeting. Paul recalled:

"The meeting was called by Liam Lynch apparently for the purpose of a general survey of the position and ... we were informed of the projected landing of an Italian cargo of arms

---

[84] *Irish Times* "The Dungarvan Ambush" 28 March 1921.

[85] Keohan, Edmond, *Illustrated History of Dungarvan* (*Waterford News*, Waterford, 1924); NLI FOD 31,150 (Activities – Waterford brigade).

which was expected to take place on the southern coast in the immediate future."

After the conference, Paul and Lennon boarded the train for Cappagh. Again Lennon found himself sharing a train carriage with British soldiers and senior officers, which according to Paul, 'made us feel rather uncomfortable for a while but they did not seem to take any notice of us and we detrained at Cappagh without incident'.[86]

In early April 1921, a party of the 'Buffs' from Dungarvan led by Captain Thomas captured Edmond Power, of the column, in Kilmacthomas, where he had been recovering from a foot injury sustained after the Burgery ambush. According to Power:

"The captain did not recognise me as being one of his captors a short time previously. When travelling in the military lorry from Kilmacthomas to Dungarvan, it was obvious that the military were very nervous of being ambushed en route; in fact, the officer warned me that I would be 'the first to go' if he was ambushed, to which I replied: 'I'll have plenty of company if I do go'. I was lodged in a cell in Dungarvan barracks and the first evening an old fellow was put in with me. He was, supposedly a tramp, but I had no doubts from his conversation that he was a spy. Then followed a hammering at the cell door and in came two Black and Tans both of whom were drunk. They proceeded to hit me and said I was to be shot next day. They were restrained from further assaulting me by a regular member of the RIC."[87]

---

86 IMA BMH WS Patrick Paul.

87 IMA BMH WS Edmond Power.

An IRA report giving names and descriptions of some of the Black and Tans based in Dungarvan in mid-1921 proves informative. Although a few were described as 'quiet' and 'inoffensive' and another was dismissed from the RIC for passing information to the local IRA, most were described as 'dangerous'. A few interesting personal details were added; 'Jock MacAllister – very dangerous' was 'expected to marry local prostitute'. 'White – ex Irish Guards' was a 'bully, brutal to prisoners, always threatening and complete rowdy. Shot boy ten years of age last June in Youghal Road'. 'Wells – very bad appearance' was a Londoner like White, while 'Skilton' was 'dangerous, officious and untrustworthy'.[88]

On 3 April 1921, a party of these Black and Tans carried out a raid on a shop in Abbeyside in Dungarvan during which, according to Jeremiah MacVeagh, an MP for the Irish Parliamentary Party who subsequently raised the matter in the British House of Commons, they carried out 'looting and overtures and acts of indecency'. The IRA report identified one Black and Tan as having carried out an act of rape in this matter. The two women involved made an official complaint to the RIC and identified one of the men concerned at Dungarvan barracks. According to MacVeagh:

"... as a reprisal for the identification, the police returned in the middle of the night on 14th April and wrecked and burned the shop and house, destroyed furniture, stock and effects, stole money, and left the lady homeless and penniless, the only

---

[88] NLI FOD MS 31,204 – 'miscellaneous undated 1st So. Division intelligence documents'.

occupants of the house being these two ladies and a child of six years."[89]

According to the *Waterford News*:

"The Strand Hotel was first visited ... soon the hotel was ablaze. The fire burned fiercely and quickly spread to a house next door ... both houses were gutted. Almost at the same time, the public house of Mr Thomas Fahey [interned at the time] was set on fire and ... completely destroyed with all of its contents. The shop of Mrs Terry, next door to Fahey's, was caught in the conflagration and burned to the ground ... The Fire Brigade, under Mr Thomas Walsh, came on the scene about 2 o'clock this morning and by its aid the fire zone was confined, so that its spread throughout the whole street was fortunately prevented. The military and RIC also turned out and assisted in fighting the flames."[90]

No Black and Tan was held to account for these incidents. Although these particular events were popularly believed to be reprisals for the Burgery ambush they were far more likely to have been a consequence of the slipping of the normally tight hold kept on the Black and Tans in Dungarvan.

At about this time, Paddy Paul in Waterford received a request for assistance from the hard-pressed West Waterford men, and dispatched a hundred rounds of ammunition to Dungarvan, all he could spare at the time.[91]

---

[89] Hansard HC 16 June 1921, Vol. 143 cc583–4.

[90] *Waterford News*, 'Shocking Scenes in Dungarvan', 15 April 1921.

[91] IMA BMH WS Patrick Paul.

On 20 April 1921, six members of the Waterford flying column carried out an attack on the British platoon based at Charles Nugent Humble's house at Cloncoskoran. According to Mick Shalloe:

"The building was about fifty yards in off the main Waterford - Dungarvan road and the ground for half a mile on either side of it was well wooded; it afforded excellent cover. Sentries could be seen patrolling the grounds. The night was dark. One shot was fired first, in the hope that this would bring out the guard on duty. In fact, the result was that the British opened indiscriminate fire from the sandbagged windows of the building without any regard as to where they fired. It was obvious that the lesson taught them on the night of the Burgery ambush had not been forgotten. They showed no inclination to come out and fight. We kept up intermittent firing for the best part of an hour – with what effect, I cannot say – and when the military showed no signs of coming out in the open, the six of us decided to move off. For fully half an hour after we had left to join up with the main body of the column, the British kept up a continuous fire with machine-guns and rifles."[92]

No representative from either Waterford brigade was present at a meeting in Millstreet on 26 April 1921, which saw the formation of the IRA's 1st Southern Division, under the command of Liam Lynch. This development was an attempt to bring the nine IRA brigades of Waterford, Cork, Kerry and West Limerick, together under the command of a tactical headquarters, closer to the

---

[92] NLI FOD 31,150 (Activities – Waterford brigade); IMA BMH WS Michael Shalloe.

fighting units than GHQ in Dublin.[93] On the morning of 29 April 1921, according to Michael Cummins of Stradbally:

"I happened to be at home at the time, sick and in bed, when George Lennon sent a message to me to come quickly to Ballyvoyle Cross ... I got ready, and bringing a rifle and revolver, met Lennon and another member of the Active Service Unit – Mick Morrissey of Dungarvan – at the appointed venue. The time was about 11 a.m. Lennon told me that he had got word that a train carrying military would be passing soon from Waterford to Dungarvan and that he proposed to have a crack at them at Ballyvoyle. We got into position on high ground at Ballyvoyle overlooking the railway line, and when the train came along we noticed military in some of the carriages and had a few shots at them. The train did not stop. We made our way across the fields eastwards for about three miles until we reached a railway crossing at Ballylinch. By now our party had increased to nine ... most of the men had rifles, the remainder had shotguns ... On reaching Ballylinch level crossing, George Lennon split the party in two on the east and west sides of the railway line ... We closed the gates at the level crossing and tied on a red flag to stop any train coming along and lay concealed in ambush."

At 6.25 p.m., the train from Fermoy pulled into Dungarvan station. Aboard were between fifteen and twenty British soldiers of the Devonshire regiment commanded by an officer, guarding the military carriage hitched to the train. It was obvious that they were anticipating an ambush. Also aboard were several nervous civilians, including a Catholic priest and two nuns from Waterford city. Circling overhead was an RAF Bristol Fighter from Fermoy. This aircraft was not delivering mail to Dungarvan barracks

[93] O'Donoghue, Florence, *No Other Law* (Anvil, Dublin, 1986), pp. 154–155.

however – it was obviously escorting the train. The RAF in Ireland were arming their aircraft with machine-guns at this time and during the First World War, the 'Brisfit' had proved itself an effective ground attack aircraft.

The train pulled out from Dungarvan and continued its journey eastwards, its escorting aircraft still overhead. It is not difficult to imagine the tension building as the train abruptly slowed to follow the sharp bend as the track turned north and into the deep dark cutting before crossing the viaduct and plunging into the dark Ballyvoyle tunnel; passengers observed British soldiers and the RIC standing guard where the ambush had taken place earlier that day. As the train reached the tunnel, the Bristol Fighter was seen to turn to the west and fly back towards Fermoy, short on fuel. The RAF pilot subsequently reported:

"Aerial escort supplied for train from Fermoy to Waterford. Escorted until compelled to return on account of petrol shortage. Left train OK leaving Dungarvan. Nothing unusual and line clear. This train was subsequently held up by rebels, who had closed gates at level crossing near Kilmacthomas about fifteen minutes after the machine had left it. Several casualties occurred on both sides."

According to the *Munster Express*:

"The train left Durrow, which is beyond the tunnel, at about 6.35 p.m., and on the gradient at Ballylynch crossing the first warning that the passengers received that anything untoward was happening was the shrieking of the siren of the engine, and apparently the crossing gates were closed."

Paddy Joe Power (Stradbally) recalled:

156

"When the train pulled in and stopped we saw she was laden with military. We opened up on them and they replied with heavy rifle and machine-gun fire. From the firebox of the engine two soldiers were using a Lewis gun and raking our position."

Mick Cummins said:

"Most of the soldiers got out of the carriages and took cover on the side of the train nearest to me. I started sniping at these soldiers. The next thing I noticed was the door of a carriage opening and what appeared to be a soldier with a tin helmet and khaki coat at the open door. I fired at him but he didn't move. I chanced a second shot but still no move. I ducked low and went about thirty yards nearer my target, when suddenly a burst of machine-gun fire sprayed the corner I had just left. I saw the smoke of the machine-gun coming from a carriage window, took dead aim at it and fired. No more machine-gun fire came from that window."

The *Munster Express* continued:

"Fire was opened from the train by a machine-gun placed in a wagon which appeared to have been entirely unexpected by the attackers. Shortly afterwards the gunner received a wound in the foot and another in the groin, and as a result the gun was rendered ineffective for a short time."

The furious exchange of gunfire began at about 6.40 p.m. and continued for half an hour. Unseen by the ambushers, the civilian passengers huddled on the floor of train in understandable terror as bullets ripped through the wooden carriages and upholstery within inches of them; the coachwork was soon riddled with bullet holes while every window in the carriages were shattered.

Paddy Joe Power was turning his head in an attempt to locate the Lewis gun when a British bullet very nearly found its mark, slicing through his neck only an inch from his jugular. Bleeding badly, Power 'continued to fire, but after some time, sent word to George Lennon, who was some distance from me, that I was wounded. Lennon crawled up to me and seeing my condition, gave orders to retreat. In any case, our ammunition was practically spent and we couldn't keep up the fight any longer ... We retired southwards'.

Mick Cummins however missed the retreat order:

"Next thing I heard was the bursting of grenades near where I lay. These were probably rifle grenades being fired by the military. I kept looking for about ten minutes or so for a sight of a soldier and then spotted the heads of two soldiers between the fence and the railway. I gave them rapid fire and the heads disappeared. I remained alone in my position for another five minutes or more (it seems I had not heard the whistle blast given by George Lennon as the signal to retreat) and then saw a British officer walking up by the carriages using binoculars. I fired at him. He gave a kind of jump and then fell back. By this time I had a feeling that our lads had pulled out as the shooting had stopped. In fact, they had done so some time previously but I didn't know it. As I had only five rounds of ammunition left and seeing no sign of or hearing no sound from our fellows, I decided to retreat ... I did not make contact with any of our boys until later that evening when I met up with them near Kilrossanty."

After the ambush party had withdrawn, the British troops began searching the vicinity. Darkness had fallen and at 8.45 p.m., the troops boarded the train which pulled out and continued the journey to Kilmacthomas. The train eventually reached Waterford city at 9.50 p.m. where the wounded soldier (Private BJ Goodwin) was finally taken to hospital. Power was brought to a house near Stradbally where Dr Walsh of Bunmahon dressed his wound; later he was brought to Kilmacthomas where he was tended to by Nurse Kate Cullinane.[94]

On the 19 May 1921, on a bright moonlit night, Pat Keating's body was lifted from its temporary grave in the Mahon Valley. According to a later memoir by his sister Lena:

"My father, Willie, Thomas and Michael [brothers], accompanied by members of the Old IRA, Mick Mansfield, George Lennon, Ned and Paddy Joe Power and local Volunteers took up the remains which they carried across the Mahon river, through Crough wood and on to the Crough Road where Fr Sheehy, CC, Marcella, Bridget, Margaret, my mother, Willie's wife Mary, Tom Cunningham and myself were waiting. Fr Sheehy led the midnight funeral in his horse and trap followed by the parents, brothers, sisters, relatives, friends and comrades in the IRA flying column. When the funeral reached the cemetery in Kilrossanty a grave was already prepared in a new plot (now the republican plot) which had been selected by my parents. Fr Sheehy blessed the coffin and led the prayers for the dead. The grave was then covered over in gravel so that it could not be distinguished from the surrounding gravel paths. Finally, a volley of shots was fired over Pat Keating's last resting place by members of the Old IRA, including some of his colleagues [Lennon, Mansfield, Ned and Paddy Joe Power]. The family went back to Comeragh that night a little happier that Pat was safely back home."[95]

---

[94] IMA BMH WS Michael Cummins, Patrick J. Power; McCarthy, Patrick, 'The RAF and Ireland 1920–22', *The Irish Sword*, Vol. XVII, Issue 68; *Munster Express*, 'Train ambushed in Co. Waterford', 7 May 1921.

[95] Keating, Lena, *The Keatings of Comeragh.*

Two of the Cullinane sisters present, Mary and Kate, set out for home in Kilmacthomas in a pony and trap, escorted by Lennon, Mansfield and Paddy Joe Power, the latter cycling. Four cyclists who were to give warning of any crown forces in the area preceded them. This was rather risky since cyclists required a permit at that time and were forbidden to cycle after dark.

On the main Waterford–Dungarvan road, just west of Kilmacthomas, a large party of the Devonshire regiment from Waterford were lying in wait. It was later whispered locally that an informer had tipped them off; while this is certainly possible, the Devons patrolled Kilmacthomas and the main road regularly, frequently raiding the Cullinane's house.

One of the British officers in the patrol later stated:

"I remember the 18 May last, at about 3 a.m. I was on escort duty on the road between Kilmacthomas and Dungarvan, at a point just beyond the first level crossing beyond Kilmacthomas. I was in the leading car and I saw two cyclists approaching – one on either side of the road. I ordered my driver to stop and we got out of the car. I ordered the two cyclists to stop and put up their hands. They did so ... I took both cyclists into custody and later handed them over to the guard at the Infantry Barracks."

Another British officer related:

"About four hundred yards past the first level crossing the convoy stopped and we heard the sound of horses' hooves along the road. We got out and met a party of thirteen civilians. There were two cyclists first, then two more cyclists, then a pony trap and a man on a cycle holding onto the side of the pony cart. Then came a second car."

Lennon and Mansfield reacted like lightning. By Mansfield's account:

"Lennon and I jumped out of the trap and made over the fence on one side of the road. I clubbed a soldier with my rifle butt and made off in the darkness into a boggy field where I was soon up to my waist in bogwater. The soldiers seemed to be panic-stricken and commenced firing wildly in the darkness. Lennon and I waded through the bog until we reached the railway line about two hundred yards inland from the main road. Meanwhile, the soldiers tried following us through the bog, and having failed, they doubled around and up on to the railway line hoping to cut us off. However, we succeeded in escaping them in the darkness."

Paddy Joe Power also reacted quickly, but less luckily. Throwing his bicycle at a soldier, he jumped over the fence on the other side of the road, but was caught in barbed wire and fell headfirst into marshy ground. He was dragged from the marsh and was subjected to a severe kicking from a furious British officer (who had also fallen into the marsh) before being taken away to the military barracks in Waterford. A British officer later claimed that:

"I went to the first pony cart in which I saw Mary Cullinane, Edmund Power and Patrick Joyce [sic] ... I searched the pony trap, the two girls being still seated in the trap. From under a rug on the floor I pulled out a service rifle. I found live rounds in the magazine. The girls had their feet on the rifle. I searched the two men who were in the cart and took an army haversack off Edmond Power. I opened it in front of him and took out a piece of fuse and saw some books and a small bottle of iodine."

Six of those captured that night, including Mary Cullinane, later received five year sentences. Ned Power received seven years.[96]

Shortly afterwards, at Lennon's request, Paddy Paul travelled to the Tay Valley for a meeting, nearly being captured in a raid by crown forces on Kilmacthomas. He later related:

"Proceeding on my way to meet George Lennon I learned from him about the arrest of Paddy Joe Power and the others and he wanted to know if I could organise any attempt to rescue Power from Waterford Prison. I promised him I would do what I could but that until I had examined the possibilities I could not say how we would operate."

An attempt to free Power from the prison did in fact take place; according to Waterford Volunteer Dan Ennis.

"At about 11 a.m. on the morning of 6 April a small group that included Willy Keane and a local IRA officer Ned O'Brien (a young accountant with the *Waterford News*) took up position outside the prison with the intention of throwing a rope ladder over the wall on receipt of a pre-arranged signal that did not come. Before Paddy Joe Power was to be tried by court-martial in late June, he developed diphtheria and was hospitalised until hostilities ended, thereby avoiding possible execution."[97]

Jack O'Mara was captured near his home by a British army patrol and was interrogated in Dungarvan barracks after which he was transferred to Waterford where he 'was again closely cross-examined by some officers, including one by the name of Yeo. This

---

[96] Keating, Lena, *The Keatings of Comeragh.*

[97] IMA BMH WS Patrick Paul, Daniel Ennis.

fellow Yeo was notorious for his ill-treatment of republican prisoners and I have certainly good cause to remember how he treated me. This man hurled abuse at me for being, as he said, "concerned in the murder of a decent man, Sergeant Hickey of Dungarvan". This blackguard, Yeo, then proceeded to beat me savagely with a stick on the head, neck, back and arms. Following the beating, I was thrown into a cell, where I had to lie on the floor on my stomach, it being impossible for me to lie on my back because of the beating I had received'.

O'Mara was being held pending the arrival of a soldier witness in connection with his involvement in the Burgery ambush, but this did not happen before the close of hostilities.[98]

In late May 1921, Kilmacthomas Workhouse was occupied by a permanent garrison, an infantry company detached from the 1st Battalion of the York and Lancaster regiment in Clonmel. They were observed to have two artillery pieces with them and began patrolling the area frequently.[99] A British army intelligence report (Weekly Intelligence Summary 6th Division 17/5/21) makes interesting reading. The introduction by Major General EP Strickland trumpeted:

"No military skill or courage was shown by the rebels, who evidently find it more profitable to shoot down unarmed men – and women – than to take the field ... the recent heavy losses among their leaders, by arrest or decease, had undoubtedly

---

[98] IMA BMH WS Jack O'Mara.

[99] NLI FOD MS 31,213 'Enemy Bases in Divisional Area'; IMA BMH WS Moses Roche.

hampered their operations, which were probably planned by organisers in their GHQ."

Interestingly, although public statements referred to the IRA as 'armed civilians', their internal intelligence summaries invariably referred to the IRA by their unit designations. A few British army units, notably the Devonshires in Waterford, even referred to their adversaries by their IRA ranks. Thus, for 'West Waterford Brigade' it was noted that 'the column has not been very active during the past week and is probably in the Comeragh Mountains north-east of Kilrossanty. Mansfield, commandant 3rd (Ardmore) Battalion, and six or eight more have been located in an empty house situated in a large wood 2½ miles north-east of Ardmore'.

Elsewhere in the report, it was stated that: 'A big drive was carried out by crown forces in the Kilmacthomas area on the 6th inst. The drive failed to round up the IRA unit which has been operating in the area, yet there is no doubt that it will have a good effect in a part of the country where crown forces are seldom seen'.

Rather perceptively, it was noticed that: 'Rebel flying columns are suffering heavily from scabies. In order to cure this disease men are returning to their homes and lying up there for a week or two. It is essential that these men be kept on the move by frequent visits to their homes, thus driving them back to the column'.

It was also noted (incorrectly) that: 'Patrick Whelan, late commandant [sic], was not wounded in the Dungarvan ambush, but is now away somewhere in the west of Ireland undergoing a course of intelligence work'.

For 'Waterford East Brigade' it was noted that:

"..from reports received there is reason to believe that a column from outside the county has come into Waterford city within the last few days. There is however no confirmation except for some vague police reports of strangers. 'F' company (Ferrybank) Waterford City battalion, mobilised on 10th at the Golf Club House, which is immediately above the goods' yard and held up a goods' train'."

It was elsewhere detailed that: 'the driver and fireman were taken off the engine and placed in arrest in a shed. The train was then driven to a bridge about 1½ miles distant. Some barrels of oil, addressed to RIC Kilkenny, were broken up open and the oil spilt out, and some bacon for the military was thrown into the river. The train was then backed into the station'. Subsequently, the military retrieved the bacon at low tide.

It was also noted that 'the Dunhill company 2nd Battalion has been active trenching roads'.

All of this seems to indicate that Paddy Paul's East Waterford brigade had been reduced to mounting nuisance raids.

On the 22 May 1921, a meeting was held which the East Waterford brigade staff and all of the battalion's officers with the exception of one company captain and Paddy Paul himself attended.[100] A letter to the IRA adjutant-general [Éamon Price] dated 25/5/21, and signed 'Brigade Council, Waterford No. 1 Bde' claimed that: 'It was the unanimous decision of the meeting that the brigadier was not competent, with the result that orders issued by the brigadier [Paul] were not carried out. At this stage a new brigadier was called for ... the senior commandant then

---

[100] O'Donoghue, Florence, *No Other Law* (Anvil, Dublin, 1986) pp. 311–326.

took the chair and an election was proceeded with ... we have now once again unity in our ranks, and we can promise GHQ the immediate full co-operation of this brigade in the great fight at present being waged by the gallant men of other brigades throughout the country'.

This letter was not however forwarded to Éamon Price by the brigade's messengers, who instead handed it to Paddy Paul.

On 27 May, Paul proceeded to Dublin where Richard Mulcahy interviewed him. He returned to Waterford the following day with the following orders:

"You will remain in command of the East Waterford brigade ... you will advise all officers concerned that inquiry in the matter is pending, and that any officer who either neglects his duty or repudiates your authority shall be deemed guilty of serious insubordination."

Mulcahy also sent a message to Jim Power:

"You will submit immediately thereon through your brigade commandant, a full explanation of the circumstances in which you (1) repudiate the authority of the latter, and (2) usurp his command."

On the same day, Mulcahy dispatched a letter to Liam Lynch, OC First Southern Division which said of Paul:

"His principle offence in the eyes of those who are now criticising him in the area probably is that he endeavours to make them do definite fighting work and that he will not agree that talking about work, or even planning work, is work."

It was obvious that not even a guerrilla army could approve of what was effectively a mutiny, but the action of the East

166

Waterford brigade posed an interesting quandary. After all, the units of the IRA elected their own officers and were presumably free to elect replacements. However, the stance being taken by the IRA leadership made it obvious that the officers in East Waterford had greatly over-estimated their standing in their eyes, Michael Bishop in particular. Their cause had not been helped by way in which they had attempted to depose Paul.

On 29 May, the uncharacteristic language in a letter from Paddy Paul to IRA director of organisation, Rory O'Connor, made his anguish obvious:

"I was not aware that SECRET NEGOTIATIONS were going on between some of the brigade officers to remove me from COMMAND, and of course their ambition was to make things awkward for me in the eyes of GHQ."

Enclosing the letter from the brigade officers dated 25/5/21, he noted:

"It says that I was not competent I will leave that to more broad-minded and experienced people who knew this brigade six months ago and the type of men I had to contend with. They also state that I was holding up the fighting I will leave that to yourself ... I wish very much if you could use your influence with the CS to accept my resignation and give me a transfer to some other unit; now that all the hard work is over I consider that the brigade would be better without me."[101]

On 31 May 1921, the neighbouring No. 1 Cork Brigade reported:

---

[101] UCDA MP P7/A /19.

"4th batt Cork No. 1 1/6/21 C Coy land mine exploded 2 miles outside Youghal beneath 250 armed soldiers. 15 killed and 45–50 wounded. Mine: 6 inch Shell – 10 lbs Gelignite – buried 3 feet under surface – set off by battery."

The official history of the Hampshire regiment recorded that:

"The worst outrage of all was undoubtedly at Youghal on the 31st May 1921, when X company and the band had gone to Youghal for a musketry course. On this particular morning the band was playing the company down to the range and when they were about half a mile from their destination a land mine was fired ... when the clouds of dust settled, some twenty men and boys were seen lying on the ground, and pitiful groans and cries for help were heard. Two corporals, two bandsmen and three boys were killed and nineteen of the band were wounded."

This was the first recorded use in the conflict of what in modern parlance would be referred to as an Improvised Explosive Device (IED).[102]

Early in the month of June 1921, a military cycle patrol from Dungarvan, led by Captain D.V. Thomas, OBE, left the town and proceeded north to Colligan Lodge where they camped for the night. The following day they proceeded to Kilbrien. On 6 June 1921, this patrol was operating in the vicinity of Stradbally, and the local IRA planned an ambush. After the death of Pat Keating, his brother Tom took his place as commander of 2nd Battalion. A subsequent report by him notes that he quickly gathered all available men in the Stradbally area and:

---

[102] UCDA MP P7/A /23 Diary of Activities 4th Batt, Cork No. 1 Brigade.

"..proceeded to Knockyoolahan with thirty-three men and took up position on railway line at a point underneath Knockyoolahan where line runs parallel to road. Our force consisted of thirty-three men, made up as follows: three riflemen, twenty-four shotgun men, six unarmed scouts."

This was a lightly armed and inexperienced party, while Captain Thomas and his men had faced several ambushes by Lennon's flying column. Mick Cummins of Stradbally noted:

"Before the ambush came off I protested against it being held as our men were very badly armed, having only a few rusty old rifles and some shotguns with very little ammunition. I myself had a shotgun and five rounds of buckshot."

Tom Keating's report continued:

"At 2.30 p.m. the enemy were reported in sight coming on road to our position. As the first file of enemy were coming into our ambush, one of the scouts apparently got excited and showing himself, ran towards our position. He was observed by the enemy who opened fire on him. The first man on our position opened fire with the result that the presence of our part y was given away, and a heavy fire opened on our party by enemy who were extended back about ½ mile on our left, and a flanking movement to envelop our position, was being carried out by them. Our party responded to the fire as best they could, but were much handicapped owing to having only three rifles, shotguns being ineffective at the range from which enemy were firing and consequently our forces had to retire."

From Keating's report it seems that Captain Thomas was leading from the front, and had a charmed life on this day: 'At the beginning of the engagement one of our shotguns would have shot enemy OC but for shotgun missing fire (sic) three times'.

Mick Cummins reported:

"Two soldiers ... fired on Jack Cummins [no relation] of Ballyvoyle as he was climbing over a wire fence on the railway embankment. I saw Cummins fall. He was shot dead, through the back."

These two soldiers have been identified as Lt G.L.B. Oliver and Sergeant Fred Barton. The latter was awarded an O.B.E. for his part in this action.[103]

Keating later suggested that Jack Cummins (23) was taken alive and put to death by the British, but this was contradicted by Michael Cummins' eyewitness account and the death certificate which stated 'Heart Failure Haemorrhage Following Gunshot Wound – Death Instantaneous'. As the Royal Marines from Ballinacourty began arriving on the scene, the ambush party withdrew across the fields, bringing two wounded with them.[104]

These British forces at Ballyvoyle nearly made a sensational capture. In the locality, and warned of the ambush just in time, was Liam Lynch and several of his staff officers. That night, he held a meeting near Stradbally that was attended by all of East Waterford's brigade staff and battalion officers with the exception of Mick Bishop who had been summoned to Dublin. Lynch 'found that any of the charges brought against [Paddy Paul] could not be proved. I insisted on all officers obeying orders of Bde OC and now believe they will do their utmost to do this'. More pessimistically,

---

[103] Flaherty, Cian, *The Ballyvoile Ambush; A Centenary Study* (Dungarvan, 2021).

[104] UCDA MP P7/A /20 'Report of Operations at Knockyoolohan 6/6/21'; IMA BMH WS Michael Cummins; GRO Death Certificate for John Cummins.

Lynch noted of East Waterford: 'This area will never get action as a separate brigade'.

On 10 June 1921, the question of the East Waterford brigade was the cause of a flurry of internal correspondence within the IRA. In Dublin, Mick Bishop was interviewed in Dublin, and bluntly stated 'that even if GHQ refused to sanction Commandant Power's appointment – the brigade would refuse to carry on under Paul'. Mulcahy sent general instructions to Paddy Paul regarding his brigade which did not mention recent events. Liam Lynch sent two detailed reports to Mulcahy regarding the Waterford brigades, which noted that:

"There are only two officers in the whole brigade capable of holding brigade or battalion rank – that is brigade OC and brigade quartermaster. Brigade OC is a capable officer in every way except his defect in hearing in action which is a result of his service in enemy army, this fault would not interfere with his working brigade, when he is a capable officer in every other way. I did not order any suspensions or dismissals, but later officers will have to be removed wholesale. Some of these officers are holding back even in minor activities and are simply a lot of grumblers. [Jim Power] might after a little training be capable to take charge of a battalion, but such a battalion would never do fighting on its own initiative."

More ominously for Mick Bishop, Lynch noted that: 'the present brigade vice OC should not hold any rank as he seems there only for his own ends'.

Ultimately, Lynch's recommendation was that East Waterford brigade be amalgamated with West Waterford brigade, with Pax Whelan commanding the new brigade. Among the reasons given for this decision was that 'Present OC No. 1 [Paddy Paul] has not the confidence of any officer in brigade, except brigade Adjutant and Qr-master. Should he have to give over command there is no officer capable to take his place'.

Paddy Paul had made mistakes in planning actions, particularly at the Tramore ambush. Whether the men who intended to replace him could have performed better was open to question. Paul later reported that:

"I was not responsible for the operation on the 28-5-21 in which the city batt was brought from its base for the purpose of demolishing bridges. During the operation, which continued until the morning of the 29-521 and enemy cyclist patrol came in contact with one of our sentries whom they seriously wounded and died the following [day] from the effects. The enemy then retired to his base, leaving outposts near the city boundary. Three of our men were captured while returning to their homes."

The dead Volunteer was John O'Rourke (23), a plumber from Waterford city. In later years Paul commented:

"The operation was carried out by instructions of the brigade vice commandant, M. Bishop, and amounted really to nothing except the blocking and trenching of roads on the Cork–Waterford road a few miles from Waterford. O'Rourke was detailed as a guard to watch for the approach of any enemy parties while the trenching was in progress, though why he should have been selected for such duty I cannot understand for O'Rourke was a man who had very poor sight and he wore glasses. Therefore, the enemy were upon him before he even saw them. The operation was carried out by night. O'Rourke was armed with a revolver but I do not think he got any chance of using it. As he was captured with arms on him, the British military party carried out the instructions that were issued to them at this time, to kill anyone found with arms in their hands."

Liam Lynch was aware that Paul's re-instalment was not an ideal solution to the situation. On 2 July 1921, he recommended to Mulcahy that 'Brigade OC should not be pressed to hold command as he is not anxious for it, also all officers and men have not confidence in him'.[105] In the end, Paul himself found the best compromise. In mid-June 1921, Paddy Paul selected fourteen men from his brigade as the nucleus of a flying column. Eleven of these men were from Waterford city and included Jerry Cronin, Jack Edwards and Mick Wylie, the latter having recovered from his wounds sustained at the Tramore ambush. The previous April, Jim Power had been instructed to construct a brigade arms dump on his farm at Ballycraddock and it was here that Paul's group assembled one evening. According to Paul:

"The rifles were a few Lee-Enfields, some Mausers and some Martini single-shot weapons ... the brigade dump ... was where the column first assembled, drew its arms and moved off. It was not intended that I should permanently command the column but I felt that as the brigade commander and as the person who had the best military training I should accompany them at first. I hoped to have a few little fights in which the column would become seasoned. It was then my intention to hand over command of the column to Jerry Cronin. Both because of the smallness of our numbers and the unsuitability of the terrain in the East Waterford brigade area, I felt that it would be unsuitable to carry out any operations on our own at first and therefore I made contact with George Lennon, the vice commandant of the West Waterford brigade and leader of the West Waterford column. I proposed that

---

[105] UCDA MP P7/A /19.

we should join forces with the West Waterford column and that between us we might be able to bring off something worthwhile."

Paul's group moved off at dusk to begin an overnight march over the darkening back roads. With his departure ended armed operations in East Waterford, with the exception of a failed attack on Tramore coastguard station. Jim Power noted: 'when the column was formed and went out of my area we had so very little arms and ammunition left that it was not possible to carry out any active engagements'. Paul's column marched west through the night, skirting the dark villages of Carroll's Cross, Kilmacthomas, Fews, and into Mahonbridge by dawn. They crossed the Tay Valley as the sun and mist were rising from the fields, passing Kilrossanty and crossing the Monavullagh Mountains over the Barnamadra Gap. Near the village of Ballinamult, they linked up with the West Waterford column and soon settled into a training routine. The weather was fine, and in contrast to East Waterford, Paul found that 'the people around were, with very few exceptions, friendly and well-disposed to us'.

Shortly after the East Waterford men had joined up with the ASU, three more volunteers from the Ballymacarbery company of the 1st Battalion, who were issued rifles when they joined the column at Kilbrien, joined them. One of these, Patrick Ryan, remembered:

"We were billeted in farmhouses in the neighbourhood and had to be on parade each morning at 8 am and again, after a break, at 10 a.m. Dinner was at 1 p.m. We paraded again at 4 p.m. and finally at 7 p.m. Our training consisted mainly in field manoeuvres, advancing and retiring under cover and general tactics in guerrilla fighting."[106]

A report from a British officer attached to the headquarters of the 16th Infantry Brigade in Fermoy (dated 17 June 1921) observed:

"As I have told you verbally the policy of reprisals is definitely off. I do not think that this decision by the cabinet has been arrived at because of the vapourings of some insignificant member of the House of Commons. I believe it have been largely due to His Majesty's influence, so in that case we can all be perfectly happy about the decision."

This report went on to discuss the court-martial arrangements for captured IRA men, particularly those captured in possession of arms, urging that such cases be tried as quickly as possible. The report however concerned itself mainly with a new development in the conflict: the British army was forming its own flying columns. These usually consisted of a company of infantry, sometimes accompanied by an artillery piece:

"I want OC flying columns to bear in mind that one of the objects of the flying columns is to get troops and police in touch with the people in a friendly way, so as to enlist the waverers on our side ... I want you to consider whether there is any possible means of getting flying columns to converge on a quarry suddenly heard of supposing you have several columns out at any particular time ... The Rebels are getting very fond of making dugouts in isolated hilly places. A search for dugouts in an isolated bit of country is therefore a suitable objective for a flying column. I hope to get air

---

[106] IMA BMH WS Patrick Paul, James Power, Patrick Ryan.

photos of suspected places. I much want (sic) to reach out into our isolated hilly places by means of flying columns."

The report included a list of IRA flying columns and their suspected locations (the Waterford column was thought to be 'East of Tallow, Monavullack (sic) Mts ... 1st Bn, 2nd Cork Bde, East Waterford Bde') and concluded: 'They form good objectives for our flying columns – our flying columns can lower their morale by chasing them out of their areas, or with luck in the shape of good information may be able to attack them'.[107]

On 29 June, James Mansfield's 3rd Battalion suffered a disaster at Piltown Cross. A unit of the Hampshire regiment based in Youghal had slipped across the Blackwater after dark and clashed with the local IRA company near Piltown Cross, site of the successful ambush eight months earlier. This 'return match' had a very different outcome, seven Volunteers being taken prisoner by the British. The lack of fatalities suggests that perhaps the Hampshires appreciated the leniency shown them when the roles were reversed the previous November.[108]

In early July, according to Paddy Paul:

"We got word that there was a troop train due to pass bringing jurors into Waterford city. At that time jurors were not inclined to serve on juries, and so they got them from outlying districts and brought them into Waterford under military escort ... the West Waterford intelligence officer [Thomas Lincoln] brought word to us about this train, and it was decided to ambush it at Cappagh

---

[107] NLI FOD MS 31,223 (3) Letter from HQ 16th infantry brigade 17 June 1921. 67 NLI FOD MS 31,150.

[108] Irish Military Archives MA/MSPC/A/9 Waterford Brigade.

176

Station, which is midway between Dungarvan and Cappoquin Station. The troop train was expected to pass there at an early hour."

According to Mick Mansfield:

"The night previous [4 July 1921], I was engaged laying mines on the roads in the neighbourhood of Cappagh. I remember we were at this work all night, the purpose being to prevent British reinforcements coming up from Fermoy or Dungarvan while the ambush was proceeding. All the men on the column together with some men from the local company were engaged. There were upwards of thirty men or perhaps more. This included scouts and those on outpost duty a distance from the ambush position. There are level crossing gates at Cappagh station, and shortly before the troop train was due to arrive, we put the signal against the train and closed the gates. The attacking party was divided into two groups in position on high ground on both sides of the station and within about fifty to eighty yards of the railway line. At the appointed time, the train pulled into Cappagh and stopped."

Mick Shalloe recalled:

"As the train slowed to a stop, it could be seen from our positions overlooking the railway that there were many soldiers aboard. The order was given to fire and we poured volley after volley into the carriages. The soldiers replied half-heartedly but, after about a quarter of an hour firing, the train began to move out of the junction. It gathered speed, crashed the local crossing gates and went on its way. I think I remember one of our lads telling me that a British officer climbed on to the driver's cabin and forced the driver, at revolver point, to pull out of Cappagh. We undoubtedly inflicted heavy casualties on the British that morning, but I am sorry to say I can give no estimate. None of our lads were hit. George Lennon was OC on that occasion."

Mick Mansfield continues:

"Following the Cappagh attack, the British sent out large columns of troops to cover the area between Clonmel and Dungarvan which was, roughly, our brigade area. We countered these moves by constantly mining the roads, blowing bridges, trenching roads and hampering in every way possible enemy plans to encircle us. In this we succeeded. At this time, the brigade headquarters were situated in tent in a wood at Ballymacmague, Colligan, near Cappoquin. There, Pax Whelan and I received reports from dispatch riders."

Pax Whelan subsequently reported to Dublin:

"Three enemy columns consisting of about one hundred and twenty men each were very active particularly in the 1st Battalion area. They travelled for the most part on foot, though there were also a small number of cavalry and a cycle column with them. They searched only a few houses in the course of their travels and for the most part seemed inclined to be friendly with the people; their advances however, were coldly accepted."

George Lennon remembered:

"Everything had seemed to be going exceptionally well recently. Twelve additional riflemen had some time before come over the Gap from the east part of the county to join us and I was moving about with a well-disciplined force of forty-two men. Our enemies had retreated into the towns and they were now only venturing out in large mobile columns complete with mounted officers and a field kitchen. We had been on the tail of one such column for three days. We just missed them coming through the Lickey position where we would have had a decided advantage. I dared not bring such a large body of troops to action in open country as they were more than twice our strength and we would have to make a capture to replenish our expended and limited supply of ammunition - to say that we were like Indians on the trail of covered wagons is not a bad illustration."

Jerry Cronin recalled:

"Word reached us that British troops in convoy were approaching the Waterford–Tipperary border from their camp in Kilworth, Co Cork. At the time the column was billeted in the Mount Mellary district. We decided to attack and moved to meet the British, who we had learned had camped in a field near Ballinamult in west Waterford. At about 2 p.m., on a bright spring day we approached to within fifty yards of the British encampment under cover of well-wooded country. We had an excellent firing position. We were close enough to take them completely by surprise and we had first class country into which we could retreat when the action was over. We were in position and awaiting the order to fire when a scout came to our lines with the news that a second British convoy was approaching our position from a westerly direction. Faced with a strong possibility of an outflanking movement by a vastly superior force, orders were given to retire. We had no sooner pulled away a safe distance when word reached us that a third British convoy was approaching from a north-westerly direction. We had no option therefore, but to retreat hastily out of the grip of the pincer movement which the British were carrying out."

According to Paddy Paul's recollection:

"We returned to our retreat in the mountains in the Ballinamult area, that is, on the south slope of the Knockmealdown Mountains.

We were not long there when we observed the approach of a strong column of British soldiers moving towards our area in battle order. I imagine there would be about a hundred in this column, roughly company strength. I estimated that figure as I watched them through my binoculars. They had a field gun with them, which I took to be an eighteen-pounder. This column was obviously searching for us and we had immediately to decide what we were going to do. They were at least double our numbers, with much superior armament, so that the possibility of attacking them in any straightforward manner was out of the question. The other possibility, of surrounding them so as to strike a blow at their rear and withdraw rapidly, was soon put out of consideration when we discovered that other garrisons of military, police and Black and Tans were moving along the surrounding roads, acting as flank guards and scouts for the British column. This force that I mentioned of about a hundred men was therefore, only part of the force which was out hunting for us. It therefore becomes our job just to elude them. To counter any intelligence they might have concerning our position, G. Lennon and I decided that we should move further in the direction of the Knockmealdown Mountains, to a place called Crow Hill in the Mount Mellary area. Our movement was unobserved and the British round up did not succeed in catching us inside."[109]

In the early hours of the 9 July 1921, there was a sudden loud explosion near the village of Kilgobnet, only a short distance north of Dungarvan. Pax Whelan's brigade staff reached the scene at dawn to witness a scene of appalling carnage. A road had been

---

[109] IMA BMH MS Patrick Paul, Michael J. Mansfield, Michael Shalloe, Jeremiah Cronin; UCDA MP P7/A/23 'Report for Month Ending July 11th'.

trenched in the area, but had been partly filled in and left unguarded. A party of the 'Buffs' took the opportunity to carefully plant landmines in the trench, which were detonated when a group of local civilians returned to open it. The official history of the East Kent regiment notes, rather gleefully, that 'one road block was converted into a booby trap, causing many Sinn Féin casualties'. Pax Whelan subsequently reported:

"During the re-opening of a trench in 'H' Coy area on night of 8th–9th inst a mine laid therein by the enemy exploded and killed two outright and wounded twelve others four of whom died later. The remainder are out of danger and will recover."[110]

George Lennon said:

"As we had had no sleep for two days running we let out enemies go and moved for rest to a place called Collagortuide (the place of the yellow fields) at the foot of the Knockmealdown Mountains. Then a dispatch carrier came running across the fields waving a paper. Quite unexpectedly a Truce had been declared.

July 12, 1921. Sleady.

"The column has been disbanded, the arms dumped and the lads have all returned home. Kirby took off with alacrity and our best Webley revolver disappeared with him.

"I am waiting for a car to pick me up. Sitting very much alone on a ditch I am overcome with sadness and I cannot shake off a dread premonition.

---

[110] Knight, C.R.B., *Historical Records of the Buffs* (Medici, London, 1951), p. 3; UCDA MP P7/A/23 'Report for Month Ending July 11th'.

"This action on the part of our leaders caused me considerable doubt and I was wondering if accepting a premature Truce was not a grave error. At no other time in our unhappy history had things seemed to be going so well. The people were all with us as we were with our people and we had the enemy apparently on the run. We were holding two trump cards, Unity and Secrecy. Secrecy was our secret weapon as the inefficient British intelligence system was convinced that all the hills were crawling with insurgents. Now we would be coming into losing the other card, our leaders would rend the country from top to bottom. True, the arms situation was by no means good but there were some signs that at last this was going to be rectified. Was it by deliberation or through incompetence that our G.H.Q. had failed to arm the Volunteers?

"The questions of unity was vital. For a guerrilla war to succeed the army must have the active support of the civil population. With a hostile, or part hostile, population the game was up.

"I had some sad premonition regarding all this as I waited for the car. What a luxury to sit in a car after the years of foot-slogging. Soon we would be all riding around in cars, little heroes, and a softening up process would begin. We would, naturally, be reluctant to go back to all that other business again.

"With no letup in hostilities our political leaders could have negotiated from a position of strength. Bargaining from a position of weakness they would have to accept the best terms they could get.

"In fact, and in effect, the war was over.

"How good it was that the sun shone (it had been a wonderful summer), that peace reigned and that the people were working happily in the fields – yet, something indefinable had gone away forever."

1 RIC / Black and Tans in Dungarvan Castle in 1920. Waterford County Museum EK178.

2 IRA training camp in the Comeraghs, during the Truce period in 1921. Mick Mansfield in foreground. Waterford County Museum UK1502.

3 Early 1922: Back row: John Power, Father Tom Power and Dr. Joe Walsh (M.D. to the Waterford Flying Column). Front row: T. Boyle, George Lennon, and Michael Foley. Waterford County Museum UK260.

4 Following IRA takeover of Dungarvan Castle in March 1922. Front Row: Mick Mansfield, Patrick Gumbleton, Mick Shalloe, Bennie McCarthy, Geoff Morrissey. Second Row: Josie Wyre, Unknown, Paddy Troy, Jim Lonergan, Jack "Mott" Morrissey, Jack Lynch, Jack O'Meara, Unknown, Bob Atkins. Third Row: John Whyte, Jim Prendergast, "Nipper" McCarthy, Jim Kirwan, Pakeen Whelan. Waterford County Museum EK187.

5 Early 1922: George Lennon, Moses Roche, James Prendergast and Paddy Power in the Infantry Barracks after the British departure from Waterford City. Waterford County Museum UK261.

6 The Infantry Barracks following the Battle of Waterford in 1922. Waterford County Museum UK 228.

7 1926: George Lennon in a group at Clonea Strand. Waterford County Museum UK3809.

8 George Lennon at the home of journalist Geoffrey Coulter in Sutton in 1939. Left, back row: George Lennon and Olive Sibbald, his wife's younger sister. Front row, l - r: Niall Coulter (Geoffrey/Ivy's son), Joyce Pierce (Cousin), May Sibbald Lennon (George's wife) and Robin Pierce (Cousin). Waterford County Museum UK3809.

9 *George Lennon and Colonel Roger McCorley crossing O'Connell Bridge in 1939. Photo taken by famous street photographer Arthur Fields. Waterford County Museum UK4492.*

10 1965: portrait of George Lennon by Ruth Carver exhibited at The Memorial Art Gallery on University Avenue in Rochester, New York. Waterford County Museum UK265.

11 1970: Friends, enemies, then friends again. George Lennon, and Paddy Paul in Rochester, New York. Waterford County Museum UK264.

12 George Lennon on a peace march in 1971. Photo courtesy of Ivan Lennon.

13 1987: Mary Mansfield, Mick Mansfield, and Ivan Lennon in the Mansfield home at The Burgery, Abbeyside. Waterford County Museum UK263

Truce & Civil War, 1921-1923

Chapter 4

During the Truce', according to Paddy Paul, 'as well as being training officer to the brigade, I was acting as deputy liaison officer. George Lennon of the West Waterford brigade was liaison officer and I was his deputy'.[111] Both sides appointed liaison officers to ensure the Truce was being complied with, although in practice both sides were guilty of violations. Although Lennon was appointed county liaison officer, he was later peripherally involved in two major incidents, having prior knowledge of them if not actual involvement. Internal IRA documentation at this time makes it clear that they had serious doubts that the Truce would last, and the organisation was willing to use this fortuitous breathing space to rearm and reorganise as best they could.

In Waterford, the first item on the agenda was the amalgamation of the brigades. In a report to the headquarters of 1st Southern Division dated 17 August, Pax Whelan announced that the East and West Waterford brigades had been amalgamated into the Waterford brigade. An area of responsibility for the new brigade was established and a new brigade staff appointed by Liam Lynch. Pax Whelan was to be brigade OC with George Lennon as vice commandant. The new quartermaster was the quartermaster of the former East Waterford brigade (Knox) while Paddy Paul was appointed brigade training officer, an appointment that he filled

---

[111] IMA BMH MS Patrick Paul.

enthusiastically. Mick Mansfield was confirmed as brigade engineering officer.

Apart from the Lismore battalion which was handed over to Cork No. 2 brigade, West Waterford's three battalions were retained and East Waterford's three battalions redesignated, while a seventh battalion was organised in the Nire valley area. The new organisation was thus:

1st Battalion: Dungarvan

2nd Battalion: Comeragh region (formerly 4th Battalion, West Waterford)

3rd Battalion: Ardmore

4th Battalion: Waterford city (formerly 1st Battalion, East Waterford)

5th Battalion: Tramore (formerly 2nd Battalion, East Waterford)

6th Battalion: Dunmore East (formerly 3rd Battalion, East Waterford)
7th Battalion: Nire Valley.

Shortly afterwards, Jerry Cronin was appointed OC of the Waterford City battalion.[112]

GHQ began providing training programmes and the IRA organised intensive training camps across the country. General Neville Macready, commander in chief of British forces in Ireland, complained that the IRA were taking advantage of the Truce to

---

[112] UCDA MP P7/A/23; IMA BMH MS Jeremiah Cronin.

turn 'disorganised rabble [into a] well-disciplined, well-organised and well-armed force'. [113]

According to Mick Mansfield:

"No time was lost in organising training camps in case of a resumption of hostilities. Brigade and battalion training classes were started by me. Munition making was begun by each battalion, dumps and dugouts – properly constructed underground ones – were started and general intensive training undertaken."

Moses Roche said:

"During the Truce period I organised billets for a company officers' course in training conducted by Paddy Paul, the brigade training officer for the Waterford brigade. About fifty men attended at Graignarush just outside Kilmacthomas where the camp was held. Following the course, an examination was held at which I obtained second place. As a result I was asked to take over the training of the 2nd Battalion (Kilrossanty) Waterford brigade."

Mick Shalloe took charge of another training camp at Kilbrien. According to Dan Ennis:

"In September 1921, I went to a training camp in Kilmovee near Kilmacthomas, Co. Waterford, together with other officers of the Waterford City battalion. Here we received instruction in the use

---

[113] Duggan, John, *History of the Irish Army* (Gill and Macmillan, Dublin, 1991), p. 71.

of the Thompson machine-gun, grenades, and rifle and revolver practice. Paddy Paul ... was in charge of the camp."[114]

George Lennon's 1934 application for an IRA service certificate mentions that at this time he was involved in 'gun-running operations terminating at Cheekpoint'. On a miserable Sunday morning in November, an exhausted Derryman named Charles McGuinness appeared at the house of Dr White, the Sinn Féin mayor of Waterford city. McGuinness was an accomplished adventurer and apart from being an experienced sailor, had served in the Great War with both the British army and navy, and latterly in the IRA. More to the point, he had just walked five miles from Cheekpoint, a point east of the city where a sturdy German tugboat named the *Frieda* was covertly sheltering with a crew of German communists and (according to McGuinness) a cargo of 1,500 rifles, 2,000 pistols and 1.7 million rounds of ammunition. McGuinness had captained the *Frieda* all the way from Hamburg via Holland to its intended landing point at Helvic Head where an IRA unit was waiting, but had been defeated by bad weather and was unable to receive any signal from land. McGuinness then brought the *Frieda* up the Suir estuary and contacted Dr White.

Jerry Cronin of the Waterford City battalion was contacted and quickly arranged for several trucks to proceed immediately to Cheekpoint, where the cargo was off-loaded and brought to the Keatings' house in the Comeragh Mountains. Later the weapons and ammunition were transferred to the midlands and the *Frieda* sold to a buyer in Cork. As McGuinness himself put it: 'So ended happily an incident which might have proved extremely awkward

---

[114] IMA BMH MS Michael J. Mansfield, Moses Roche, Michael Shalloe.

for the Irish envoys negotiating with Lloyd George in Downing Street'.[115]

On 6 December 1921, the Anglo-Irish Treaty was signed in London. Although this gave Ireland independence on the level of an autonomous dominion, it did not grant the status of a full republic. Many aspects of it were unacceptable to some republicans; the head of state would be the king of England, represented by a governor-general, members of the Irish parliament would swear allegiance to the king and six counties of north-east Ulster would remain part of the United Kingdom. Because of the Treaty, IRA prisoners began to be released from Ballykinlar camp and various prisons, most of the Waterford men and women returning in December. On 7 January 1922, George Lennon was present at the meeting of Dáil Éireann in the Mansion House when the Treaty was ratified in by sixty-four votes to fifty-seven. There was cheering in the street outside when the result was revealed, but the mood in the building was far more sombre. De Valera announced his resignation; an attempt at reconciliation by Michael Collins was prevented by a shrill denouncement by Mary MacSwiney. Ireland had taken its first step on the road to Civil War. Lennon subsequently remembered:

"Liam Lynch, Charlie Daly, Fitz and I have come to Vaughan's Hotel from the Mansion House where a majority has just voted to accept the Treaty. We are greeted by a drizzly rain and a solitary kilted piper who is marching back and forth in the street dreeing his weird. We go upstairs to the familiar room. In the dining room below some prominent Free State supporters are happily playing

---

[115] IMA BMH MS Dr Vincent White; McGuinness, John, *Nomad* (Methuen, London, 1934), pp. 173–178.

a game called 'Put and Take'. The four of us are silent and depressed."

In January 1922, the British army began to withdraw its forces from Ireland. On 8 February 1922, the Devonshires left Waterford aboard the ships *Great Western*, *Great Southern*, and the cattle transport *St Patrick*. Lieutenant Yeo later transferred to the Royal Ulster Rifles; he retired from the British army in 1940. The York and Lancaster regiment temporarily manned the military barracks in Waterford. Later that month, the Buffs departed Ireland.[116] Captain D.V. Thomas was no longer with his company when it pulled out of Dungarvan. The previous autumn he had left Ireland to attend training at the British army small arms school in England, where he suffered a leg injury in a motorcycle accident that October. By 20 May 1922, Thomas had re-joined his battalion at Shorncliffe, when his army career was abruptly terminated by a letter from the war office that stated:

"I am commanded by the army council to inform you that they regret it has been found necessary to dispense with your services, and in consequence your retirement will be carried out 10 days from the date of this letter ... I am to inform you that your compulsory retirement is not the result of misconduct on your part, and in no way reflects upon your character or conduct in the army, and I am to convey to you the regret of the army council for this action, which is due to the reduction of the army, following the necessity for a curtailment of national expenditure."

---

[116] Archives of the Devonshire regiment, Wyvern barracks, Exeter; *London Gazette, 14 June 1940;* Knight, C.R.B., *Historical Records of the Buffs* (Medici, London, 1951), p. 3.

It appears that Thomas had nominated himself for the OBE by exaggerating his conduct during the Burgery Ambush, something that the British Army would not have been happy with. Certainly his personal file was weeded of almost all references to the medal. Although Thomas was retired with a very handsome gratuity of £1,900, a fortune at the time, he appears to have left the British army an unhappy man, failing to settle an officer's mess bill of £12 which was a practice much frowned upon. A wine merchant in Dungarvan was also pursuing Thomas with regard to an unsettled bill for £5. Thomas is known to have emigrated to New Zealand later that year, and in 1923 he moved to South Africa where he died a few years later.[117]

By the Second World War, Captain F.A.J.E. Marshall rose to the rank of Major-General and at one point commanded an infantry brigade on the vital fortress island of Malta.[118] He died of natural causes shortly after the war.

The Royal Marines evacuated Ballinacourty coastguard station and this was taken over by an IRA party of about sixty under the command of Paddy Paul. At this time, Lynch's 1st Southern Division were experiencing difficulty obtaining weapons, when, as Moses Roche noted:

"Information reached us from a friendly Black and Tan that a convoy was proceeding to Gormanston Camp, County Meath, for disbandment and that the convoy would consist of about eighty

---

[117] UKNA WO339/8667 (Personal file Captain D.V. Thomas).

[118] Knight, C.R.B., *Historical Records of the Buffs* (Medici, London, 1951); *London Gazette,* 14 March 1947.

armed RIC and Black and Tans in Crossley tenders with a Lancia armoured car."

According to Paul:

"I was still in Ballinacourty at this time ... when I was informed by George Lennon one night that the divisional commander, Liam Lynch, had decided to hold up the RIC party, disarm them and relieve them of all their ammunition and arms' stores which they would be carrying with them to Gormanston. Apparently I had been ordered to carry out this job, though I had not been a party to the discussions about it, and I pointed out to George Lennon on the spot the difficulties surrounding such an undertaking. First of all, it would be a breach of the Truce, and if the RIC resisted and someone got killed or wounded, there was liable to be a very awkward situation created. Besides all this, it was now ten o'clock at night and I was in bed and would have to travel the thirty miles to Waterford and make the necessary arrangements for the ambush before nine o'clock the following morning ... Having collected the men, we went by Portlaw and across Fiddown Bridge into South Kilkenny ... selecting a spot three miles from Waterford: Dunkitt in south Kilkenny."

It was the morning of 3 March 1922. Michael Cummins of Stradbally recalled:

"I had a rifle, a revolver and three grenades. Paddy Paul ... was in charge of the operation, which of course, was unofficial as the Truce was on at the time. We waited on the roadside at Dunkitt from 4.30 a.m. until 10.30 a.m. when the Tans came along in nine Crossley tenders and a [Lancia] armoured car. Paul had given strict orders that we weren't to shoot unless compelled to do so."

Moses Roche remembered:

"The convoy came along in due course and stopped at the barricade. We shouted: 'Put them up, ye are all covered'. A Black and Tan (probably the man who had given us the tip off) shouted: 'Stop, boys, they are too many for us'. I remember these words quite well. All the men in the convoy dismounted and put up their hands. They put up no opposition. We seized the Crossley tenders with cases of ammunition, rifles, machine-guns, revolvers and grenades. The Lancia armoured car was also taken and all the enemy cars were manned by our own drivers and driven up to Comeragh in the mountains where the captured stuff was carefully hidden."

According to Paul:

"I had arranged that we would have our own drivers to take over the cars but, as the Tans were inclined to be friendly at this stage, we let their own drivers stay on the lorries, with our drivers sitting beside them ... at Portlaw our drivers took over the vehicles."

Lynch and Lennon had entrusted Paul with an important mission, the consequences of which could have been disastrous, and he had performed well, although the Black and Tans proved very co-operative. Perhaps a 'deal' had been done, but it is likely that with their demobilisation and evacuation imminent, they had not been inclined to risk their lives.[119]

On 4 March 1922, Dungarvan barracks was evacuated by the RIC garrison and handed over to the IRA. According to an eyewitness:

"The evacuation of Dungarvan barracks took place on the 4th March 1922. The large square of the enclosure had been used for

---

[119] IMA BMH MS Moses Roche, Patrick Paul, Michael Cummins.

the purpose of keeping the motor lorries and motorcars, and it is from here that the military used issue forth on their raiding expeditions. The Black-and-Tans had gone away some days before the military had left the town, and the Castle was occupied solely by sixty-five members of the RIC. They were under the command of Captain [sic] Sheehan, an officer who had fought in the Great War.

"Before the police left some conferences were held in the barracks. An application was made to Captain Sheehan for possession in the name of the IRA. He asked for credentials from the Provisional Government, for now, under the Treaty, the Irish Provisional Government was in power. Captain Sheehan did not consider those produced satisfactory. As a consequence, the giving over of the barracks was delayed until the 12 train came from Waterford, when a commissioner from the Provisional Government arrived, and, driving in a motor to the barracks, he had an interview with Captain Sheehan. Captain Sheehan, being satisfied, handed over the control of the fortress to the representative of the Irish government, and in a few minutes afterwards he formed his men four deep in the square, and giving the order 'March', the men filed out of the castle, passed through the massive gateway, and thus was ended, apparently for evermore, the symbol of British rule in this historic fortress.

"There were many onlookers at their doors and windows as the body of police marched up the street, headed by their captain, en route for the railway station, to leave the old town forever. Some of the men smiled greetings to their friends as they passed them by, others appeared to realise the changed position of affairs. A musical instrument was being played by one of the party, and the air 'Good-Bye-ee' only indicated too well the meaning of the proceeding. Their departure was regarded with mixed feelings, and perhaps at the moment the mind was filled with kindly recollections. For, until the strife, these men and the public had got on very well together. They were regarded by the ordinary citizen as the protectors of the people's rights, and, apart from their position as representatives of a foreign power, they were, on the whole, held in high esteem

"It might have been two hours later that three motorcars drove down the street. In them were members of the IRA. They entered the barracks and installed themselves there, and within a few minutes the Tricolour floated from the ramparts of the building. These incidents in themselves were of tremendous significance, in as much as they emphasised the change that had taken place, that the rule of which the people had so long complained was at an end, and that the affairs of the country were now in the hands of their own representatives."[120]

"On 9 March, the British army with a show of ceremony evacuated Waterford military barracks. Captain Wedgewood of the York and Lancaster regiment handed over the barracks to an IRA delegation which included Pax Whelan, Mick Mansfield and Gerry Cronin. Formalities over, 200 British troops were formed up on the square of the Infantry Barracks and preceded by their regimental fife and drum band, marched through the gate and to the quays, locals cheering or booing depending on their political persuasion. The Great Western ferry brought this group to Fishguard after which they were returned to England."[121]

---

[120] Keohan, Edmond, *Illustrated History of Dungarvan* (*Waterford News*, Waterford, 1924).

[121] *Munster Express*, 'Waterford Military Barracks Evacuated', 11 March 1922.

Lennon led the Irish unit that took over the military barracks in Waterford, using the vehicles seized at Dunkitt.

"Early in 1922, after the elapse of 750 years it was our proud privilege to enter the city with native troops and take it back for the Irish nation.

"We did not come to the city with any ceremony but drove into the back of the town in lorries and took possession of the Infantry Barracks just vacated by the Devon regiment (sic) of the British army.

"The main building of the barracks was the officers' quarters, two long wings connected from here enclosing a very large barrack square. Other buildings comprised the married quarters, the hospital, the transport shed, the magazine and some other buildings for stores. Just inside the barrack gate was a small building marked 'Early Treatment Station'. This, we speculated was for the precautionary treatment of Venusian diseases; needless to say, we had no use for this exotic place.

"Our maintenance party, as we were modestly first described, was a company of eighty-two men. The right half company was composed of men with column service (the Old Guard.). The left half of picked men from the brigade. I had four junior officers, one who acted as barrack quartermaster and another who looked after our paper work.

"And I had a prince of a sergeant major who ran the whole internal show for me. Sergeant Major Jim Power had been a non-commissioned officer in the Royal Scots and had waded through half the mud in Flanders. On being de-mobbed at the end of the war he had immediately joined the Volunteers. He was most competent and quite indispensable and never liked to be far away from my right elbow.

"Next I rate in importance the famous Nipper. The Nipper was just a nipper as he was quite young and small in stature – that is, physically. His column service was from the very beginning.

"The 'Nip' was my driver and he followed me around like a shadow.

"We acquired a most admirable chef, John Phelan, who had been a ship's cook; he always referred to his kitchen, which he was quite proud of, as 'the galley'. John usually wore spotless ducks and he had only one failing, if it could be called that, he had a strong addiction to grand opera. Sometimes on returning to the barracks at night, in a gay mood, he would start his arias at the guard-house and would continue his high notes all through the barrack square and far into the night. We remonstrated and he quit in a huff and only returned after we had humiliated ourselves. Afterwards he sang to his heart's content.

"In addition we had four bugler boys as well as four stray dogs that the men adopted. The boys received lessons from an old ex-service man and in time became quite proficient in the various bugle calls.

"For transport we possessed three Crossley tenders, a battered Lancia armoured car (a death trap) and a Buick touring car.

"There was quite a lot of cleaning up to be done after the Devons and then we got the men into uniform. The sergeant major gave them all the basic drill, and plenty of it, and after that slow-motion guards' drill. Soon we had a company of crack troops.

"Next to the officers' quarters was a room I used as an office and which was at times the orderly room. Here minor breaches of discipline would be punished with confinement to barracks and extra fatigue duties. I also read the men a lecture on the moral dangers involved in speaking to girls they might meet in the street. The poor fellows took it all in good part.

"My position was an anomalous one. The country was as yet without a government, or had five different governments, and bitter dissension was going on all over. I almost forgot to add that across Barrack Street was the Cavalry Barracks, which we occupied with thirty temporary police. So I became, under the circumstances, a kind of military governor on my own without the benefit of any civil advice or instruction.

"When the Nipper drove me outside the town we changed places and he gave me driving lessons. When I wanted to create an impression on the populace I sat in the back of the car, with my driver and my batman in front. I must have looked like a twenty-one year old brass hat and if at this tender age I had a mild case of swelled head who would blame me.

"There were, of course, a number of trying incidents and I will confine myself to just two as both had happy endings.

"It became necessary for me to place a section sergeant's guard in the central post office. For one thing, all telephone calls between the headquarters of the Free State army in Beggars Bush barracks and their forces in Kilkenny had to pass through our post office telephone exchange where I had agents to tap the messages and keep me informed as to what was in the wind. (The Kilkenny troops were always threatening to move in on us.) As soon as the guard was posted the postmaster called the staff together and led them out of the building. Now the city was left without a postal service, a telegraph service and a telephone service. After the lapse of three days the citizens got very irate indeed. And there was another disruption; Waterford had a large number of British ex-service men whose war pensions were processed through the post office. A deputation of the ex-soldiers waited on me and in very impolite terms demanded to know what I intended to do about it. This was the last straw and I was very annoyed, in fact, I was quite mad. My driver drove me over to Newtown, the residential section of the city where the postmaster lived, and we had a brief interview. The postmaster said hastily that he would go back and I returned my Luger to its holster. Everybody was happy again.

"One Sunday when I was communing with myself, having no one else to consult with, the telephone rang. The man on the line said there was a strike of farm labourers and that they had taken over possession of his town. I said so what and he said quite a lot what. To this he added that I was now 'the competent military authority' responsible for law and order and that I had better do something about it quick. I told Power to fall in the right half company, ready the three tenders and have the men bring their bayonets with them.

"[Kilmacthomas] was one of those country towns consisting mainly of one long street running up the side of a hill. More than half way up this hill a dark mass of men was gathered. Dismounting the forty men from the trucks we fell them in, fixed bayonets and advanced up the street.

"Two lines of twenty men each, bayonets to the front, not a hair out of place, boots crashing on the street. So we advanced steadily up the town. Halt. A dark glaring man, seemingly the leader, was standing in front of the farm labourers, his eyes staring me.

'What is going on here, my man.' said I, in my best officer manner.

'---- you,' said he.

"The sergeant major moved from my side and felled him with a blow. Some of the men broke ranks and knocked down a few of the strikers with their rifle butts. A pause and a boy rushed forward to confront me. Calling me by name he said bitterly, 'What is the matter with you I thought you would be the last person in the world to do this to us'. We pushed the strikers back to the end of the street and held them there at the bayonet point. Then a truck came up with the labour organiser who was to preside at their meeting. He glared also. I told him if everything was going to be orderly they could hold the meeting, otherwise no meeting. He angrily assented and we marched off quite a ways to the old Union buildings nearby so as to be on call. From here we heard cheers but no other sounds of trouble.

"I sat on a stone wondering what the boy meant. You and Us... Then it began to dawn on me. No wonder they were mad. In the past, lancers had ridden them down, redcoats had marched against them, bluecoats had marched against them, now men in green jackets were putting them back in their place. Poor landless men, people of no property, betaghs.

'Sergeant'.

'Fall in the men, we are going back to barracks'.

"About this time a prisoner was reported [as] being held in the guard-house. On going to investigate I discovered it was Kirby. He said he had been arrested after leaving Beggars Bush barracks where he had been spending some time giving the new regime a look over. He was anxious to get back to the river and we parted most warmly.

"Towards the end of our occupation we suffered some marauding visits from our own side. On one occasion they presented the manager of the Bank of Ireland with a demand that nearly gave the poor man a heart attack; on another they stripped the ships in the port of their wireless sets. It was almost a relief when the pro-Treaty forces attacked us."

The majority of the Waterford men were against the Treaty. The few exceptions included Paddy Paul, Michael Bishop, Matt Knox and young Ned O'Brien, all of whom had had joined the pro-Treaty government's emergent army. Michael Cummins, the captain of the Stradbally company [not the same Cummins who had fought at Ballylinch], also took the pro-Treaty side; having been warned to leave the village at the end of June, he was arrested and held in Fermoy. He later escaped and made his way to Waterford on foot.

In May, Commandant Paddy Paul arrived in Waterford on a mission to take command of the city for the pro-Treaty forces. He was promptly arrested by Jerry Cronin and began a hunger strike in protest. After ten days without food and three days without water, he was hurriedly moved to the County and City Infirmary where he was kept in a room under armed guard. When two nuns from the Sisters of Charity paid a visit, the sentries naturally did not search them and bade them a polite good evening when they left. The two 'nuns' walked to a waiting car which soon drove them at speed to New Ross. One of the 'nuns' was Paddy Paul; the other was a member of the Cumann na mBan, as was a young woman left behind in the infirmary, having provided her borrowed nun's habit to allow Paul's escape. The scheme had the backing of Monsignor Kearney, dean of Waterford.[122] The following day, Paul was driven to Kilkenny, then under the command of pro-Treaty Colonel-Commandant John Prout, where he spent most of June recovering from his hunger strike. Born in Tipperary in 1880, Prout had emigrated to the USA as a boy. On

---

[122] Neeson Eoin, *The Civil War in Ireland* (Mercier, Cork, 1966), pp. 97–98.

America's entry into the First World War, he joined the famous 69th regiment and spent five months attached to the French command staff. Among several decorations he was awarded the Croix de Guerre. Returning to Ireland in 1919, he became involved in the IRA in his native Tipperary, where according to the pro-Treaty army newspaper:

"He rendered very valuable services as Divisional Instructor and Intelligence officer in his area. Later he was appointed divisional Instructor at the Divisional Training Camp, Galtee Castle, having previously acted as training officer for the 3rd Tipperary Brigade."[123]

The increasing friction between pro-Treaty and anti-Treaty factions in Ireland erupted into outright warfare on 28 June 1922 when the National Army began an artillery barrage on the anti-Treaty garrison of the Four Courts in Dublin, opening heavy fighting in the capital in which the pro-Treaty faction were victorious.

Anti-Treaty strength was concentrated in the province of Munster, and Liam Lynch (now the commander of all anti-Treaty forces) chose to establish a front line along the 'Limerick–Waterford line' which one commentator noted 'held no more substance than the equator'.[124]

It was necessary to bring up troops from Cork and Kerry to reinforce this 'frontline.' The arrival in Waterford city of reinforcements from the 1st Cork Brigade brought the numbers of the anti-Treaty garrison to three hundred although a

---

[123] *An tÓglach*, 'Major-General Prout GOC Waterford Command', 14 July 1923.

[124] Younger, Calton, *Ireland's Civil War, (Mercier Press 1966).*

proportion of this number were armed only with pistols. The latter were probably mainly members of the local IRA who had been earlier occupied in police duties. The Waterford men who had opted to fight against the Treaty were still wearing their green uniforms although they had discarded the headgear and replaced them with civilian caps.[125]

The anti-Treaty garrison began preparations for the assault on Waterford city. Redmond Bridge spanning the River Suir featured a central drawbridge wide enough to allow a small ship through, and this was raised at midnight every night. Vehicles, provisions, clothing and other items were commandeered from the civil population which did nothing for their popularity. The Corkmen stripped the radio equipment from three of the cargo vessels in the harbour and assembled them in the Infantry Barracks, apparently in hope of communicating with Lynch's headquarters in Fermoy.

Some accounts of the subsequent battle have criticised the Waterford men for not attempting to secure Mount Misery, the high ground on the north bank of the Suir overlooking the city. Any attempt by them to have done so would have meant exposing their force to a battle on open ground with a larger and better-equipped enemy, with very limited avenues of retreat back to the city. Few military commanders would not have opted for positioning their force in a well-protected built up area under the circumstances.

In fact, the anti-Treaty forces had a better scheme in mind for the defence of the city. It had been agreed that when the pro-Treaty

---

[125] *Munster Express*, 'The Battle of Waterford', 29 July 1922; Murphy, Seán and Síle, *The Comeraghs: Refuge of Rebels* (Kennedy Print, Clonmel, 1980), p. 59.

forces began their assault, a force of one hundred and fifty men under the command of Denis Lacey would move out from Clonmel and would attack the attacking force from the north. This force would be divided into three columns: a column of Corkmen under the command of Jim Hurley, a Tipperary column led by Michael Sheehan and a third column of Kilkenny men under Andrew Kennedy. This counteroffensive was to be launched from Mullinavat, which would be held by a reserve force of one hundred men led by the famous guerrilla Dan Breen.

On Sunday 16 July, the central span on the Redmond Bridge was raised at eight p.m., unusually early. It was intermittently lowered to allow passage to civilians. Two ships that were moored at the north bank of the river were ordered to move to the south.

On Tuesday 17 July, the bridge remained closed all day, except when a funeral was allowed to pass through in the early afternoon. Later that day, the post office on the quays was seized by the anti-Treaty forces and fortified. The building was garrisoned by Waterford city men, one of whom – Jack Edwards – was obliged to chase away his younger brother. Young Frank Edwards had to wait until the Spanish Civil War to fight, as a sergeant with the famous XV International Brigade. The post office was a formidable position, constructed of massive stone walls and commanding open ground. Other buildings already occupied by the anti-Treatyites included the Infantry and Artillery Barracks, the County Club, the Adelphi Hotel, Reginald's Tower, the Granville Hotel, the *Munster Express* newspaper offices, and Farrell's Corn Stores. The Imperial Hotel was designated a hospital and a Red Cross flag flown outside it. In the city jail at Ballybricken, a detachment of fifteen men led by George Lennon and Jim Power were taking possession. Like the post office, this building had not been designed as a fortification, but its thick walls and positioning, in this case commanding the quays and Redmond Bridge, made it certainly worthwhile using it in this role. There had been thirty-two prisoners 'in residence' at the time; half of these who were on remand were released; the remainder who had been convicted of various offences were dispatched to a local workhouse under the custody of four warders. The governor however proved reluctant to leave and had to be evicted at bayonet point! The jail cells facing the river were quickly adapted as firing posts and a machine-gun was placed in position.

Back in Kilkenny, Colonel-Commandant Prout was marshalling his force of four hundred and fifty men. Almost all were equipped with Lee-Enfield rifles and four Lewis machine-guns were also being carried. Some of the officers had valuable local knowledge. Apart from Commandant Paddy Paul, there was also Captain Ned O'Brien, of the East Waterford brigade, and Captain Ned Mackey, in civil life a chairman of the Clonmel Board of Guardians

Utilising both horse and motor transport, Prout moved his column out onto the dusty road to Waterford. Towed by horses was his most valuable asset: an 18-pounder artillery piece, of the same type that had bombarded the Four Courts. Ironically, given the fact that most of the anti-Treaty forces in Waterford wore uniforms, the gun crew (led by Gunner Kavanagh) were still wearing civilian clothing although they displayed some espirit de corps by wearing leather bandoliers and white lanyards. Prout's column also included a party of engineers, who removed many obstacles encountered on the road to Waterford, including trenches in the road and breached bridges without much difficulty. These troops had been continually deployed in the weeks since the outbreak of Civil War, most having been involved in the fighting around Blessington and County Dublin.

The pro-Treaty column made good time and by 3 p.m. reached the south Kilkenny village of Ballykeoghane. A much appreciated rest halt was called and rations distributed. A local priest administered general absolution – a Catholic ceremony providing absolution for a large group of people in imminent danger, where there is insufficient time for individual confession. Fr Green of Kilmacow carried out the ceremony while the officers and men knelt in a large circle around him. The column proceeded through the village and then was split into three separate columns to advance on Waterford city itself. The horses were unhitched and left under guard, while the infantrymen advanced on foot, proceeded by small reconnaissance parties. The 18-pounder was hitched up to a Crossley tender and later conveyed to its intended firing position.

In the city, in the balmy early afternoon, two lorries full of exuberant anti-Treaty troops and a car carrying Red Cross markings drove along the quays and up to Bilberry Rock where they took up position, much to the interest of the large numbers of curious citizenry gathering at vantage points. Several boats, including city corporation ferry boats, were still ferrying civilians across the river including those who had arrived on the trains which were still running. Other boats were even ferrying perishable goods from the railway station to the cross channel ferries still in port. News was received that the pro-Treaty forces were advancing via Kilmacow.

At 6.50 p.m., a small group of pro-Treaty soldiers were seen to break the skyline on Mount Misery. Local citizens were startled to hear the stutter of the machine-gun being fired from the jail, Lennon's unit firing the first shots of the battle. Other weapons, including Lewis and Thompson guns were soon being fired from the Infantry and Artillery Barracks, a waste of ammunition at that range. It was likely to have been the detachment on Bilberry Rock that drew first blood. The pro-Treaty soldiers on Mount Misery ran for cover, but one of them, Volunteer Costello, was shot through the chest. He was rescued under fire and carried to safety by Captain Ned O'Brien and Sergeant Murphy; the wound proved fatal and Costello died two nights later. Crowds of civilians on the quays watched all this with 'complete *sang froid* and absolute lack of panicky fear … the wonder in this is that this stage of the assault was not marked with many casualties amongst the civilian population'. This was a feature of the early fighting in Dublin where crowds of civilians gathered on O'Connell Bridge to watch the battle along O'Connell Street. After this initial exchange of fire, both sides confined themselves to individual riflemen sniping at each other, while parties of pro-Treaty troops worked their way down the hill to the railway line alongside the river Suir.

By 8 p.m., enough pro-Treaty troops had occupied these positions to begin firing volleys at the anti-Treaty positions along the quays.[126]

At this time Pax Whelan sent a message from the Infantry Barracks to his divisional headquarters in Buttevant:

"Free State forces of about four hundred are at present attacking city from far side of the river (Ferrybank). All posts occupied by our men, and heavy firing is at present on. Try and get Tipperary three to get on their flank in Co. Kilkenny. We are very short of ammunition, send on some."

Firing continued until 10 p.m., when darkness fell and halted proceedings. At daybreak on the morning of Wednesday 19 July,

---

[126] Neeson Eoin, *The Civil War in Ireland,(Mercier 1966)* pp. 100-101; *Munster Express*, 'The Battle of Waterford', 29 July 1922 – this is a particularly detailed and unbiased account of the battle.

anti-Treaty forces within the city recommenced sniping at targets across the river, accompanied by several bursts of fire from Ballybricken prison. Their attention and ammunition were soon directed to an important target: anti-Treaty troops were manhandling the 18-pounder over the skyline at Mount Misery and across the golf links there. The gun crew grimly huddled behind their armoured gun shield as bullets cracked around them, some cutting the branches from a small grove of trees nearby. Paddy Paul was nearby, to guide the 18-pounders' fire.

At 10.40 p.m., the first shells were fired by the gun crew into the city. Two shrapnel shells were fired to begin with; although these tended to do little damage to buildings, they emitted a puff of smoke as they exploded, allowing the gun crews to judge the range to their targets. Thirty-four high explosive shells, four of which smashed into Ballybricken prison causing some damage to the roof, followed these. The remaining thirty shells were directed at the Infantry Barracks. The shelling was generally accurate, although a few houses suffered near misses; one of these, to Commandant Paul's chagrin was his family home near the barracks. Two shells landed in the grounds of the Ursuline Convent without causing damage.

Throughout the initial barrage, which lasted until after midday, the crackle of rifle and machine-gun fire from both sides echoed along the Suir River. When the boom and crack of the artillery barrage ceased, the small arms' fire intensified. The main target of the pro-Treaty infantrymen was the post office, which became a particularly dangerous position for John Edwards' garrison, the building's large windows somewhat negating the protection offered by its thick walls. At one point, young John Doyle unwisely chose to peer through a window in an attempt to locate pro-Treaty positions. A pro-Treaty sniper found his mark and Doyle was thrown back into the building, blood gushing from wounds in his hand and mouth. He was quickly evacuated to the County and City Infirmary. According to the *Munster Express*:

"At times a hurricane of bullets swept the streets and one could not pass through the area without being hit. Any of the streets running to the quays, such as Keyser Street, Barronstrand Street, Gladstone Street and Hanover Street were dangerous to cross. Reginald's Tower, another stronghold of the republicans, was the object of much concentrated fire from the Free State troops."

This heavy fire inevitably inflicted civilian casualties, including two fatalities: one local man was shot near the Catholic church, while a native of Portarlington was shot dead near the Franciscan church. By this stage, many civilians had decided to flee the city for the town of Tramore, using the Waterford–Tramore railway. Extra services were laid on and were quickly booked out. Those who could afford hotel rooms in Tramore were charged extortionate rates. Those who could not were provided with shelter at the Hibernian Hotel and Piper's cinema, and even in tents pitched along the beach. Those refugees who could not even make their way to Tramore were seen in large groups walking along the Cork Road, where 'they provided a pathetic spectacle'.

At 5 p.m., the 18-pounder's crew began firing again, concentrating on both of the military barracks. This continued until after 9 p.m. when the anti-Treaty garrisons ordered the evacuation of both positions. As soon as the Infantry Barracks was abandoned, crowds of desperately poor civilians rushed through the open gates to find the buildings had been set on fire; the looters nevertheless went to work. Ironically, one of the items stolen was a portable fire engine. At 11 p.m., the Artillery Barracks were also discovered to be burning. By midnight, both barracks were blazing and the huge conflagration could be seen for miles outside the city. Suddenly an explosion (possibly ammunition) ripped through the Infantry Barracks and the crowd of looters inside, four of which were badly injured (one fatally.) The injured were taken to hospital and the civilians hurriedly left both barracks.

At about this time, a party of a hundred pro-Treaty troops were in hiding by the river outside the eastern suburbs of the city. Led by Commandant Mackey and Captain Ned O'Brien, this unit had crossed the River Suir in boats after nightfall, three miles to the east of the city. They then stealthily approached along the river bank towards the city, dodging an anti-Treaty patrol that was driving along the road.

They remained under cover until 1.45 p.m., before silently occupying a house, a hundred yards behind the County Club, and placing a Lewis gun to cover the adjoining Adelphi Hotel, while a patrol led by Captain O'Brien advanced quietly on both buildings. Although they were ready to storm these anti-Treaty positions with gunfire and grenades if necessary, this proved unnecessary. Captain Mackey was able to slip into the County Club through the back door, surprising the sentry and the sleeping garrison without firing a shot. A breach was discovered in the wall and a pro-Treaty party slipped through and captured the Adelphi garrison in the same way. Soon afterwards, the adjoining steamship offices were similarly captured. Twelve pro-Treaty troops then captured the Imperial Hotel; although this had been declared a hospital and there were unarmed personnel wearing Red Cross armbands, there was no evidence of any doctors or patients within. Shortly after this, the pro-Treaty unit took possession of Reginald's Tower, which was unmanned although there was a quantity of arms and ammunition left behind. Mines and explosives were discovered at Reginald's Tower and the Adelphi Hotel which were quickly made safe.[127]

Thus, when the morning of Thursday 20 July dawned, the pro-Treaty force had taken all the buildings on the east end of the quay without firing a shot. The abandoned military barracks were still blazing. A witness in Kilmeaden described the city as 'looking like an erupting slag heap. A great pall of smoke, visible for many miles, hung over it and was lit from time to time by dull tongues of flame shooting up through it'.[128]

George Lennon's group still held Ballybricken prison, while other anti-Treaty units held the post office and some sniping positions along the quay. There was no sign of the counter-attack from Clonmel. That morning the anti-Treaty forces in the city received general absolution from local priests.

The next pro-Treaty objective was the post office, where 'a determined stand was anticipated'. This building was surrounded by open ground and its design allowed its defenders a commanding field of fire. Already being kept under fire by the pro-Treaty troops firing from the railway line three hundred yards across the river, the post office was soon under attack from the infantry advancing along the quays. Captain Ned O'Brien led one party to within twenty yards of the position but these were driven back by fierce defensive fire. In turn, 'severe fire was opened from the jail and sniping posts at Ballybricken, Thomas Hill and the quay as well as from behind the post office' at pro-Treaty positions in the Ferrybank area. Shortly after 4 p.m., the

---

[127] *Munster Express*, 'The Battle of Waterford', 29 July 1922; *Waterford News*, 'The Siege of Waterford', 28 July 1922.

[128] Neeson Eoin, *The Civil War in Ireland,* p. 102.

18-pounder was observed being manhandled into position across the river from the post office. It soon came under a storm of small arms' fire, the crew having an unnerving experience as they huddled behind the gun shield, ears ringing from the deafening clang that occurred every time an enemy bullet struck it. Soon the gunfire began to ease and the pro-Treaty forces observed that the gun crew were lying on the ground around their artillery piece. In fact, they had only been estimating a gun line to the post office, and soon jumped into action. As a tempest of bullets were fired at the building from pro-Treaty positions on both sides of the river, the gun crew loaded and fired six shells in rapid succession through the upper windows of the building. Two of these exploded inside the building, forcing the garrison to evacuate the upper floors. The pro-Treaty infantry launched an assault and captured the building, but only a few of the occupiers. Most of the garrison escaped through the front of the building, and dashed along the quay for five hundred yards under a hail of bullets to the safety of the Granville Hotel. It was a brief respite; the pro-Treaty infantry quickly followed up with an assault on the hotel and the anti-Treaty forces soon had to evacuate this position too. While most escaped under heavy fire to another position in a butcher's shop on nearby Barronstrand Street (already under attack), eighteen were captured including Jerry Cronin: 'whose heroic demeanour throughout the entire conflict had evoked the intense admiration of those who fought and worked beside him'. Explosive charges were discovered in the Granville Hotel and quickly neutralised.[129]

---

[129] *Munster Express*, 'The Battle of Waterford', 29 July 1922; *Waterford News*, 'The Siege of Waterford', 28 July 1922.

A significant incident had occurred in Mullinavat during the afternoon. A small group of eight pro-Treaty soldiers led by Captain Clifford were travelling from Waterford to Kilkenny when they came under attack from a sizeable anti-Treaty force led by Denis Lacey. Escaping to a farmyard, Clifford's men were surrounded and were forced to fight off their attackers for three hours until reinforcements arrived. The anti-Treaty force withdrew and Clifford's men continued their journey. Unknown to them, they had actually encountered the vanguard of the planned anti-Treaty offensive from Clonmel. Despite his orders to the contrary, Michael Sheehan had ordered his column to attack the little pro-Treaty unit. However, contrary to the subsequent opinion of the anti-Treaty leaders, the element of surprise was still intact. Commandant Paddy Paul first learned of the proposed anti-Treaty counter-attack against Prout's force when he was informed of it by writer Eoin Neeson forty years later. Yet Lacey's force remained in situ only a few miles from Waterford city, making no preparations to attack.[130]

As one Cork column was withdrawing from Waterford, another arrived in the city. According to a report of the battle later forwarded to Liam Deasy: 'Reinforcements to the number of one hundred and fifty arrived in the city about 6.30 p.m. having landed at Maypark'.

The pro-Treaty forces continued to consolidate their gains. As darkness fell, all was quiet but for an occasional shot fired by anti-Treaty snipers. By the morning of Friday 21 July, the only remaining anti-Treaty positions in the city were Ballybricken prison, a few nearby houses and sniper posts near the quay, one

---

[130] Neeson Eoin, *The Civil War in Ireland*, p. 101; *Munster Express*, 'The Battle of Waterford', 29 July 1922; UCDA MP P7/B/63. 22 UCDA OMP P17a/ 96.

of which was particularly active near the Protestant cathedral. In the prison, the floors of the cells were covered with brass cartridge cases while pro-Treaty bullets, from across the river, broke several windows.

At dawn, the pro-Treaty forces opened heavy rifle and machine-gun fire on the prison, still manned by George Lennon's unit. At 7.00 a.m., the Cork column that arrived the previous afternoon 'moved in direction of Maypark and the Island, with the attention of attacking the enemy on the rear'. Maypark was a few miles east of the city, near to where Commandant Mackey's force had crossed. Such an attack with the intention of cutting off the pro-Treaty force in the city might have caused them problems, although the outcome of the battle was not in doubt by this stage. However the blow fell on empty air: there was no real supply line here – Mackey's unit was in the city and was fighting toward the bridge.[131]

The cross-channel ferry from Fishguard to Waterford sailed into the harbour later that morning, but diverted to Rosslare having been warned (by megaphone) of the fighting.

"That afternoon, the 18-pounder was brought into position near the Ferrybank railway bridge to fire on the jail. As it was doing so, 'snipers from the jail opened a devastating fire upon the gun crew with machinegun and rifles … For a time the gun crew was compelled to take shelter behind the shield which was repeatedly struck by bullets'. One bullet found an aperture in the gun shield and wounded Gunner Kavanagh in the throat. A Lancia armoured car was quickly moved into position to protect the gunners, a

---

[131] Neeson Eoin, *The Civil War in Ireland,* p. 101; *Munster Express*, 'The Battle of Waterford', 29 July 1922; UCDA MP P7/B/63. 22 UCDA OMP P17a/ 96.

similar manoeuvre having been carried out during the shelling of the Four Courts. Young Sergeant Howlett from Duncannon in Wexford mounted a Lewis gun on the vehicle and began firing upon the prison, ignoring the bullets that were striking the armour all around him. Suddenly he fell back, a bullet from the jail having struck him through the eye. He died instantly."

But the brief respite for the artillerymen had been enough:

"The gunners then opened fire on the jail, from which dense clouds of smoke and dust could be seen to rise as the shells burst in the centre of the prison. In all five shells were poured into the centre of the jail, but the second had the desired effect, and the garrison of fifteen evacuated and retreated via Chapel Lane."[132]

George Lennon later recalled:

"On the last day of our occupancy of the city we had a spirited exchange of fire with the Free State troops across the river who were trying to get a gun into position to start shelling us again. Their troops were already well into the town and getting uncomfortably close to our position in the prison. Just as we sat down to get a bite to eat a shell landed in with a terrific bang, quickly followed by another. Power poked his head in the door.

'Yes Sergeant'?

'The Staters are quite close outside'.

'All right, call in the two outposts, we're leaving, have a look outside first

---

[132] *Munster Express*, 'The Battle of Waterford', 29 July 1922.

Power came back shortly to say that we could get away if we left quickly. As we crossed the road outside we were peppered with rifle fire but we soon got to the comparative safety of Barrack Street. Some irresponsible person or persons had set fire to the fine barracks during our absence. John, the chef, was waiting outside the main gate weepily surveying the remains of our former home. He called out to us plaintively 'The galley is burned, the galley is burned'.

"The men from the outposts had already arrived so we fell them in and marched away, almost casually, followed happily by the barrack dogs who were delighted to be with the company again. Everybody felt disgusted."

According to the *Munster Express*:

"It is a striking tribute to the heroism of those engaged in the defence of the jail that notwithstanding the fact that the building was struck at least five times on Wednesday with accurately directed shells the garrison did not vacate their positions until Friday afternoon, when the holding of the post became an utter impossibility. The machine-gunner in the jail was the first to open fire on Tuesday evening, and kept up incessantly during the siege and was the last of the strongholds to cease fire on Friday afternoon."

Lennon's unit had barely departed the jail when 'large crowds of men, women and children gathered in the vicinity equipped with handcarts, sledgehammers, iron bars, etc. and before the last of the irregulars had withdrawn they had rushed and looted the building'. Some prison officials tried to intervene and were assaulted by the looters, among whom were some of the convicts who had escaped from the workhouse where they had been sent at the start of the battle. One was seen to be carrying a revolver.

Pro-Treaty troops were on the scene soon afterwards and were fired upon, one soldier being shot in the knee. Although an anti-Treaty sniper was initially blamed, it appeared far more likely to have been the armed looter, unless the anti-Treaty forces in the city included an individual callous enough to also shoot two civilians, one of whom was a ten year old girl. Both were shot in the stomach, a particularly agonising wound from which they both later died.

Ironically, the civilians looting the jail are thought to have done more material damage (£5,000 worth) than the eleven shells that struck it during the battle. Furniture and fittings were rifled, the contents of the two chapels ransacked and an attempt was even made to steal a huge prison bath. Pro-Treaty troops had to fire warning shots to eventually disperse the crowd.

After the capture of the prison, only isolated shots were heard around the city, apart from a short period when pro-Treaty forces raked Bilberry Rock with machine-gun fire to protect the soldiers who had reached Redmond Bridge and were working on lowering the central span. This was a tedious business since vital machinery had been removed, and took several hours.[133]

The anti-Treaty forces withdrew to new positions to the west of the city. The Dunhill men returned to their own village, while Lennon and his men marched to Mount Congreve, a stately home not far from Kilmeaden. Others were made their way to Butlerstown Castle and Whitfield Court. The former RIC barracks in Tramore, Dunmore East and Portlaw were set on fire and abandoned.

---

[133] *Munster Express*, 'The Battle of Waterford', 29 July 1922.

By evening, all was quiet in the city. Sightseers were already gathering at the sites at the fiercest fighting; the post office proving a particularly popular attraction. Although the windows were broken and one shell had damaged the wall on the upper floor, the building was otherwise intact and the postal staff were already back on duty, working on a huge backlog of mail to be delivered. Later observers spoke about the low number of casualties incurred in the battle of Waterford and concluded that both sides had been reluctant to fight the other. It is doubtful that the combatants on either side subscribed to such a view, particularly not the 18-pounder crew or the garrisons of the jail or post office. The low casualty figure was far more likely due to thick walls and armour. Also, a claim by the National Army's newspaper that the city 'could of course have been taken in an infinitely shorter space of time but for the desire of the army to ensure the safety of civilian life and property as far as possible' had some credibility.

At 9 p.m., the central span on Redmond Bridge was finally lowered, to a long volley of gunfire and much cheering from the pro-Treaty forces. Later that night, the pro-Treaty forces to the north of the river crossed over and linked up with their comrades in the city.[134]

"When we got to Mount Congreve the sergeant major begged me to try and get some rest and the quartermaster went off to see the housekeeper about provisions; she assured him there was enough food in the larders to feed eight men for three days, but no longer.

---

[134] *Munster Express, 'The Battle of Waterford', 29 July 1922; An tÓglach, 'Major-General Prout, GOC Waterford Command', 14 July.*

"The four junior officers, the Doctor [Joe Walsh] and the local commandant retired with me to the library and somebody went off to inspect the wine cellar. The cellar was well stocked, mostly with vintage brandy and in a session that lasted three days and three nights we drank it out completely. The library apart from the books was equipped with a gramophone and just one record, 'Humoresque' by Dvorak; we kept playing it until the needle or the record wore out. The doctor was something of a demoralising influence as he kept pacing the floor cursing the Civil War and whoever was responsible for it. From time to time runners would come in with reports from 'the front' but we immediately chased them out."

While some might be inclined to regard such conduct as symptomatic of a breakdown in discipline, this behaviour was not untypical of fighting men withdrawing from the frontline.

The pro-Treaty forces in Waterford city quickly consolidated their position. The anti-Treaty troops taken prisoner during the battle were moved by train to Kilkenny and quartered in the prison there. Colonel-Commandant Prout set up temporary headquarters in the Imperial Hotel and troops were billeted in the prison building in Ballybricken. Prout was already preparing to continue his offensive up the Suir to Carrick and on to Clonmel. Commandant Paul was charged with protecting Prout's flank and moving west into the county. To achieve this he had to raise a force in Waterford; weapons were quickly made available on 22 July when the armed trawler Helga arrived from Dublin with a cargo of 500 rifles and 100,000 rounds of ammunition. Personnel were a different matter; normally the training of a soldier took a minimum of several weeks, but Waterford had been a particularly fertile recruiting ground for the British army in the First World War and there was no shortage of war veterans willing to sign up on short service contracts. According to a later account by Paul:

"After the capture of the city, I set up headquarters in Waterford Prison, from where I conducted operations in the Waterford brigade area. I had the great advantage of knowing every inch of Waterford city and county. I also knew most of the people and the officers who were opposed to me."[135]

On 26 July, Paul forwarded the following report to National Army headquarters:

> "I beg to report that the general situation in Waterford city is normal. Small bands of irregulars are now roving about in the eastern portion of the area.
>
> The majority of the [anti-Treaty] city battalion are returning to their homes in ones and twos.
>
> The main body of Irregulars that previously occupied the Infantry Barracks, are moving as a column and are retreating slowly towards the west. They are committing all the destruction possible, blocking roads, destroying bridges, etc.
>
> The '*Helga*' arrived here on Saturday morning at 7.30 a.m., cargo intact. She was detained here on [Prout's] instructions. We utilised her for patrol work, and her searchlights were brought into action during curfew hours. The 'Helga' is due to arrive in Dublin between the hours [of] 4-6 a.m. [on] Thursday.
>
> We are badly in need of short arms, as policing the city is very difficult. An armoured car would greatly facilitate in keeping the city and surrounding districts under control.

---

[135] NLI FOD MS 31,423 (19).

I am expecting Col Comdt Prout to return to Waterford this evening and I will give him my necessary requirements.

We are recovering a lot of loot.

We have also started recruiting here."[136]

George Lennon was still at Mount Congreve:

"The poor Nipper brought me food from the kitchen and begged me to eat or he would help me upstairs, cover me with blankets and try and get me to sleep. One night of our stay I was shaken awake to consult with a pale delicate looking man who said his name was Erskine Childers, in charge of publicity; he wanted an interesting account of 'the siege' for a republican paper he was printing in the field.

"The Doctor suggested a game of golf and one of the buglers offered to caddy for us but we were interrupted in our play by two stately looking ladies advancing up the avenue. 'My God,' said Joe, 'it's the Cumann na mBan.'

'What, again?'

"Half of the men were at the moment searching through the strawberry beds and the other half were parading before the front of the mansion dressed in a most extraordinary variety of uniforms and costumes borrowed from the big house's many wardrobes. The house had a tradition of military service going back beyond Waterloo. Some of the men were dressed as admirals, others generals, and one lad was arrayed in a blazer from Eton or Harrow.

---

[136] UCDA MP P7/B/63.

"The ladies were very disapproving of all this and informed us they were looking after the welfare of the troops. They said the men should have clean socks every day and should have porridge every morning for breakfast. They caused great hilarity and we returned to our play as the two women stalked off looking very angry. It was a scene of tragic comedy. The hilarity was mostly forced and there was a ground swell of disgust, at times almost despairing."

The anti-Treaty Waterford brigade staff had withdrawn to Dungarvan. According to a report from Mick Mansfield dated 25 July; 'I have been informed by OC Operations that our columns are moving on towards the original Mount Congreve–Tramore line'. This was the first recorded mention of such a frontline which proved more ethereal than the 'Waterford–Limerick line'. Tramore had already been occupied by pro-Treaty forces while Mount Congreve was a stately home and offered nothing in the way of a defensive position. Jim Power would have been particularly aware of this – in early 1920 he and a small group of IRA men had raided the house to confiscate the shotguns known to be there. The residents at first refused admission obliging the IRA men to shoot in the windows and force entrance. This initial unpleasantness over, the house owner handed over two valuable silver-inlaid shotguns on the proviso that they be returned in good order. Jim Power did indeed return them in excellent condition in 1923.[137]

The other 'positions' on the 'Mount Congreve line' were Whitfield Court, Butlerstown Castle and Dunhill, all occupied by Waterford men who had withdrawn from the city. None of these offered

---

[137] UCDA OMP P17a/ 96; IMA BMH MS William Keane.

anything in the way as a defensive position, particularly not against artillery.

A report from one of Pax Whelan's staff officers dated 30 July 1922, claimed that 'we occupy the same line as reported in last dispatch: Mount Congreve to Annestown'. Another report the following day from Mick Mansfield noted a 'list of demolitions on the Mt Congreve–Tramore line'. Acting on orders, Mansfield's engineers had demolished seven road and railway bridges between Mount Congreve and the village of Fenor. This action did not impede the advance of the National Army but added to the increasing misery of the local population. At about the same time, Pax Whelan referred to the 'Mount Congreve–Knockeen line', Knockeen being a small district near Dunhill.[138]

For his part, divisional OC Liam Deasy makes no mention of any 'Mount Congreve line' in his account of this time:

"After the occupation by Free State forces of Waterford on 23 July (sic) I spent two days in Dungarvan looking at the proposed defence of west Waterford. In theory it looked like an excellent plan. It was mainly based on the defence of the Colligan river and we expected the added strength of a column from the 1st Cork brigade under Pat Murray and a smaller unit from the 3rd Cork Brigade under the well-known leader at Crossbarry, Tommy Kelleher. Yet in spite of the excellence of these experienced officers and men their defence could not withstand the attack or prevent the Free State forces from taking Dungarvan and the rest of West Waterford.[139]

---

[138] UCDA OMP P17a/ 96.

[139] Deasy, Liam *Brother Against Brother* (Mercier, Cork, 1998), p. 69.

Anti-Treaty reports describe the disastrous state of affairs among the anti-Treaty forces in Waterford at this time. When one of Liam Lynch's senior officers visited Dungarvan barracks on 28 July, he found no security arrangements in place for the Waterford brigade headquarters and no scouts posted to warn of any pro-Treaty advance. Although he was provided with a list of the brigade's officers, he later discovered that some of these had joined the National Army! He found Tom Keating's 2nd Battalion to be 'in a very bad state' with Keating and twenty-five of the battalion's ninety men away fighting in south Tipperary. He concluded that: 'I do not consider that it is possible to restore the organisation in the brigade. The most that can be expected is that we will be able to reorganise the battalions so that they will be able to assist in doing scouting and dispatch riding for the columns'."

Another anti-Treaty staff officer compiled a more detailed assessment which proved to be scathing. Dated 31 July 1922, this report began:

"No member of the brigade staff is competent enough to fill the position he holds. The absence of officers however makes it necessary to retain them. The post of brigade vice OC is vacant and I would suggest that the divisional engineer [Mick Mansfield] who is presently in the area, be appointed. None of the battalion OCs are capable of filling the position."

James Mansfield, a capable leader during the War of Independence, was found to be particularly demoralised, and the three battalions in east Waterford had all but collapsed. Only the 7th (Nire Valley) Battalion was judged worthy of promise; it was recommended that Jack O'Mara be recalled from the fighting in south Tipperary and appointed vice OC.[140]

There were by now 300 anti-Treaty troops in Dungarvan, mostly men who had retreated from Waterford and Carrick-on-Suir including a large contingent from the 1st Cork Brigade. These men were not making themselves popular locally, having requisitioned local hotels and evicting paying customers, and requisitioning thousands of pounds worth of provisions from local traders without payment.[141] Back in Mount Congreve, Lennon and his men had had enough:

"After all the clothing had been returned to the wardrobes and everything put back in place we said goodbye to the household staff and left. We were not at all sure where we were going to next. One thing we agreed on, we were not going to live off the good country people again."

Pax Whelan subsequently reported (to Liam Lynch) that:

"On arriving back in Waterford this morning I learned that the Waterford column had vacated its position on the Mt Congreve–Knockeen line and as a result of the action the Cork columns were returning to the Div HQ, their OC stating that the Waterford column commander was retreating without informing them, and that this left them in a very awkward position so that they decided to return; the Cork column also complained of the lack of co-

---

[140] UCDA OMP P17a/ 96.

[141] Keohan, Edmond, *Illustrated History of Dungarvan* (*Waterford News*, Waterford, 1924), p. 61.

operation by our brigade, and that they had no proper scouts to keep them informed of enemy movements."

There were obvious recriminations between the Corkmen in Waterford and the natives. For his part, Lennon stated 'that the Cork units had evacuated twelve hours before he moved and that they must have got windy'.

It is interesting to note that Lennon's column had withdrawn to Portlaw, a few miles away. The Cork columns were withdrawing to their divisional headquarters which was then in Buttevant.[142]

Having left Mount Congreve, George Lennon resigned his command. According to a later account:

"Owing to a difference of opinion with the HQ of the 1st Southern Division as to the stand to be taken and with the tactics to be employed in the Civil War I resigned to Liam Deasy on or about the 1st of August 1922."[143]

Many of Lennon's men chose to resign with him. 'Nipper' McCarthy's account is particularly poignant:

"We again retreated back to Kilmac[thomas] and finally back to Dungarvan. I decided that I was finished. I would do no more. They asked me why and I told them that I didn't want anymore trouble. I had enough of it now. They asked me if I could give them the gun. 'I won't, that gun is mine, I earned that and I fought for it and with it,' says I. I gave them the parabellum that I had. Liam

---

[142] IMA (Captured Irregular Documents) Whelan to Lynch, undated.

[143] Statement made to Military Service Pensions Board, 7 January 1935.

Lynch was in charge at this time. They accepted my withdrawal."[144]

Liam Deasy later acknowledged:

"The reluctance of so many Volunteers to face up to the harsh realities. They seemed to have no heart in the fight and the knowledge that they were fighting against their kith and kin, even brother against brother, must also have influenced them very much. The divisional staff and the senior officers tried to maintain morale and to rally them at various points even where there was no fighting, but it was becoming increasingly clear to me that a cessation of hostilities then would have been the better policy. I knew at that time that this was the feeling of many senior officers, but Liam Lynch remained adamant and would not entertain any suggestion. He was to the very end an idealist with the highest principles as his guide and it was not in his nature to surrender or to compromise. He ultimately gave his life for these principles."[145]

There was a historical precedent for Lynch's situation: the American Civil War. In April 1865, with Grant's army of the Potomac advancing on the confederate capital of Richmond and the south all but defeated in conventional battle, General Robert E. Lee gathered the generals of the confederacy for a council. Although the actual outcome of this was Lee's surrendering his army of Northern Virginia to Lee at Appomattox, one of Lee's generals suggested (as did confederate President Jefferson Davis) that the remaining 175,000 men of the confederate armies scatter like 'rabbits and partridges' to the vast forests and swamps of the

---

[144] Murphy Seán and Síle, *The Comeraghs – Gunfire and Civil War* (Comeragh Publications, Kilmacthomas, 2003), p. 141.

[145] Deasy, Liam *Brother Against Brother* (Mercier, Cork, 1998), p. 73.

south and carry on a protracted guerrilla war. Lee would have none of it; with a definite end to the war and Abraham Lincoln's strategy of reconstruction of the southern states, reconciliation between North and South advanced enough for the USA to enter the twentieth century as a unified nation.

Lee was the product of a nineteenth century military caste; Lynch was a guerrilla leader by experience and temperament. There would be no quick end to the Irish Civil War.

Commandant Paddy Paul was preparing his force to move out of Waterford city and begin capturing the countryside. A pro-Treaty intelligence report dated 3 August 1922 made his task appear daunting:

"Every road leading from Waterford to Carrick and Dungarvan are trenched, blocked with trees or bridges broken ... the railway bridges at Mount Congreve on the Cork and Waterford line have been badly damaged. Railway men were prevented from repairing same by enemy."

Although the report noted that:

"Beyond the above there has been no enemy activity in East Waterford ... Irregulars were very short of petrol in County Waterford but this week their lorries are going again; they may be using paraffin."

It went on to claim that as enemy forces are billeted on farmers all over the area between Dungarvan and Waterford it is impossible to give an accurate estimate of their numbers, but they cannot be far short of 1,000.

Estimated strengths of anti-Treaty positions were given as follows:

Butlerstown Castle: 1 officer, 15 men. 15 rifles and one machine-gun.
Mount Congreve House: 2 officers, 40 men. 35 rifles
Whitfield House: 30 men. 30 rifles.
Pouldrew House: 25 men. 25 rifles.
Curraghmore House: 100 men. 80 rifles.
Kilmacthomas Workhouse: 70 men. 60 rifles.
Robert Murphy's, Dunhill. 50 men. 50 rifles.[146]

In fact, Mount Congreve had already been abandoned, and on the morning this report was issued, according to a statement issued by National Army headquarters: 'a party of troops, under Commandants Paul and Heaslip, captured eighteen irregulars occupying Butlerstown Castle near Waterford city, together with ten rifles and one Lewis gun'.

The castle was captured without a shot being fired. Anti-Treaty forces abandoned Whitfield Court shortly afterwards, the garrison retreating to Mount Congreve and then to Kilmacthomas. On their way, they changed their green uniforms for civilian dress. There is little doubt that Paul's battle against anti-Treaty forces in Waterford was made a great deal easier by the absence of George Lennon from the anti-Treaty ranks. Lennon was now living as a civilian in Dungarvan and was a witness to subsequent events.[147]

On the evening of 4 August, a series of loud rumbling explosions were heard from the vicinity of Ballyvoyle. Mick Mansfield's engineers had detonated explosive charges on the road and rail bridges, in each case destroying a central arch. A few days later, another arch on the railway bridge fell and in the coming days the

---

146 UCDA MP P7/B/63.

147 *Irish Times,* 4 August 1922.

238

entire bridge collapsed, filling the valley floor with rubble. The road bridge was saved from a similar fate by the intervention of the county surveyor who carried out an energetic salvage operation.[148]

On 5 August 1922, John Doyle, who was wounded in the post office during the battle for Waterford, died in the County and City Infirmary. He was buried in the Republican Plot in Ballygunner cemetery, alongside Thomas O'Brien of Dunhill and John O'Rourke of Waterford City, killed in the War of Independence.[149]

A report from the Waterford brigade to Liam Deasy dated 7 August 1922 optimistically announced that

"We hold the Dalligan Line. All bridges including the Railway Bridge are down".

The same report also noted F[ree] S[tate] troops in Whitfield Court and Portlaw'. Anti-Treaty forces hoped that a defensive line could be held along the Dalligan 'river' and Mick Mansfield's engineers demolished several bridges along its length. This may have seemed feasible enough on a map, the Dalligan running from the Comeraghs south to the coast, but the Dalligan is better described as a stream and can easily be stepped across for much of its length. The destruction of the bridges proved to be no impediment at all to the pro-Treaty advance.[150]

---

[148] Keohan, Edmond, *Illustrated History of Dungarvan* (*Waterford News*, Waterford, 1924), pp. 63–66.

[149] Whittle, Nicholas *Waterford Remembers* (*Waterford News*, 1948), p. 28–29.

[150] UCDA OMP P17a/ 96.

On the night of 7 August, two ships (the *Arvonia* and *Lady Wicklow*) quietly entered Cork Harbour carrying five hundred pro-Treaty troops under the command of Colonel-Commandant Emmet Dalton. At 0200 the following morning the two ships berthed at Passage West and Dalton's force began disembarking. At the same time, another two hundred troops landed at Youghal without opposition, while another one hundred and eighty landed at Union Hall. By the evening of 8 August, Dalton's force were involved in fierce fighting in Rochestown, which continued for much of the following day.

That evening, it became apparent that the anti-Treaty force in Dungarvan was preparing for evacuation, and locals were startled to see smoke, then flames, rising from Dungarvan Castle. A crowd gathered around the castle walls and particularly around the ancient tower. An eyewitness recalled:

"When the smoke was seen to ascend from its antique windows there was an indescribable feeling of sadness among the crowd – the most striking token of their ancient history was about to be destroyed. But the superior masonry of this old tower would not yield to the assaults of desperation, and though the stairway was burned, and other woodwork, though the ancient door-posts were torn from their position, the old tower still stood. The fire died out, and still looking out over the river and the sea rose the circular, conical roof, the work of those who lived a thousand years ago.

"The former RIC barracks building however was reduced to blackened walls. Soon after Dungarvan barracks had been fired, flames and smoke were seen rising from the coastguard station at Ballinacourty.

Later that evening, the Corkmen who had been part of the anti-Treaty garrison in Dungarvan boarded a special train to take them to Cappoquin. After they had crossed the elegant railway bridge across the Blackwater, explosives also demolished it."[151]

Shortly before 4.40 p.m. the following afternoon, the inhabitants of Dungarvan were startled to hear the drone of an aircraft engine high over the town, something not heard since the departure of No. 2 Squadron RAF from Fermoy four months previously. Although the aircraft in question was a Bristol Fighter and its pilot (Commandant Charles Russell) was a former RAF pilot, this aircraft was painted with the Irish tricolour and belonged to the newly formed air service of the National Army, and was carrying out vital reconnaissance missions for the pro-Treaty forces. Having taken off from Baldonnel Aerodrome less than four hours previously, the aircraft landed at Waterford Racecourse at just after 2 p.m., taking off again two hours later. Describing weather as 'fair' and visibility as 'poor', Commandant Russell later reported:

"Kilmacthomas all quiet. Awaiting occupation by our troops. Youghal – everything quiet. Troops moving about town freely. Passage West – two ships drawn up to landing stage with a number of troops aboard. All quiet in the vicinity of the ships. No sign of fighting anywhere. People moving freely about on streets. Railway bridge crossing Lough Mahon blown up at Fota Castle. Road bridge crossing Belvelly Channel strongly barricaded."

---

[151] Keohan, Edmond, *Illustrated History of Dungarvan* (*Waterford News*, Waterford, 1924), pp. 69–72; *Munster Express*, 'Dungarvan Evacuated', 12 August 1922.

It was as Russell described his approach to Cork at 4.50 p.m. that his report became dramatic:

"Cork city – one would imagine to see Cork city from the air that the whole town was enveloped in flames. Closer examination revealed the fact that all barracks, police and military, were on fire. Also what appeared to be a private house, half a mile north of Victoria barracks was on fire. Victoria barracks was, in spite of the smoke and flame, a scene of great activity. Large numbers of men were moving about in a very excited manner."

Having carefully observed the city for thirty minutes, Russell and Stapleton began their return flight. At Midleton, the Bristol Fighter came under fire from the town and the observer Captain William Stapleton (a veteran of Michael Collins' famous Squad) returned fire with a Lewis Gun.

Returning over Dungarvan, the aircraft was observed to be flying so low and slow that it seemed to hover at times. Rifle shots were fired at it by the few remaining anti-Treatyites, without effect. Russell and Stapleton then flew back to Waterford, landing just after 6 p.m. and taking off again for Baldonnel at 8. p.m., landing at their base shortly before sunset.[152]

By 11 August, pro-Treaty forces had captured the cities of Clonmel and Cork. On that date, Liam Lynch ordered the burning of the barracks that housed his headquarters in Fermoy, thereby ending the conventional phase of the Civil War. On the same day, John Dobbyn (24) of Butlerstown, serving with the anti-Treaty forces, died in a shooting accident. He was buried at the

---

[152] UCDA MP P7/B/63; *Munster Express*, 'Dungarvan Evacuated', 12 August 1922.

Republican Plot in Kilrossanty, alongside Jack Fitzgerald and Pat Keating.[153]

The loss of the bridges at Ballyvoyle and Cappoquin and the destruction of the vital railway line effectively cut off the town of Dungarvan from the outside world. Attempts to bring in supplies by road proved unsuccessful; the roads were dangerous while trucks were few in number and prone to interception by anti-Treaty forces who would requisition their contents, all of which did nothing to endear their cause to the locals.

Eventually, local traders acquired two small steamers which brought in vital supplies from Britain without which life in Dungarvan would have been impossible. One of these steamers was the *Lady Belle*, a familiar sight in Dungarvan harbour for many years.[154]

After the capture of Waterford city, Ned O'Brien had been promoted to commandant for his bravery during the fighting. On 15 August, he was shot dead in his home town. According to Paddy Paul's later account:

"I left the barracks [Ballybricken jail] on duty about half-past ten on Tuesday night. Shortly after I had gone out word came to headquarters to the effect that Shortcourse police barracks were on fire. Commandant O'Brien arranged immediately for a patrol to go out and proceed to the scene of the fire, subsequently leaving the prison himself and coming with the patrol at Mayor's

---

[153] Whittle, Nicholas *Waterford Remembers* (*Waterford News*, 1948), pp. 30–31.

[154] Keohan, Edmond, *Illustrated History of Dungarvan* (*Waterford News*, Waterford, 1924), p. 73.

Walk. Comdt O'Brien, who was accompanied by another soldier, then went in advance of the patrol, and arriving at the barracks they were successful in forcing an entrance by bursting the door off its hinges. As they did so a shot rang out and retracing his footsteps Commandant O'Brien returned to meet the patrol to hurry them along ... at this moment a volley of revolver fire opened from the direction of Upper Barrack Street and Commandant O'Brien was then seen to fall. He had been shot from behind ... other members of the patrol rushed to the scene, and Father Thomas O'Donoghue, CC Ballybricken, arrived within a few minutes and administered the last rites. The moment Commandant O'Brien was struck his first request was for a priest, and his last words just before expiring were: 'I am a soldier anyway'. This words were uttered as he handed over his revolver to a man at his side."

An inquest returned a verdict of wilful murder and observed that a bullet of a particularly destructive nature had been used. Ned O'Brien was laid to rest in Ballygunner cemetery (but not in the Republican Plot) with full military honours and a large crowd attending. He was only twenty-one.[155]

On 16 August, a small reconnaissance party of the National Army arrived in Dungarvan, now abandoned by anti-Treaty forces. A convoy of military vehicles arrived at midday, to a warm reception by the townspeople, and the pro-Treaty troops took up positions in Church Street, the Town Hall, the Union Hospital and the Provincial Bank.[156]

---

[155] *Munster Express*, 'Sensational Occurrence in Waterford', 19 August 1922.

[156] Keohan, Edmond, *Illustrated History of Dungarvan* (*Waterford News*, Waterford, 1924), p. 72.

The remaining men willing to fight on against the Treaty in Waterford were divided into three flying columns: one was placed under the command of Tom Keating and another under Jack O'Mara, both of whom had returned from south Tipperary. Paddy Curran led the third. On the morning of 19 August, Tom Keating's column carried out an attack on the National Army outpost at Whitfield Court, withdrawing before reinforcements from Waterford city (led by Commandant Paul) arrived. Paul's troops began a sweep of villages in the area, and there were two further clashes with Keating's column at Kill and Gardenmorris before the antiTreaty force withdrew to the Comeraghs.

On that same day, Jack Edwards, formerly of Lennon's column, was killed. Edwards was captured by Prout's force during the battle for the city was and subsequently held in Kilkenny Prison. He was shouting from a window to a friend outside the prison when he was shot dead by a sentry.[157]

By 26 August, the National Army had occupied the Workhouse in Kilmacthomas. One of the new garrison was Michael Cummins of Stradbally, now a captain in the National Army. On that night he strolled the short distance into the village for tea at a friend's house. As he stepped out into the rain afterwards, he was shot in the back by local men who almost certainly were known to him. Having ascertained that he was unarmed, his assailants left him alone. Critically wounded, he was lucky to survive.[158]

---

[157] Whittle, Nicholas, *Waterford Remembers* (*Waterford News*, 1948), pp. 34–35.

[158] *Munster Express*, 'Shooting at Kilmacthomas', 26 August 1922.

Paul had learned from the British the value of a garrison in Kilmacthomas, only five miles from the refuge afforded by the Tay Valley. On the night of 2 September, a pro-Treaty unit from the Workhouse moved out and took up positions a mile south of Kilrossanty where Tom Keating's column was known to be based. At 06.30 a.m. they moved in to attack and after forty-five minutes of fierce fighting ten of Keating's column were captured, the rest escaping into the mountains. A month later, eight more members of the column were captured near Ballylinch, finishing Keating's unit as a fighting force.[159]

This left Curran's column in the Ardmore area and Jack O'Mara's column operating in the Nire Valley, the latter comprising thirty men armed with rifles and a Lewis gun. O'Mara noted: 'We fought actions with Free State troops at the Halfway House, Ballymacarbery and Mullinahurka. There were four enemy casualties in those encounters. We suffered no losses'. Paddy Paul later observed: 'During meeting engagements in the open country I noticed that the opposition always withdrew when the attack was pressed home. John O'Meara's column and one of the Tipperary columns did put up a good fight on a couple of occasions. The odds however were against them.'[160]

In Dungarvan on the night of 7 September, a bomb was thrown at a National Army outpost in the town at a time when the nearby street was crowded with pedestrians. Two soldiers were wounded, as were three local girls, two of them seriously. Locals were outraged and it did nothing for the popularity of the anti-Treaty cause. On 22 October, a National Army patrol was

---

[159] *Irish Times*, 'Ten Irregulars Captured', 4 September 1922.

[160] NLI FOD MS 31,423 (19).

ambushed near Millstreet, a few miles north of Cappagh. Two young soldiers, one from Waterford city and another from Kilmacthomas, were killed.[161]

Pax Whelan was captured in November. Throughout the winter of 1922-23, the guerrilla war continued and more young men were buried in the graveyards at Kilrossanty and Ballygunner. The anti-Treaty cause was crippled by the lack of support from local civilians. In 1921, almost every door in Waterford had been open to Lennon's column. In 1923, there were very few open for O'Mara's.

On 25 January 1923, two young men from the anti-Treaty 1st Cork Brigade who had been captured in Waterford a month previously, were executed by firing squad in Waterford city. Patrick O'Reilly and Michael Fitzgerald went to their deaths bravely, singing as they were marched from Ballybricken prison to the parade square in the burned out Infantry Barracks and even sharing their cigarettes with the firing squad. Although the official reason for the execution was for bearing arms and waging war against government forces, some noted that these two men had carried out the bomb attack on British forces in Youghal in May 1921. Mercifully, these were the only two such executions in Waterford during the Civil War. A subsequent report from the National Army director of intelligence, Colonel MJ Costello, dated 12 October 1923, stated:

"I have the honour to submit for your information the following report from one of our officers, who is in touch with Mick Sheehan, Adjutant of the 2nd Southern Division (Irregulars), who

---

161 *Irish Times*, 'Dungarvan Outrage', 9 September 1922; *Irish Times*, '2 Killed, I wounded in County Waterford', 28 October 1922.

was arrested by officers of this Department a few days ago ... with reference to the executions in the Waterford command, Sheehan states – 'We may thank Prout for the fact that they were so few'."[162]

In February 1923, Paddy Ormonde was maimed by a National Army bullet near Ballylemon. Although pro Treaty troops brought him straight to Dungarvan hospital, he was crippled for life. Jack O'Mara was with Liam Lynch when he was fatally wounded:

On April 9th 1923, I went to Glosha, two miles west of Ballymacarbery, with Bill Quirke and Seán Hayes and met Frank Aiken and Liam Lynch. We went on to Newcastle and at about 4 p.m. on April 10th scouts informed us of advancing Free State troops. We started up the mountain at daybreak and saw the troops. When about 400 yards ahead of them they opened fire on us. Firing ceased for a while, then one shot rang out. Liam Lynch, who was fifty yards to our rear, shouted he was hit. We went back and carried him for twenty yards or so, but he begged us to leave him down as he was suffering too much from a wound on his right side. We took his papers and gun from him and left him. He was subsequently taken by the Free Staters to Clonmel, where he died that same night.[163]

With the death of Liam Lynch, the anti-Treaty leadership began making moves to end the fighting. But there was still time for men to die. On 11 April 1923, Tom Keating was fatally shot at

---

[162] Whittle, Nicholas *Waterford Remembers* (Waterford News, 1948), pp. 46–7; UCDA MP P7/B/91.

[163] IMA BMH WS Patrick Ormonde, Jack O'Mara.

Coolnasmear, two miles north of Dungarvan. According to an account by his sister Lena:

"Free State soldiers tried to capture him as he ran from a house in Coolnasmear, intending to escape across the mountain. He was helping a companion, Paddy Landers, over a fence when he was hit by a volley of shots from the soldiers and badly wounded. The soldiers took him to Wade's house in Coolnasmear where Mrs Wade made him as comfortable as possible but still in great pain. She sent for Fr Burke ... from whom he received the last rites and further attention to his wounds. Fr Burke then requested the soldiers to bring Thomas to his house until such time as he could be taken to hospital and receive proper medical attention. The soldiers would not agree to this so they threw him onto the back of a lorry and drove to Cappoquin, stopping at every public house on the way."[164]

The evidence is that, other than the execution of O'Reilly and Fitzgerald, no anti-Treaty prisoners died while in the custody of troops commanded by Paddy Paul. Tom Keating however had been captured by pro-Treaty troops based in Cappoquin, not Paul's 14th Infantry Battalion. Dr Moloney of Dungarvan was directed to Cappoquin where he found Tom Keating and immediately ordered an ambulance which brought him directly to Dungarvan hospital where he was operated upon to remove a bullet lodged in his body. The treatment came too late and Keating died during surgery. It was Dr Moloney's opinion that Keating could have been saved had he received medical attention sooner.

The Catholic priests in Dungarvan were hostile to the anti-Treaty cause but allowed one mass, during which a guard of honour was

---

[164] Keating, Lena, *The Keatings of Comeragh* (undated).

mounted over the coffin by tall men in blue uniforms. These were members of the Garda Síochána, the new Irish police force, who had taken up duties in Dungarvan the previous January. Unlike the RIC, this new force upheld the law without weapons; the honour guard for Keating was a conciliatory gesture and was greatly appreciated by the Keating family.

Tom was subsequently laid to rest beside his brother Pat in the Republican plot in Kilrossanty.[165]

On 30 April, Frank Aiken ordered a suspension of anti-Treaty military operations. This however was not a surrender or armistice and the fighting slowed rather than stopped. According to Mick Mansfield:

"After Liam Lynch's death, conditions became very bad, and even after the 'cease fire' order, it was almost impossible to get sleeping accommodation. It was also difficult to get sufficient food. Most of the time we slept out in the open with a waterproof covering. The Free State round ups were continuing and it was a whole time job to evade capture. One day in the early morning in company with Mick Shalloe, Seán Wade, and [Paddy] Cashin, I approached my home in Old Parish in the hopes of getting some badly needed food and clothing. I received a signal (pre-arranged) from my sister warning me that Free State troops were in the vicinity. We all went to a point about a mile further back overlooking the road and lay down in a field. Some children going to school saw us and on being questioned by Free State soldiers, said that they had seen men in this field. We knew nothing until a number of cattle in the field with us began to mill around and look

---

[165] Keating, Lena, *The Keatings of Comeragh* (undated). IMA BMH WS Michael J. Mansfield, Jack O'Mara.

over the fence. On looking over the fence, we found ourselves surrounded by Free Staters. We were unarmed, as the cease fire order had been given some time previously. After a hurried consultation, we decided to make a dash for it. The chances were that we would be shot anyway, if we were captured where we lay. We dashed through a gap in the hedge and the military opened fire on us. Luckily, we all got through without being hit. We were then chased and fired on for over three miles, but we succeeded in getting away."

From 1923 onward, several former members of the Waterford flying column left the country. Shortly after the Civil War, a small group that included Mick Mansfield and Mick Shalloe, succeeded in covertly arranging transport to Britain, from where they worked their passage to Canada. They worked for a while as lumberjacks in the freezing conditions of Quebec, thereafter slipping over the border to New York in 1924. Jack O'Mara, as a former US soldier, was able to emigrate legally to the USA in 1923.[166]

---

[166] IMA BMH WS Michael J. Mansfield, Jack O'Mara.

The Years Between, 1923-1971

Chapter 5

A hint of Lennon's future life philosophy was indicated by a verse written in the autograph book of the sister of a former comrade of the flying column. This was on the occasion of the girl's 'American Wake,' the social occasion held on the eve of an Irish person's emigration to the United States and so-called since they were as unlikely to return as the dead.

> *Be kind to little animals*
> *Wherever they may be,*
> *And give the stranded jelly fish*
> *A push into the sea.*
> (13 September 1923)

It was not until late 1924 that the railway bridge at Ballyvoyle was rebuilt and trains could run again between Dungarvan and Waterford. The infrastructure throughout the country had been similarly devastated by anti-Treaty forces, wrecking the new state's economy. Employment was scarce and emigration high.

George Lennon's older brother, James, had already emigrated to Wales by late 1924. On 7 November that year George's mother, Ellen, died of cancer of the liver and was subsequently buried beside her deceased husband in St Mary's of Dungarvan.

In May 1926, George's two younger sisters and younger brother emigrated from Cobh on the Cunard liner *Samaria*, arriving and settling in New York city. This left George as the last member of his family in Dungarvan; he was not to remain for long:

A warm October day in 1926: I am passing through Cork on my way from the American consulate in Cobh with a visa to enter the United States in my pocket. Like many thousand others I am forced to emigrate to seek a living abroad.

On January 1927, George Lennon boarded the Cunard liner *Ascania* at Cobh, arriving in New York city on 1 February. Reunited with his siblings and sharing a New Jersey address with them, George quickly secured a position with the Prudential Insurance Company for whom he worked until December 1928. The following month (January 1929) he took a position as a night auditor at the Pennsylvania Hotel in Manhattan.[167]

On October 1929, the US Stock Market crashed, triggering the Great Depression of the 1930s:

"How did I exist through those seven Depression years? Being fairly capable and having a genius for survival I clung to the job. Twelve hours a day, sometimes seven days a week. I was being ground in the white satanic mills of America. In the rare moments of blessed relief from office slavery I lay in Central Park, read Marx, and became an ardent communist."

In later years, George openly admitted to being a card carrying member of the American Communist Party for a short period. Later deciding that 'the CP was not the answer' he left, although he remained avowedly left wing in his political views. George Lennon's brief flirtation with communism should be taken in its proper context. 1930 was a long time before the deaths of millions

---

[167] Lennon, Ivan, *Lennons in Time,* unpublished family history.

of Russians in Stalin's gulags or the starvation of millions of Chinese in 1959, the full details of which have only emerged in quite recent years. 1930 even preceded Stalin's deliberately engineered Ukrainian Famine of 1932–32 which killed at least three million people. Immediately after the Wall Street Crash and economic disaster for the United States and much of the world, communism genuinely seemed to offer a viable alternative to the capitalist system. The Soviet Union actively sold itself as a beacon of hope; a primer for Stalin's 'five year plan' became a bestseller in the US while the New York office of Soviet trade agency Amtorg reported over 100,000 emigration applications. Thousands of Americans did emigrate to Russia, at least 3,000 of whom are thought to have died in Stalin's subsequent purges.

At the end of 1931, Lennon received a letter from Leningrad from Charles J. McGuinness who was in charge of the Cheekpoint gun-running in 1921. McGuinness' references to the Lennon siblings suggest that the pair had been friends in New York during the prohibition years. McGuinness at this time had been using his nautical skills to command a small ship smuggling rum across the Canadian border, having previously participated in Admiral Byrd's Antarctic Expedition. The letter (rather appropriately written in red ink) announced that McGuinness was:

"..now semi-permanently settled in Leningrad and am thoroughly enthused with the Socialist system in Russia. Russia is all and more that we have conjured about it and the mystifying thing to me is that the remainder of the world should voluntarily suffer the oppression of Capitalist grafters. My position is rather interesting. I am inspector in the port of Leningrad of loading, discharging and handling of cargoes introducing where necessary foreign and modern methods to speed up dispatch. The Russians are a pleasant hospitable race and my life here is extremely pleasant. I have made many acquaintances and feel thoroughly at home, something I never really felt in the US."

McGuinness went on to enthuse about the Red army and navy, and to claim that organised religion in Russia was not being persecuted, but was nevertheless being abandoned. He also claimed that he was planning to join a Russian polar expedition the following year.

Another letter written in January 1932 (which mentioned that his 'Russian name' was Karl Ivanovitch) continued to extol the virtues of the Soviet Union:

"Russia is a most interesting country and the progress of these past few years is undoubtedly much finer than the States and all of it practically organised and run by the workers ... Life is not the drab affair we were given to understand rather the reverse with clubs, concerts, theatres and the incomparable Russian ballet."

Despite this, there were admissions in the same letter that 'there is at present an absence of many articles' and of a 'present housing shortage'. McGuinness admitted that some luxury items could only be obtained in 'Foreign Stores' which did not accept Russian roubles. He requested a loan of American currency from Lennon and extended an invitation for him to come to Russia, one Lennon did not avail of.[168]

McGuiness quickly became disillusioned with the reality of life in the USSR and later left, publishing an account of his time there entitled Behind the Red Curtain. McGuinness remained sympathetic enough to Communists to briefly fight alongside

---

[168] Tzouliadis, Tim, *The Forsaken* (Penguin Group, New York, 2008); NLI UT MS 35,699.

them during the Spanish Civil War. He had evidently changed ideology by 1942 when he was interned by the Irish government for consorting with the German intelligence agency.

In 1932, the Fianna Fáil republican party, led by Éamon de Valera and comprised mainly of persons who had opposed the Anglo-Irish Treaty in the Irish Civil War, were elected to power in Ireland. De Valera began several reforms, including the abolition of the TDs oath of allegiance to the king.

On 22 April 1934, George Lennon became a citizen of the United States with Certificate of Naturalisation No. 3815157 and that September was issued US Passport No. 240298. Occupation was noted as 'Cashier'.[169]

In 1934, through George Sherwood, husband of his sister Eileen, Lennon became the business manager for *The Irish Review*, a short-lived magazine of Irish expression printed at Albany in New York State. In May 1934, this journal carried an article on the newly-established Irish Volunteer Force, a military reserve force established by the Fianna Fáil government partly to encourage Irish republicans to serve in the Irish army. 'George Crolly' wrote the article – since George Lennon had a strong family connection with that name (his father alone was named 'George Crolly Lennon') this was almost certainly a pseudonym for Lennon. The article was enthusiastic and detailed, demonstrating that Lennon still had a keen interest in military affairs. It was noted that the Volunteer Force would be organised in regiments based on ancient Irish territories (Waterford would be part of the 'Regiment of Ossory'.) and would be organised in three 'lines'. The First Line comprised under 25s, but it was noted that the Second

---

[169] US Passport 240298 issued September 1934 to George Lennon.

Line would be made up of men aged under 45 while the Third Line would comprise 'men of recognised national service'.[170]

Also in 1934, the Irish parliament passed the Military Service Pensions Act which provided for the payment of pensions to those who had fought on the anti-Treaty side in the Irish Civil War, pro-Treaty veterans having been provided for by the Army Pensions Act of 1923.

With a republican government in power and the pension providing a basic income, several veterans of the Waterford IRA returned home. James Mansfield had returned from Canada in 1931, setting up a knitting industry in Dungarvan and subsequently working for the Dickens Leather Company in the town. Mick Mansfield returned in 1933, commencing a spectacular career in the Garda Síochána, attaining the rank of inspector by 1938. Jack O'Mara also returned from the US in 1933, Mick Shalloe in 1934. Michael Cummins returned from England in 1936.[171]

A letter to the Military Pensions Advisory Board dated 13 September 1935 indicates that there was in existence a Waterford Brigade Old IRA Men's Association, contact address for which was Lennon's address at 14 West 74th Street. The president of this association was James Fraher, while George Lennon was named as secretary. Other members included Patrick Cashin, Augustine Donovan and Richard Mooney.

---

[170] 'Crolly, George', The *Irish Review*, 'An Irish Volunteer Army', Vol. 1, No. 2.

[171] *Capuchin Annual,* 1970, p. 645; Garda Archives Dublin Castle; IMA BMH WS (various).

"I am taking advantage of my sick leave to go to Ireland and hope to be in Dublin on or about the 1st October. I would be glad to have an opportunity to go before the Board for a hearing on my own claim and also to testify on the claims of all the active Waterford brigade men who were compelled to emigrate and who are now resident here."[172]

Lennon was obliged to fill out a sixteen-page application form detailing 'continuous active service' for a series of periods from 1 April 1916 to his resignation on 1 August 1922. His application had the address of 11 Mitchel Terrace in Dungarvan, instead of his New York address.

In October 1935, Lennon went before the pensions board on his own and his comrades' behalf. The board granted Lennon his pension on 10 December 1935, recognising his service except for the 'weighted' period of Easter Week 1916. This amounted to an annual pension of £93, 6s d.[173]

He subsequently returned to New York, terminating his employment with the Hotel Pennsylvania in March 1936; his passport indicates that he then returned to Ireland, landing at Cobh on 4 August 1936:

"There is a muting of the sound from the ship's propellers. The motion of the ark is slowing down. The three of them are sitting motionless in the main lounge long after all the other passengers have retired to bed: Mrs Worthington, he and Vivian. Mrs Mowthington has a house in Mayfair and she wants them to come

---

[172] Letter from George Lennon to Military Pensions Advisory Board, 13 September 1935.

[173] Award Certificate, Department of Defence, 10 December 1935.

and stay with her sometime but they know they will never see each other again. He is on his way to give aid to the Spanish republicans – and where is she going to now? The kind lady administers words of practical English wisdom and leaves them alone. They, are both of course, mature people, but this does not seem to help very much. Is this the end of their enchantment ... They go up on deck to face a most unfriendly looking dawn ... In no time at all he is off on the tender, the ship gives a most mournful sounding hoot ('Outward Bound') and quickly, disappears over the watery horizon. Some fellow on the tender is playing 'Come Back to Erin' on a battered instrument. It sounds like Taps. He steps ashore and gazes about in dismay. What on earth ever brought him back to this place?"

The Spanish Civil War erupted in July 1937, when a group of right wing Spanish army officers launched a rebellion against the democratically elected government. While the war would eventually be recognised as a democracy fighting fascism, the distinction was not so clear in 1936, particularly when extremists supporting the government committed atrocities against Catholic churches and clergy. The Irish Catholic Church declared support for the Spanish republicans' battle against the 'Reds', as did Nazi Germany and Fascist Italy.

This viewpoint prompted George Lennon to pen the following forthright letter to the *Irish Times*:

"There has been such confusion created in the minds of the Irish people by the propagandist reports in the British daily press and its Irish equivalents, on the situation in Spain that it seems of some importance to restate the actual position. The war between the 'Reds' and the 'Patriots' is in reality a Fascist revolt against a lawfully elected democratic government. Heretofore in Ireland we were taught that all power came to governments from God through the people. Since when has this teaching been discarded?

"The Spanish government is a coalition government composed of all the democratic elements in the country. In its struggle for life it has called to its aid and armed those of its loyal subjects that were willing to serve. Is this a disgraceful or unprecedented proceeding?

"Opposed to this government in armed revolt are the Fascists, composed of the landlords, the nobles, the militarists. One fails to see how the enthronement of this Fascism in Spain is to be considered a triumph for Christianity. Fascism, whose philosophy is to sweep away all the gains of democratic progress, to subdue all men to its will, and wage war for plunder or for glory, and under whose regime the gas mask shall be the soother for the newly born and the rifle the toy of the school child.

"The atrocity campaign has unfortunately for the propagandists, come so soon after the similar campaign in the Great War, that it is not likely to deceive many. Indeed, as one opens the newspaper each morning, one involuntarily looks for the resurrection of the story of boiling down the corpses to make candles.

"The Catholic Church has undoubtedly received a heavy blow; but not because it is the Catholic Church. It has suffered because its ministers in Spain, as in other countries, have thrown in their lot with the powerful, the monied, the privileged, and turned a deaf ear to the just demands of the toiling masses. The real danger to Christianity does not come from the workers, but from the un-Christ-like practices of its ministers in allying with the powerful against the poor.

"If the churches, and particularly the Catholic Church, wish to retain the respect and support of the world they will have to respect the fundamental truth that you cannot serve God and Mammon."[174]

It took great moral courage to speak out against the Catholic Church at this time. To put Lennon's comments in perspective, it is necessary to appreciate the enormous influence on Irish society then enjoyed by the Church. In 1932, ostensibly the 1500th anniversary of St Patrick's mission to Ireland, the International Eucharistic Congress was held in Dublin. For five days that June, hundreds of thousands of fervent worshippers attended a series of open air masses in the Phoenix Park, culminating in a high mass attended by an estimated one million people, during which the pope broadcast live from the Vatican, over the most extensive PA system ever assembled, and turned Dublin into a virtual open-air cathedral. In 1937, De Valera's constitution, which removed most of the provisions of the Anglo-Irish Treaty, was carried by a national referendum. This constitution was influenced by Catholic teachings, due to the participation in its drafting by Dr John McQuaid, then president of Blackrock college (de Valera's *alma mater*) and later archbishop of Dublin. This was most obvious in the recognition of the 'special position' of the Catholic Church, the prohibition of divorce and the express intention 'to ensure that mothers shall not be obliged by economic necessity to engage in labour to the neglect of their duties in the home'.

The Catholic Church in Ireland had not even reached the zenith of its power. In the 1920s, it had been unsuccessful in its opposition to the world-leading Shannon hydro-electric power scheme. In 1951, the Church successfully opposed the Mother and Child Scheme (with the assistance of certain politicians and doctors), which proposed state-funded healthcare for mothers before and

---

[174] *Irish Times*, 'Spain's Civil War', 18 August 1936.

after pregnancy, in a nation with the highest child mortality rates in Europe. Today, there is a growing consensus that the Catholic's Church's relentless interference at every level of Irish society was to prove greatly detrimental to the new nation's social development.

On the weekend of 12–13 September 1936, Lennon participated in a meeting at 41 Parnell Square which saw the foundation of the All-Ireland Old IRA Men's Association. Although Liam Deasy, formerly leader of the anti-Treaty 1st Southern Division, was appointed president, both sides of the Civil War divide were represented in the new organisation. Vice presidents included Roger McCorley and Frank Thornton, both former officers in the National Army. George Lennon was appointed to the association's executive, and later became the association's secretary.

Much of the rhetoric was naturally stridently republican: The only speech reported was by an unnamed northern delegate who warned that whatever the likelihood of nationalists achieving a majority of the population in Northern Ireland, the 'Imperialists' would seek to make the partition of Ireland 'a permanent thing'. It was agreed at the meeting that:

"In moving towards the establishment of the republic proclaimed in 1916, the full weight of the old IRA would be thrown into the field to prevent any further growth of Imperialism, to awaken full national consciousness, and to emphasise that the old IRA had regained the position which was lost after the Truce, and are now preparing plans for a resumption of genuine national advance, based on present circumstances, in the knowledge that the old army which fearlessly dealt smashing blows against overwhelming British forces bent on extermination of the people, is again re-organised to realise the national objective.

"The conference demanded:

..that no public representative attend the Coronation of Edward VIII of England in London next year [it was highly unlikely that the Fianna Fáil government would have contemplated such a step anyway].

"Another resolution deplored the 'extent to which alien interests have been permitted to secure control of our industries', and called upon the government to take adequate steps 'to prevent further foreign penetration, and to bring all existing industries under complete national control within ten years'.

"It was significant that the group had adopted the term 'Old IRA' to distinguish themselves from the extremists who now also claimed the name IRA. This group had emerged after the defeat of the anti-Treaty forces in 1923, but by 1936 were concentrating its efforts against the Irish government, largely in the form of gun attacks on the unarmed Garda Síochána. In 1936 a young man was shot dead on the streets of Dungarvan. His 'crime' was to attempt to leave the IRA without permission, a privilege that any member of the Old IRA had enjoyed as of right.

"It was announced at the inaugural meeting of the Old IRA men's association 'that President de Valera had agreed to receive a deputation to consider a scheme adopted by the conference, for alleviating distress among old IRA men, providing free hospital and sanatoria treatment for men physically disabled, and giving preference in the various spheres of employment for men with national records'."[175]

---

[175] *Irish Times*, 'New Organisation for All Ireland', 14 September 1936.

On 16 October however, the Irish government committed itself to equal employment opportunities for all, 'regardless of creed, class or political affiliations.'[176]

In January 1938, Lennon published a long and detailed article entitled 'National Defence' in a popular but short-lived magazine named Ireland To-Day. It described Lennon as 'identified with system of flying column organisation Anglo-Irish conflict and engaged in action against British forces; associated in United States with League Against War and Fascism and Irish Cultural movement; Secretary Nat. Assoc. Old IRA'.[177]

This article was an informed assessment of Ireland's defence options in the face of the deteriorating situation in Europe. Colonel Des Travers (retired), a former Commandant of the Military College who reviewed this article observed that:

"Oftentimes the litmus test of a piece of analyses such Mr Lennon's is the degree to which this analyses withstands the test of time. While Ireland's security circumstances and indeed that of Europe's has sustained a sea-change post-Cold War, the assessments here would have a validity in 1938.

"What does also impress is the reach of his analyses. Unlike many military analysts who frequently rail against the parsimony of government towards military expenditure, Lennon produces strong arguments as to why a Free State such as ours then was,

---

[176] Kissane, Bill, *The Politics of the Irish Civil War* (Oxford University Press, USA, 2005), p. 195.

[177] Lennon, George, 'National Defence', *Ireland To-Day*, Vol. III, No. 1.

could ill afford the expense of a modern standing army. He then argues for what might reasonably be expected of us in order to:

> '... strengthen the national defence machinery to the point where it would make it a very costly business for any foreign power to again attempt a conquest of our liberated territory ...'

"Lennon of course does argue for and against alliances with 'England' on the basis of mutual interest. This too is a very mature assessment given both countries antagonisms which were then within memory. It is therefore a testament to his abilities to reason strategically without being hampered by the historical burdens when the geographical realities were the issue.

"His assessments at the 'war fighting' level are less sure especially when he argues for the primacy of mass infantry in preference to tanks, aircraft and artillery. It must be said here however that his views were de-rigueur at that time as only some German officers observing manoeuvres in the Soviet east were able to see the potential of mass armour.

"Crucial to Lennon's thesis is his argument on the need for a defence policy. He returns to this theme again and in his concluding comments. How right he was; for it was not until years later that the Defence Forces did eventually form such a policy."[178]

The same edition of this magazine carried a review of the novel *Dead Star's Light* published by Methuen and written by Una Troy under the *nom de plume* Elizabeth Connor. In 1931, Dr Joe Walsh, formerly doctor to Lennon's old flying column, had married Una,

---

[178] Colonel Desmond Travers (retired).

the daughter of a solicitor and later a prolific novelist. In 1936, her first novel, *Mount Prospect* was published and was promptly banned in Ireland. This was at a time when, according to Irish playwright Hugh Leonard, 'to find one keeping company on the banned list ... one needed hardly do more that put pen to paper'. *Dead Star's Light* avoided this fate, but it was not to avoid censure by the Catholic Church.

Apart from some obvious poetic license, John Davern, the hero of the novel was transparently based on George Lennon. The teenage Davern, leaves his home town of 'Kilvane' to fight with the IRA in the War of Independence:

"..he joined his country's rebellion with the idealism of a crusader – and participated in it with the zest of a schoolboy ... often afterwards, looking back on those months of 1920 and 1921, he thought they were perhaps the happiest of his life, for he lived much in action and little in thought ... only some things were imprinted on his memory for ever, small sharp cameos formed in keener sensation; his first ambush, the jar of the rifle against his shoulder and a figure twisting and falling in the road ... hurrying at night bent behind hedges, from a farmhouse, while the searchlights of a military lorry beat down the lane after him."

Later, he leads the garrison of the city jail in the Civil War battle of 'Fordtown':

"When finally the attack was launched and shells began to drop on the barracks and jail from the opposite side of the river ... later, the defending force was concentrated in the jail ... the shells were falling more rapidly and more surely, and as the building began to crumble about them, their position was becoming untenable. At last O'Brien ordered a retreat."

Withdrawing from the city:

266

"..he enjoyed the long warm days when Hurley and he wandered about with their aimless brigade ... they chose their lodgings well, seeking only the largest and most comfortable houses abandoned by their alarmed Anglo-Irish owners, and whiled away the hours by recourse to well-stocked cellars."

Here they are visited by the 'Cumann na Monsters' who are cruelly ridiculed. Later:

"John was silent, remembering a haggard man he had seen drinking tea in the Kilmacthomas Workhouse, while Erskine Childers walked up and down ceaselessly, coughing ... coughing ... coughing. Pity warred with anger; youthful contempt for untidy failure fought with youthful admiration for hopelessness. 'I'm chucking it,' he said. 'I'm going home'."

In 1924, Davern emigrates to the USA:

"At first, in that false harvest of prosperity, work was to be had for the asking ... he had been on the staff of an enterprising and unsuccessful newspaper ... for six weary years he had served an adding machine in an insurance office."

He returns to Ireland in 1937 (Davern's parents both live until this date – Lennon was orphaned by 1924), where his left wing views and refusal to attend Catholic mass brings him into conflict with the local clergy, particularly Fr Gleeson, the villainous parish priest who is concerned less for Davern's spiritual salvation than for the money he is expected to contribute to the parish:

"..this man who was reputed never to have done a kind or disinterested deed in his life, who was notorious among his parishioners for wringing the last penny from the poor, who was gross and paunchy from too much food and drink."

In a clash with another priest, Davern clearly exhibits Lennon's own point of view:

"Do you believe your Christ is always an ally of the rich – never of the poor? Must that always be a coincidence? You tell me I must not say this or that – you tell the Irish people they must not think in such and such a way … do you think you can have a country of artificial, cloistered virtue? And even there – have you not failed – has the Catholic Church not failed?"

Rather melodramatically, Fr Gleeson whips his parishioners into a frenzy and sends them to burn down Davern's farm. But the novel ends on an upbeat note, when Davern opts to stay in Ireland:

"These people are mine! I'm theirs! We have the same blood – we have the same faults and virtues. I don't want to stay aloof on mountain-tops – I want to be down there where I belong."[179]

Dead Star's Light was a success and received mostly favourable reviews. One exception was the heavily pro-Catholic *Sunday Independent* who objected to the novel's 'spiteful caricature' of Irish life, claiming that

"Davern is … less a character than a peg on which the author hangs her own savagely disillusioned ideas of present-day Ireland. All the outworn notions of the anti-clerical rag-bag are brought out anew to deck this embittered idealist – a lapsed Catholic, of course, as the tradition demands – for his struggle."[180]

---

[179] Connor, Elizabeth, *Dead Star's Light* (Methuen, London, 1938).

[180] *Sunday Independent*, 'Caricature of Irish Life', 4 March 1938.

Dead Star's Light certainly continued in this way. On page 244 in the novel Davern states:

"Our patriotism ... our religion ... The shadows of our two allusions ... Patriotism - our new Irish synonym for jobbery; our Church – the best run and most powerful business institution in the country ... I had a dream ... I saw a country of beauty and courage ... and I saw a people wandering in the darkness of the two shadows ... blinded by a wrong conception of national pride ... blinded by superstition and ignorance ... Ireland must take her place in the sun ... I must fight ... I must change it."

These sentiments evidently angered Fr W. Byrne, pastor of SS Peter and Paul's in Clonmel, as evidenced in a letter, quoting scripture, to Una Troy Walsh, dated 18 March 1938:

"I am truly appalled and grieved by the anti-religious and anti-clerical spirit which the ... book reveals. I was utterly unprepared to find that such views as, for instance, are set forth on p. 244 and following would be propounded as the views of the hero and heroine of the book, and I fear the impression will be inevitably taken that these views are the teaching of the book and represent the mind of the author, and that as a consequence, the author must be regarded as having lost the faith ... consider the terrible course on which you have entered and the most serious responsibilities in which you are involving yourself."

Una Troy Walsh's reply was prompt, criticising the silence of the Roman Catholic Church about the murderous air attack on the undefended Spanish town of Guernica by Franco's German allies. In a second letter dated 20 March 1938, Fr Byrne stated:

"In regard to Guernica, I suggest you have come under the influence of the 'Red' propaganda so largely spread in England and nearer home. Are you aware this 'Red' account is simply ...

complete falsification by numbers of those who have given the matter thorough investigation? I have before me at the moment the estimate of one ... who is satisfied that the place was bombarded by the nationalists as a military objective and was burned by the 'Reds', enraged at having to abandon it."[181]

Through his work for the Old IRA Men's Association (which became the 1916–21 Club in the late 1940s), Lennon met Geoffrey Coulter who then worked for the *Irish Press* and had been editor of republican newspaper *An Phoblacht*. Coulter introduced Lennon to his wife's sister, May Sibbald, who was then secretary to the minister for finance Seán MacEntee. Lennon left Ireland for the winter of 1938 to work at the Princess Hotel in Bermuda as chief cashier. He returned in early 1939 and married to May Sibbald on 14 July, in the York Road Presbyterian Church in Dun Laoghaire. Due to the 'marriage ban' then in effect (made possible by Article 41 of the 1937 Constitution) May was obliged to resign from her civil service post. There was only a small crowd in attendance: Catholic friends of the couple would have been prohibited from attending any ceremony in a non-Catholic church.[182]

The Tourist Traffic Act of 1939 established the Irish Tourist Board, a five man permanent committee, to look after the development of Irish tourism and empowered to appoint staff to achieve this. The outbreak of the Second World War naturally crippled any hope of establishing a significant tourist industry in the short term, but planning and preparations could be made for the post-war era. In 1940, George Lennon was appointed an

---

[181] NLI UT MS 35,686 (2).

[182] Lennon, Ivan *Lennons in Time*, unpublished family history.

inspector for the Irish Tourist Board and threw himself into his new role with enthusiasm. In a long article for the *Irish Times* he later noted:

"My own point of view is that, discounting all the windy talk about tens of millions to be obtained from foreign visitors, the fact remains that a healthy revenue can be obtained from this source in the years immediately ahead. We paid growing, but even then too little, attention to this source of revenue before the war. The possibility is that we actually lost money on the holiday traffic, inasmuch as so many Irish holiday-makers spent their vacations abroad that the balance more than offset the gains from visitors to our own shores. It is pertinent here to observe that Great Britain's adverse balance on the tourist traffic amounted before the war to no less than £10,000,000 a year.

"Our post-war problem, then, it to create a healthy credit balance by retaining, as far as possible, our own holiday-makers, and by enticing all the visitors we can from overseas.

"How are we to set about it? First, let us disabuse ourselves of certain false notions and ideals ... the ideal holiday centre requires the sunshine and the warmth that we do not possess. The holiday-maker who looks for perpetually sun-drenched beaches can go hunt for them in other latitudes; he will not find them in Ireland. And we are just as badly off in respect of the beauty of history. The ruins of Cashel and Clonmacnoise furnish a link with the glorious past, but in themselves they compare very badly with the cathedral cities and medieval towns of continental Europe. Let us not shut our eyes to these facts.

"Have we anything then to offer? We have. We have a countryside which is often beautiful, generally unspoiled and – outside the precincts of South Dublin, Killarney and a few other centres –

open. In other words, scenery. And that is just what the 'dynamic' holiday maker – if I may employ the adjective – desires.

"By the dynamic holiday maker I mean the one who likes to travel from place to place – the motorist, the cyclist, the hiker, the canoeist. These people are easily pleased. They are satisfied with good roads, and most of our roads are good enough, though many of them might be bettered. What they need is places in which to stop the night. Let us face the fact that some of our visitors, and the great bulk of our native holiday-makers, will be people in search of a cheap holiday. How many of them can pay the prices demanded by even a modest Irish hotel today?

"The State is already spending a lot of money – and will spend still more in the post-war years – on Irish tourist development, mainly for hotel improvement, publicity and resort developments. Much more can be done with that money. What is wrong for instance, with the purchase of a fleet of caravans, fully equipped with furniture and maps, and if so desired, fishing rods, the lot to be available at a reasonable charge for hitching on the back of your holiday makers car? Or of a fleet of more or less luxurious vessels for hire on the Shannon and other rivers? There may be a theoretical complaint that this 'sleep-where-you-are' traffic would do harm to the hotels. The complaint is not soundly based. Experience on the Continent has proved that the growth of 'auto camps' and trailer services have been an all-round encouragement to the general tourist traffic, and that perverse as it may seem, the hotels have benefited from them.

"But the real problem is that what one may call the 'static' holiday maker. This is the fellow who has only a week, a fortnight, or a month to spend, and prefers to spend it in the one place. He may or may not have a family. If he has small children, they may be satisfied to dig over the same square yard of sand day after day, but he and his wife are apt to be bored. Let us face the fact that far too many Irish resorts are apt to be boring in the ultimate degree. There is nothing to do except have too much to drink, which may lend a sort of evanescent lustre to scenery which otherwise, however beautiful, is apt to pall. Is it any wonder that so many Irish people crossed the Channel for their holidays before the war? On this side they found exquisite scenery, digs that were often uncomfortable and very often expensive, and an almost complete lack of any form of amusement. On the other side was little or no scenery, but a well organised system of hotels and lodging houses and in a hundred watering places, an almost endless variety of entertainments, often cheap and gaudy, but sustaining. Is it any wonder that the Isle of Man attracted its tens of thousands from Ireland? And how many Irishmen have spent a two or three weeks holiday in France or Germany at less expense than would have been needed for a vacation of equal length not more than twenty miles from their own home town?

"I come ... to the essential point. Our job, as I see it, is not so much to attract tourists from abroad as to furnish decent holidays for our own people. And with that end in view, we must provide them with good and cheap accommodation."[183]

Nearly thirty years later, Lennon recalled his work for the Tourist Board:

"Some considerable years gone by I had been employed by a government Board to direct a topographical survey of the twenty-six counties of our land and Brian was most capable and enthusiastic assistant ... the different learned societies offered all their facilities which we were most happy to avail of. Brian, who

---

[183] *Irish Times*, 'The Tourist Traffic', 30 January 1945.

is an architect as well as an archaeologist, did the drawings and plans for a conjectural scheme of restoration of Cashel and we planned a dig and model recreation of the once great monastic settlement of Holy Island on the Shannon. We had many other ambitious schemes such as further excavations at the sight of the great 'Stone Age' mound at Newgrange.

"The great burial mound was searched for plunder by the Norsemen during their depredations but they must have come away disappointed as no golden loot was available. The entrance to this remarkable place was rediscovered in 1699 by a local planter or landlord and from his description the interior was then much the same as it appears today."

George Lennon continued to meet interesting people:

"John Betjeman took me to lunch at the University Club and gave me most useful advice."

John Betjeman, future poet laureate of Britain, was posted to Ireland as British press attaché from 1941–1943. It is claimed that he was working as a low-level spy at this time and that the IRA were only dissuaded from assassinating him by an admirer of his poetry within their ranks! There was a Dungarvan connection here; during his stay in Ireland, Betjeman was a regular visitor to the Yellow House at Helvic Head, the fishing lodge of the Villiers-Stuart family and in later years composed a poem of unrequited love: *The Irish Unionist's farewell to Greta Hellastrom in 1922* part of which reads:

> *Gales along the Comeragh Mountains*
> *Beating sleet on creaking signs*
> *Iron gutters turned to fountains*
> *And the windscreen laced with lines*
> *And the evening getting later*

And the ache – increased again
As the distance grows the greater
From Dungarvan in the rain

The identity of the mysterious woman of the poem, referred to by Betjeman as 'my Swedish beauty' was only revealed in recent years to be Emily Sears who subsequently married Ian Villers-Stuart, the poem's date and the Swedish beauty being an elaborate disguise.[184]

In March 1943, Irish Tourist Board suspended its activities 'for the duration', since it was now obvious that no tourists could be expected from outside the country for the near future, although the Irish Tourist Association for domestic tourism continued to operate. Lennon soon found alternative employment: a letter to the office of the Taoiseach dated 8 April 1943 and carrying the letterhead of 'The National Planning Conference' is signed by George Lennon, the group's 'Acting Honorary Secretary':

> I have the pleasure to enclose herewith for the Taoiseach's information:
>
> (1) Outline of Agenda for tomorrow's meeting, and
>
> (2) Memoranda covering notes of what Senator McGee (President) Mr Condon (Chairman of Executive committee) and Mr Richards Orpen propose to say.

The stated aim of the National Planning Conference was 'to present the result of Research, Conferences and Studies of Planning Problems'. The genesis for the National Planning originated in June 1942 when a meeting of town planners and

---

[184] *Irish Times*, 'Betjeman's Mystery Woman Revealed', 10 July 2007.

engineers, presided over by Fr J. Canavan in his capacity as chairman of the Civics Institute, recognised the importance of economic planning for the post-war era. In the words of Fr Canavan, 'the main object is the appointment of a body of men in whom they would have confidence, to organise an exhibition next year in Dublin, to collect data and plans, and through lectures and conferences, educate the public to the necessity and importance of national planning'.

On 9 April 1943, the Taoiseach (Éamon de Valera) attended a meeting of the National Planning Conference at the Mansion House in Dublin. Presided over by Senator J.T. McGee, and including representatives from the Irish Tourist Association, the agricultural and labour sectors, the Town Planning Institute and Muintir na Tire. Erskine Childers (later President) also attended.

Éamon de Valera made a long speech, dutifully recorded in *The Irish Press*, in which he made his own agenda clear: 'Planning,' said Mr de Valera, 'is a very interesting but a very seductive occupation. It can very easily become little more than day-dreaming or building castles in the air, unless you get down to earth, and still have in mind the practical application of your plans'.[185]

De Valera was keen to improve living conditions in the country (at this time most Irish homes were without electricity or running water) and in particular to arrest the 'flight from the land' – the continuing depopulation of rural areas. This was in keeping with de Valera's own vision for Ireland as a rural society as outlined in his much- quoted and subsequently derided speech the previous

---

[185] *Irish Press*, 'Taoiseach on Purpose of National Planning', 10 April 1943.

month, anachronistic even for that time, in which he followed the Irish Catholic Church's stance of spirituality over wealth:

The Ireland which we would desire of would be the home of a people who valued material wealth only as the basis of a right living, of a people who were satisfied with frugal comfort and devoted their leisure to the things of the soul; a land whose countryside would be bright with cosy homesteads, whose fields and valleys would be joyous with the sounds of industry, with the romping of sturdy children, the contests of athletic youth, the laughter of happy maidens; whose firesides would be forums for the wisdom of old age. It would, in a word, be the home of a people living the life that God desires that men should live. For many the pursuit of the material life is a necessity. Man to express himself fully and to make the best use of the talents God has given him, needs a certain minimum of comfort and wealth. A section of our people have not yet this minimum. They rightly strive to secure it and it must be our aim and the aim of all who are just and wise to assist in that effort. But many have got more than is required and are free, if they choose, to devote themselves more completely to cultivating the things of the mind and, in particular, those that make us out as a distinct nation.[186]

In June 1943, May Lennon gave birth to a boy at the Rotunda Hospital in Dublin. Four months later, George's son (Ivan) was baptised as a Presbyterian at the York Road church in Dun Laoghaire. This was in blatant defiance of the Catholic Church's destructive *Ne Temere* decree which required the children of mixed marriages to be raised as Catholics and contributed greatly to the decline of the Protestant population of independent Ireland. The *Ne Temere* decree was so widely enforced in Ireland

---

[186] Radio Éireann broadcast, 17 March 1943.

at this time that it was often (falsely) assumed to be the law of the land, even before the decree was actually upheld by a 1950 high court ruling. The most infamous example of the damage that the decree could do occurred in the Wexford town of Fethard in 1957; when a Protestant mother of a mixed marriage absconded with her children the local Protestant population was ostracised by their Catholic neighbours, as was the father when he opposed the boycott. The case received worldwide attention and *Time* magazine wondered whether 'fetharding' would enter the English language as 'boycott' had.[187]

The 1943 meeting of the National Planning Conference in the Mansion House was a relatively low-key affair, achieving little of note. But by early 1944, this body was preparing a major exhibition in the same venue. From March 1944, Lennon in his capacity of secretary of the National Planning Conference sent a series of letters from his Nassau Street office in connection with the National Planning Exhibition being planned for the following month. Several were sent to the office of the Taoiseach, beginning with an invitation for de Valera to open the exhibition. This correspondence gives some idea of the level of preparation involved, for example on 17 April 1944:

> A Chara,
> The following arrangements for the opening ceremony on Tuesday the 25th inst at 3 o'clock are submitted for the information of An Taoiseach –
> (1) Senator McGee, President of the Conference, will welcome An Taoiseach
> (2) An Taoiseach will open Exhibition.

---

[187] *Time*, 'Fethardism', 10 August 1957.

(3) Vote of thanks will be moved by Senator General Mulcahy and seconded by Mr William Norton TD.

Platform accommodation will necessarily be limited and the committee therefore would be glad if An Taoiseach would indicate the names of any individuals he would like to have seats reserved for.

I may mention that invitations are being sent to all members of the Government.

As accommodation in the Round Room will be limited to the platform and gallery, arrangements have been made to have An Taoiseach's speech relayed to other apartments in the Mansion House and to the adjoining garden.

A copy of the official Programme and Handbook on National Planning will be forwarded to An Taoiseach prior to the opening of the exhibition.

The committee hope that these arrangements will be fully in accord with An Taoiseach's wishes. Mise le Meas

George Lennon

The *Irish Times* gives further details of the enthusiastic efforts of a wide range of people to make the exhibition a success:

"The tremendous amount of preparatory work necessary for the launching of the twelve days National Planning Exhibition in the Mansion House, Dublin, on April 25th, is nearing peak point.

"Architects, architectural students, engineers and others from all over the country are putting the finishing touches to detailed models of schools, farms, play centres, holiday camps, etc. Statisticians are making last minute additions to elaborate graphs and charts. Cartographers are busy on a wide range of maps. Photographs are being mounted and captioned. Some of the best American and British [films] (16mm sound) on planning have been secured for showing each evening through the efforts of the

Irish Film Society. Every aspect of planning has been touched on, and as the date of the exhibition approaches, the completed picture is beginning to take shape, with section after section neatly dove-tailing into position.

"The most ambitious project yet undertaken by the National Planning Conference, the exhibition is being made possible by the voluntary work of members of many organisations in the country. By means of these models, films, graphs and charts it is hoped to impress on the public that the planning of the future really means the betterment of the individual, that their interest, their energy and even their criticism will be of help."

Evening lectures would be given over the twelve days of the conference by experts in the fields of agriculture, industry, transport, public health, nutrition, education, town planning, rural life and education. Also involved in the exhibition was the Ulster Planning Group which had carried out a similar effort in Belfast.

In a loft in a Dublin side street, architects and students from the National University of Ireland had spent many weeks painstakingly preparing detailed models of schools, farms and even youth hostels. The most important of these projects was a huge relief map of Ireland, which required the assembly of a hundred different parts. On the eve of the exhibition, these young enthusiasts worked late into the night to assemble these models in the Mansion House. The massive relief map was the centrepiece of the display, featuring proposed motorways, airfields, agricultural belts, forestries, electricity generating stations, industrial regions, national parks and hospitals.

The exhibition opened on the afternoon of the 25 April and was a lavish affair by the standards of 1940s Dublin. The Army No. 1

280

Band was in attendance, as were Taoiseach Éamon de Valera, finance minister Seán MacEntee and even the leaders of the opposition parties.

De Valera however cast an ominous note with his speech:

"It was the government that had the duty of planning, and carrying out its plans, and it was of great assistance to the Government and the officers of State who were at work on planning to know what the people outside were thinking and what plans they had in mind. Of course, it was easy to plan, if one had not to carry out the plans, and it was only when one had the direct responsibility of carrying out those plans that the difficulties began to appear."

For his part, Senator McGee:

"..said that the Exhibition was only intended to suggest what the Conference thought might be done in the way of post-war planning. They had deemed it their duty to bring grist to the Government legislative mill. They could however, only propose; the decisions had to be taken by the Government."

An *Irish Times* editorial subsequently commented:

"We decline to believe that Mr de Valera, the idealist of 1916 and the curiously far-sighted politician of fifteen years ago, has acquired so cautious an outlook as to assume that all hope of a more comfortable and efficient country is outside the bounds of reason. That hope can be realised. Of so much we are certain, and we have little doubt that every person who visits the Mansion House in the next ten days will share our certainty."

Any hopes that the exhibition might favourably influence government policy were dashed on its final night when Seán MacEntee spoke at an informal dinner and discussion at the Royal

Hibernian Hotel, making it quite clear that the responsibility of post-war planning would lie with the government alone. The *Irish Times* commented:

"It sounded almost as if he had been sent there by his Cabinet colleagues to administer a grandfatherly rebuke to the host of distinguished engineers, architects, farmers, doctors and other practical men who have gone so far as to profess enthusiasm for the physical reconstruction of Ireland."

To have claimed that the National Planning Conference could have brought about a Celtic Tiger economy for the 1950s would have been an exaggeration. Not all the schemes were practical – one wonders what the well-heeled residents of Killiney would have made of the holiday camp proposed for their area – and there does not seem to have any provision for training and education that was the cornerstone of the Seán Lemass strategy from 1958 onward. Yet at the very least the conference comprised a think tank of the very people that could have provided a comprehensive economic strategy, the lack of which was to result in the collapse of the Irish economy in the post-war years.[188]

An appropriate summation of the whole affair was made in Dáil Éireann by an opposition TD on 12 June 1944, during the reading of a Finance Bill:

"Quite recently an effort was made by a group of outsiders calling themselves the National Planning Conference, who showed a variety of ways their ideas for dealing with the big problems of production and development in agriculture and industry with a view to securing a better future for our people. Deputy MacEntee

---

[188] INA Department of the Taoiseach S 13469.

was very piqued about the matter, and indicated that, so far as the government were concerned, they had no belief in the capacity of people outside the government and outside Government Departments, to use intelligence and ability in planning a better future for our people."[189]

Rather symbolic of the entire enterprise was a proposed Youth Hostel in the isolated Wicklow valley of Glenmalure. The concept, as illustrated in meticulously prepared models and diagrams, was for a beautifully appointed two storey circumlinear building with modern facilities. The reality was a tiny cottage without electricity or running water, as were sixty per cent of Irish homes until the 1960s. In this cottage incidentally, Dorothy Macardle had spent years compiling *The Irish Republic*, her history of the struggle for independence and something of a hagiography of Éamon de Valera.

On 8 August 1944, the Army Pensions Board granted Lennon, then living in Rathfarnham, a wound/disability pension for £120 per annum, because of severe psychological problems due to what would quickly be recognised today as Post Traumatic Stress Disorder. According to Professor Diarmaid Ferriter:

"An updated medical report in 1944 suggested he was suffering from 'reactive depression (psychasthenia) and pulmonary disease attributable to military service in IRA,' and he was estimated to have an 80 per cent disability. He had 'recurrent depression, occasional bouts of insomnia and feeling of constriction and nervousness in upper abdomen.' He could only do work of 'limited responsibility' such as casher jobs. What was most interesting about Lennon's application was that it included

---

[189] Dáil Éireann, Vol. 94–12 June 1944; Finance Bill 1944 – Second Stage.

substantial testimony on post-traumatic stress disorder, absent from many other applications. Ironically it took the evidence of a former British Army captain to impress on the Army Pensions Board the debilitating nature of a condition that was not widely understood at that stage."[190]

Lennon had also been awarded the 1917–1921 Service Medal instituted in 1941. This was a bronze medal on a black and brown ribbon, with a bar engraved 'COMRAC' indicating combat service. Unfortunately, his infant son subsequently dropped Lennon's medal into a stream near his home. Ivan made amends in 1984 by obtaining a replacement medal for his father.[191]

In January 1945, Lennon wrote to the *Irish Times*. Although commending them for a series of articles they were running in relation to post-war reconstruction, his disillusionment is clear:

"The National Planning Conference ... have reason to know something about the difficulties of the task you have undertaken, and more especially about popular indifference to issues which are of deep and pressing importance to the lives of this and coming generations of Irish citizens. If you can do anything to suspend the current lethargy, your efforts will merit the gratitude of an indolent public, who are more disposed to indulge in destructive criticism of official activities than to contribute their quotas to constructive thought and action."[192]

---

[190] Ferriter, Diarmaid, *Between Two Hells; The Irish Civil War* (Profile Books, London, 2021).

[191] Award Certificate, Department of Defence, 8 August 1944.

[192] *Irish Times*, Letter to Editor, 31 October 1944.

In 1949, Ireland was declared a republic. The first decade of the new republic's existence saw the collapse of its economy and the emigration of over half a million of its citizens. Although most of the waves of emigrants were unskilled youngsters with only a primary level education, by 1958 young professionals were also leaving in search of a better lifestyle. At a time when western Europe was booming, Ireland was as poor as any of the communist nations. Most senior Irish politicians at this time were septuagenarians; an aging leadership for an aging population. But Lennon was not in Ireland to see any of this.

On 20 February 1946, Lennon was sitting aboard a big four engined aircraft preparing for flight at the newly established Shannon airport. The Lockheed Super Constellation, bearing the blue and white livery of Pan American Airways, had flown in from Heathrow airport in England and was preparing for a transatlantic flight carrying only eleven passengers. This was significantly less than the sixty passengers that the aircraft could carry; at $250 for a one-way ticket, a transatlantic flight in those days was not cheap, nor was it particularly safe – later that year all Lockheed Super Constellations were temporarily grounded after two crashes.

One by one, each of the four powerful Wright R-3350 propeller engines roared to life, belching flames and smoke to the consternation of onlookers who may not have realised that this was entirely normal for this type of engine. Having taxied to the top of Shannon's main 7,000 foot runway, the pilots applied brakes while running the engines up to maximum revolutions, each one emitting a long tongue of purple flame. Then the Constellation surged forward, covering most of the length of the runway and building speed to one hundred and twenty knots before the nose-wheel lifted, then the rest of the forty ton aircraft. Retracting its massive undercarriage, the Constellation began its slow climb, passing over the mudflats of the Shannon River and towards the coast near Ennis to commence the twelve-hour journey over the Atlantic:

"As the plane took off from Shannon I wanted to shout 'Higher, higher. Faster, faster'. The plane had a minor accident half way across the Atlantic and had to come down in the outer reaches of Newfoundland."

It was quite normal for one of the Super Constellation's engines to fail over the Atlantic, the other three being capable of carrying the aircraft for the long flight. It was apparently not made clear to the first passengers that the flight would land to refuel at the isolated airport at Gander before continuing to New York. George Lennon was beginning the second half of his life.[193]

Taking up residence at 180 Riverside Drive in New York city, Lennon began work as a cashier in the Hotel Lexington in New York city in March 1946.

In May 1947, *The Dark Road*, Una Troy's stage adaptation of her novel *Dead Star's Light*, opened to a successful run at Dublin's Abbey Theatre. The most striking aspect of this adaptation is the almost complete absence of any criticism of the Catholic Church; even the villainous Fr Gleeson gets only a very fleeting mention. 1947 was evidently a more cynical time than 1938; when Davern returns from the US in *The Dark Road*, he is told:

"Perhaps you left the returned hero stuff rather late. Heroes are out of fashion. Well, you could be an Inspector of something ...

---

[193] George G. Lennon, *Trauma in Time*, extracted from 'Trauma in Time' (1971) the unpublished memoirs of George G. Lennon.

done a bit of writing too, haven't you ... some nice articles on Spain I believe. Wrong viewpoint, though. Tut, tut!"[194]

The real life inspiration for Davern had already left the country whose independence he had fought for. His young family would follow later that autumn when they boarded a liner in Southampton, bound for New York where they would be reunited.

In April 1948, Lennon was fired from the Hotel Lexington after he was elected as a representative for the Hotel Workers Union. Later that year the Lennon family moved to Rochester in upstate New York. With a population of 330,000, Rochester was thriving; the city's leading industrial employer was Eastman Kodak which dominated the world's film and camera industry, while the Haloid Corporation, holding the patents on the revolutionary 'xerography' process invented by Chester Carlson, was to expand into the multinational Xerox Corporation.

Eastman Kodak hired George Lennon on 15 November 1948 as a shipping clerk. According to a later account by son Ivan:

"George began his study of religion and philosophy in the late 1940s and early 1950s. Of particular interest to him were the writings of Gurdjieff, Ouspensky, and the philosophy of Zen Buddhism. Through his interest in the latter, he made the acquaintance of Chester Carlson, inventor of 'electrophotography'. Along with Haloid's Joseph Wilson and others, Chet was attempting to make what was to become known as 'Xerography' a viable commercial enterprise."[195]

---

[194] NLI UT MS 35,687 (3), *The Dark Road.*

[195] Lennon, Ivan *Lennons in Time,* unpublished family history.

At this time, George started to attend meetings of the Religious Society of Friends, popularly known as 'Quakers' and well thought of in Ireland for their important relief work during the Great Famine. This denomination eschewed formal rites for worship and a religious hierarchy, no doubt attractive facets to a disillusioned former Catholic.

In the summer of 1950 May and Ivan spent a holiday in Ireland, staying in Dun Laoghaire with May's mother and sister. A short time was also spent at the home of Mick Mansfield, now married and retired from the gardaí, and living adjacent to the site of the Burgery ambush.[196]

In 1947, the Bureau of Military History was founded by Irish Defence Minister Oscar Traynor (himself a veteran of 1916, War of Independence and Civil War) to chronicle the events of the 1916 Rising and the Irish War of Independence. A staff of civilians and army officers were trained in interview techniques and over the following ten years 1,773 witness statements were taken. Information was given under a guarantee of confidentiality and the statements were only made public in 2003. Prominent in the BMH was Lieutenant-Colonel Flor O'Donoghue, formerly Liam Lynch's proficient intelligent officer until 1921. Most 1919–1921 veterans in the Waterford area were interviewed in 1955 – the majority of George Lennon's old comrades paying full tribute to his role at that time.

One of those interviewed was Lieutenant-Colonel Paddy Paul who in correspondence with O'Donoghue informed him that Lennon had emigrated to the USA. He later noted that: 'I have now got George Lennon's address and I am communicating with him'.

---

[196] NLI FOD MS 31,423 (19).

There is no statement from George Lennon on record with the BMH; it is unclear whether he was ever contacted in this regard. In another letter to O'Donoghue, Paul paid this tribute: 'I am satisfied that George Lennon was not a party to the scheming that went on. I always found George to be a true Irishman, a good fighting officer and loyal comrade. I have no hesitation in placing him No. 1 as regards IRA activities in the Waterford brigades'.[197]

George Lennon did provide a fictionalised account of some of his experiences. In 1952, Lennon wrote a play named *Down by the Glen Side* which was completed in September that year. This play is set in November 1920, in 'a disused hunting lodge situated at the termination of a wild glen in the Irish mountains', clearly modelled on Sleady Castle. The main character is Henry Rogan, the leader of an IRA flying column, 'extremely young and boyish for a position of responsibility and command but he generates a more than youthful enthusiasm ... he has obvious qualities of leadership'. Rogan is charged with the custody of a captured British officer, who is being held as a hostage for an IRA man under sentence of death. British soldiers of the 1st Battalion of the Devonshire regiment are searching the mountains for them. A friendship grows between Rogan and the sympathetically portrayed Captain Robert Harley, making the play part of a particular genre of which the most famous example is Frank O'Connor's short story *Guests of the Nation*.

As the Devonshires close in on their position, Rogan receives word that an IRA man has been executed and that Harley is to be shot in reprisal:

---

[197] NLI UT MS 35,699 (1).

Harley: 'This is cruel to you also ... we will give each other courage. But there is something I must say to you.

Rogan: 'Yes, Captain'.

Harley: 'It is within your power to save my life!'

Rogan: (Sincerely) I would give almost anything – but – I cannot –

Harley: 'You mean you dare not? ... Forgive me, I am making it hard for you.

Moments later an IRA sentry rushes in with word that the Devonshires are invading the valley and are almost upon them. Rogan orders his men to retreat, remaining behind with Captain Harley:

His humanity and his generosity are in wild conflict with what he conceived to be his duty. But, in spite of his youth, he is a person with an understanding beyond the ordinary. A deeply rooted instinct, an instruction, as it were, pulls him out of his dilemma.

He decides, picks up his rifle, and goes towards the rear exit. A whistle shrills. Just as he is about to leave he turns and looks towards Harley.

Rogan: (With assumed coldness) 'Goodbye English officer'.

As he exits there is a sudden burst of rifle fire interspersed with excited and angry shouts outside ...

Cut to exterior.

Rogan runs forward into a hail of rifle fire. As he is hit he stops, drops his rifle and throws his arm over his head, turns and staggers in the opposite direction. He trips and pitches heavily on his face.

Rogan chose a dramatically different course of action than that taken by George Lennon on the morning of 19 March 1921. Captain Harley, reprieved from death, tears up a letter he has written to his wife and refuses to identify his former captors who have been captured by the Devonshires. In his last words in the play, Harley espouses a philosophy actually adopted by Lennon:

Fighting! Killing! It has been going on and on, and there is more to come – but it cannot go on forever – I take it upon myself to refuse – to say No! It is my personal choice![198]

George's wife and son paid another visit to Ireland in the summer of 1954, staying with May's sister in Dun Laoghaire and again paying a visit to the Mansfield's home at the Burgery.

In 1958, Lennon wrote the following piece to the *Rochester Democrat and Chronicle*:

Dr Goebbels Still Living?
Evidently Dr Goebbels is not as dead as we thought he was; we were all startled to read in your newspaper that the communists were behind the bombing of Jewish places of worship in this country.
Could it not be possible that they are also responsible for keeping the children out of our schools in the South?
GEORGE LENNON
31 Grassmere Pk

---

[198] *Down by the Glen Side.*

This apparently displeased a former acquaintance from the Quakers, who had known Lennon from some years earlier and had been angered by his openly left wing political views. On 20 October 1958, this individual contacted the Federal Bureau of Investigation with the allegation 'that George Lennon told him in approximately 1944 [*sic*] that he had been a 'card carrying communist at one time'. He admitting that 'he asked Lennon why he had severed from the organisation, and Lennon remarked that 'the CP is not the answer' and that he therefore, had dropped out'. He also admitted that 'he had never noticed any CP literature in subject's house' and that while alleging that the Lennons 'had often made praising remarks concerning the Russians ... he was unable to recall any statements'. The FBI noted that the individual making the allegations 'appeared to be an excitable person and displayed a strong bitterness toward the Lennons'.

Under the provisions of the Internal Security Act of 1950, the FBI investigated on the grounds that 'because subject is employed in a Key Facility, and because of the allegation that he once was a card carrying communist, it is suggested this case be opened for development of background and contact with informants'. The Kodak Park Division was included on a US Department of Defence 'Key Facility List' with the US Air Force holding security responsibility. The FBI carried out a thorough background check into Lennon's past employment and residences (most beneficial from a biographers point of view!) and made discreet enquiries among a wide network of informants on communist activities and the police, none of which had any record of Lennon.

The Kodak employment office informed the FBI that they had employed Lennon since 15 November 1948 with a favourable record and that he 'does not have access to classified information or areas'. It is significant that on 26 February 1959, it was recommended that the FBI interview Lennon personally with regard to the allegations.

On the 9 April 1959, an FBI agent knocked on the door of 31 Grassmere Park. May Lennon at first refused to admit him (a detail the agent graciously omitted from his report), but George did speak to him. It was subsequently reported that 'during interview on 4/9/59, subject appeared friendly, co-operative and volunteered to assist this Bureau where ever possible. It was not indicated that he has any current potential as a possible source of information or PSI [Potential Security Informant]. Re-contact with him is not contemplated at this time'.

This appeared to be the end of the matter as far as the FBI was concerned. Under the provisions of the Freedom of Information Act, Ivan Lennon filed a request to review FBI file 100-16497 (Subject George G Lennon) in 1999; Lennon's later suspicions of a file dating to 1927 or photographs from peace marches were unfounded.[199]

In 1965, Lennon retired from Eastman Kodak; he and May were able to live quite comfortably on George's IRA and Kodak pensions, two social security cheques and their savings.

In April 1966, George Lennon returned, alone, to Ireland on the fiftieth anniversary of the Easter Rising, his first visit in twenty years. Son Ivan, now studying at New York University, remembers this being a short visit and noticed that on his return to Rochester, Lennon began work on a short memoir entitled *Trauma in Time*.

1967

---

[199] Federal Bureau of Investigation File 100–16497 (George Gerald Lennon).

"Buffalo. Four hundred of us are come to the Peace Bridge to bring hospital supplies and money for the suffering people of Viet Nam. The night before we all met together for a subsistence meal of rice at the Universalist Church and for a briefing as to what we should do if arrested. Afterwards we went to the motel and following on the moment of silence we sang, 'No Man is an Island/No Man Stands Alone'. We brought our compassionate gift across the bridge and handed them over to the Canadian Friends for shipment to Indochina. We were not arrested. In fact, the police and the different customs officials were most courteous.

"Rochester. Seven hundred or more people – Friends, Hippies, Catholic nuns – we all walk peacefully along the pavements of the city holding lighted candles. The hundreds of lights are stars in the darkness. The flower children lift up their young voices and plaintively sing 'All We are Saying is Give Peace a Chance'.

"We also protest and make our plea in the public press."

By October 1967, US casualties (killed, wounded and missing) in Vietnam had exceeded 100,000. Theodore G. Sorenson, former special counsel to Presidents Kennedy and Johnson, publicly stated that the lives of American soldiers 'are being given for a war which we are not "winning' in the traditional sense and cannot ever expect to "win".'

Lennon was moved to write a Letter to the Editor printed in the *Rochester Democrat and Chronicle* of 21 October 1967; this makes it clear that although Lennon was a pacifist, he still retained his Irish republican principles:

> Dear Sir:
> Heated appeals to partisan emotionalism do little to resolve the present appalling situation in Viet Nam but a

careful study of past and recent historical trends might lead to a more sane appraisal, agonising or otherwise.

Since the end of World War I and the breaking up of old regimes, the predominant historical motivating force has been the upsurge of new emerging nationalisms and freedom movements, many of them not only seeking national independence but striving for a socialist form of economy.

Ireland and Algeria may be taken as classic examples of the military factors involved and useful analogies may be drawn from the popular uprisings in those countries, both of them directed towards the expulsion of an alien army of occupation. A system of guerrilla warfare supported by the great majority of the population, proved to be the deciding factor in determining the future of those two small nations. In the historical cases mentioned comparisons may appear odious but they can also be fruitful and informative.

Someone more closely informed can deal with the case of Algeria, but I feel competent to give information about the Irish struggle and to note similarities to the present war in Viet Nam.

When, in the early months of 1920, it was decided to resort to guerrilla warfare in Ireland, the active service units, or commandos, in the field amounted to not more than 150 men in opposition to an occupation army of 50,000 troops, plus an armed police force (native and auxiliary) of 10,000. At the termination of hostilities, the Irish armed commandos did not exceed 1,000 trained guerrillas and the British troops were holding only the towns and cities where they were under considerable attack. In July 1921, Mr Winston Churchill told the British Cabinet:

'One hundred thousand new special troops must be raised, thousands of motor cars must be armoured and equipped;

the three Southern Provinces of Ireland must be closely laced with cordons of blockhouses and barbed wire; a systematic rummaging and questioning of every individual must be put in force.'

Alas, does not this have a familiar ring to us today as we open our morning newspaper – more and more troops, more and more blockhouses. Luckily, in the case of Ireland, the British government in its wisdom – not being concerned with prestige and saving face – withdrew its troops and peace eventually descended on the beleaguered countryside.

During the last year of the Irish war, the alien military force found itself frustrated in dealing with a native population sullenly hostile and an elusive army it could not catch up with. Terror was resorted to: towns were burned, prisoners were mistreated, and thousands put in prisons or internment camps. The only result of this mistaken policy was to stiffen the resistance of the people who became determined not to surrender.

I think the few comparisons between the past war in Ireland the present war in Viet Nam should be obvious. The only sure way to win such a war is by a policy of genocide. Surely such a policy will not have the assent of conscientious and genuinely patriotic citizens of this great nation. A country has the right to protect itself from outside interference and the right of self-determination be it Red, White, or Blue. Decency and magnanimity never harmed any great nation and it cannot harm ours – we will have to withdraw from Viet Nam sooner or later, so why not now?

GEORGE LENNON

Late Brigade Vice Commandant Irish Volunteers (IRA)[200]

The most fascinating detail of George Lennon's later life was his involvement in Zen Buddhism which began with his involvement with a Zen meditation group which included Chester and Doris Carlson. In 1966, this group invited the noted Philip Kapleau, author of *The Seven Pillars of Zen*, to visit Rochester. As a young court reporter, Kapleau had covered the Nuremburg war crimes trials in 1946, after which he had covered similar trials in Tokyo. His attempts to come to terms with the appalling atrocities perpetrated by the guilty parties led the former atheist on a spiritual search which eventually led to the study of Zen.

Hugh Curran from Donegal, today a lecturer in peace studies at the University of Maine, became the head monastic at the Rochester Zen Centre for the first five years of its existence. He later recalled of George:

"George was originally involved with a Vedanta group (Vedanta means the end of knowledge and attainment of self-realisation or cosmic consciousness) in Rochester. The group was led by Doris Carlson, wife of Chester Carlson, the inventor of the Xerox process and one of the wealthiest men in America at that time. George had joined the Vedanta group a few years before the formation of the Rochester Zen Center which had come about when Doris and Chester read a book (this was in 1965) called The Three Pillars of Zen. The author of the book was Philip Kapleau (PK), an American who had lived for thirteen years in Japan, a couple of years of that time in a Zen monastery. The Three Pillars of Zen has since become the first Zen book to sell over one million copies. Doris and Chester Carlson invited PK to Rochester to guide their

---

[200] *Rochester Democrat and Chronicle*, Letter to the Editor, 21 October 1967.

meditation group so it was initially called the 'Zen Meditation Center'.

"George was a highly valued member of the Vedanta group which had about twenty members. He subsequently became a valued member of the Zen Meditation Center on Buckingham Street after PK arrived in 1966. PK had been offered a house as well as a regular stipend and it was at Buckingham Street that the Rochester Zen Center was founded.

"For the first couple of years Doris and Chester financed the Zen Center and George undertook the job of helping PK on a day-to-day basis by driving him to do errands such as shopping, attending meetings, etc. He also helped out around the meditation center and assisted PK in evening meditation sessions as well as weekend retreats.

"I arrived in the early months of 1967 from Toronto where I had been working as a counsellor at an orphanage while meditating in the evening with a Zen group. I had begun my Zen training with the Zen Studies Society in New York city under Yasutani Roshi in 1965. After a year in Toronto I heard that PK was looking for a young assistant to help him so I resigned from my job and travelled to the other side of Lake Ontario.

"PK accepted me right away as an assistant and almost immediately I met George. His presence made an enormous difference to me since we shared the same heritage, both of us having been born in Ireland and both of us with Irish republican backgrounds (my father had been a member of the Old IRA). Both of us also tended to an instinctive scepticism where organised religion was concerned. As a result we became good friends and I would visit his home near Lake Ontario on a regular basis where his wife, May (also from Ireland) would make wonderful meals.

When problems arose, as they often did at the Zen Center, it was to George that I turned for advice.

"George not only helped out by driving me on errands but also attended twice weekly evening meditation sessions as well as monthly retreats. He had an incurable irascibility and humorous cynicism that I found familiar and appealing. At this time George was on the Board of Directors and, as the first monastic, I was asked to attend meetings as well. George had a compelling way of using his thick brogue to cut through vague conversations and delve into the heart of the matter while also deflating anything he found pompous.

"The Vietnam War was in full swing and we began to see the first of the returning veterans as well as a movement of young people in their early twenties, who like myself, were desperate to embrace an authentic spiritual tradition. Within a year and a half our small Zen Center had to move to a larger building on Arnold Park which entailed considerable efforts in renovations. On top of that a devastating fire took place which required an enormous amount of rebuilding with up to thirty young volunteers each day working on the site. I assumed a supervisory role as well as being the 'Jiki' who looked after the Zendo (meditation hall) so felt somewhat overwhelmed with the seven day a week efforts involved in keeping up with all these responsibilities. In those times George was my refuge and the one who readily listened to my complaints with sympathetic patience.

"George continued to attend most of the weekend retreats, although due to an arthritic condition, it was excruciating for him to sit in meditation for any extended period of time. As a result of this he was unable to attend longer retreats which were held at the Gratwick estate, about thirty miles south of Rochester.

"During this time (1968), and prior to our move to Arnold Park, Doris and Chester Carlson decided to halt further support of the Zen Center in reaction to PK having taken issue with some of her strongly worded directives. George maintained his individual mind-set and kept up a balancing act of staying on with the Zen Center while also participating with Doris and her Vedanta group. Doris funded a small bookstore and library in downtown Rochester and I'd often find George there talking with visitors and providing tea or coffee and fascinating conversations.

"The following year (1970) I got married, and my wife, who had become very fond of George, asked him to 'give her away' since her own father was no longer alive. George did so with aplomb and dignity and walked her down the aisle at one of the first weddings to take place at the Rochester Zen Center. By this time the word 'meditation' had been dropped from the title.

"George and May were kindness personified and my wife, Susan and I, felt honoured to be invited to their house to enjoy their generous hospitality. Susan had spent over a year in the Dublin area learning hand weaving design so both of us felt a wonderful sense of nostalgia whenever we were freed up enough to spend the afternoon with both of them.

"George Lennon was an integral part of my life, and in retrospect, I don't believe I could have survived the responsibilities and the psychological adjustments I had to make in order to live as a Zen monastic and practise a radically new way of experiencing life. I now view the Zen way as having considerable kinship with the ancient Celtic spiritual tradition and I teach courses and guide retreats in Zen with this in mind. I feel George, in his humorous and irascible way, would be in complete agreement with this Celtic-Zen approach to spirituality."[201]

In April 1969, George was visited in Rochester by old comrade Paddy Paul who had retired from the Irish army a decade previously, and was visiting a son who had emigrated to the United States. Paul had earned something of a reputation as a martinet in the army; any of the young artillery officers under his command who had got on his wrong side would gleefully pass on the story of how the artillery had destroyed Paul's house in 1922![202]

Rekindling their old friendship, Lennon and Paul went to see a film together: The Killing of Sister George which they had assumed to be a murder mystery. The two septuagenarians were mildly disconcerted to discover that it was in fact an adaptation of a stage play notorious for a graphic scene of lesbian lovemaking that caused the film to be banned in several locations.

In October 1970, Lennon received another visitor – Geoffrey Coulter, Irish journalist and former subeditor of *An Phoblacht*. In a subsequent article in the *Irish Times* Coulter related:

"My trip to America, limited only by slender finances, was purely one of pleasure. I went to visit my daughter Barbara, a sultry but incredibly Celtic-looking beauty who works as a research biologist for Eastman Kodak in Rochester, my wife's sister May who in her youth was secretary to 'Old Mischief MacEntee' and

---

[201] 'My Memories of George Lennon', personal account by Hugh Curran, February 2009.

[202] Duggan, John, *History of the Irish Army* (Gill and Macmillan, Dublin, 1991), p. 77.

her husband – George Lennon, onetime OC of the West Waterford Brigade IRA [*sic*] and now deeply immersed in research into the history of Ireland in the days of the first Elizabeth.

"Almost every day George Lennon used to drive me out fifty or sixty miles, as my daughter did at weekends, and every beautiful place, as well as historic places, was liable to have been made a park by some Authority. One thing I noticed right away was that once you got out of the suburbs you were in the country with smallish picturesque towns, farms with enormous long narrow fields, ranges of low hills and acre upon acre of lovely, misty woodland. There were many lakes and rivers."

Coulter recorded his impressions of Rochester:

"..an industrial city half the size of Dublin on the shore of Lake Ontario, one of the Great Lakes. Most of its inhabitants work for Kodak which is just as paternal a firm as you can get. There are about 40,000 Negroes and some hundred American Indians around. Irish visitors to Rochester are shown the grave of Mrs Catherine Wheelwright, President de Valera's mother. There's no denying it – mid town Rochester looks rough enough and once you leave the few palatial shopping plazas it looks like an Irish industrial estate that has been given a strong dose of fertiliser ... in Rochester there are both a Buddhist seminary and a Hindu seminary and the majority of the students are native born White Americans. There are literally hundreds of churches in Rochester catering for dozens of creeds including Buddhists, Hindus, Mormons, Jews, Albanian Orthodox, Ukrainian Catholics, Lutherans, Christian Scientists and many others. It seemed to me far more given to religion than any Irish city, including Belfast, and the small towns throughout the state weren't far behind."[203]

In May 1971, George and May Lennon returned to Ireland.

The Years To Come, 1971

Chapter 6

In the summer of 1971, George Lennon returned to Waterford city.

"The first name of Waterford was Cuan-na-Grioth, i.e. the Harbour of the Sun. The name that followed was Gleann-na-Gleodh, i.e. The Valley of Lamentation; this sad title was conferred on the place after the native Irish were defeated in a most sanguinary battle by the Norsemen, who took over. For some reason it got back an Irish name from the Horse and was known as Port-lairge. The English called it Waterford and conferred upon it the title of Urbs Intacta as a reward for its continuous loyalty to the English crown. Different English monarchs lavished fulsome charters on the city in return for this unswerving loyalty, for it was indeed to the English 'the one bright spot'."

Redmond Bridge was still standing over the river Suir, but was only to do so for another ten years, being replaced by the current construction named for Edmund Ignatius Rice, the locally born founder of the Christian Brothers. The cross-channel ferry services had ceased in the 1950s, but this decade had also seen

---

[203] *Irish Times*, 'Americans at Home', 25–26 December 1970.

the establishment of an industrial park in the city which provided badly needed employment, in particular, the foundation of the famous Waterford Crystal plant.

In the 1920s, the Ballybricken jail reverted to its intended purpose as a prison. It had ceased this function by 1940, when it briefly became a barracks again, housing units of the greatly expanded Irish defence forces during the Emergency years. In 1943 disaster occurred when one of the jail's high walls collapsed onto a nearby row of houses, killing ten local people and injuring many more. In February 1949, work began on the final demolition of the building and by 1971 only a vacant plot of land marked its ever having been there. Today, the site is the location of the city's main Garda station:

"Waterford prison (or gaol), which I first looked for, is now no more and the landscape is much improved by its absence."

By 1971, the old Infantry Barracks was home only to a company of FCA part-time military reservists, possessing not even an armoury and only open on a weekday night and an occasional weekend.

"My next visit was to the Infantry Barracks which has been rebuilt and looks almost exactly the same as when I left it. I wanted to see the office again where I used to worry on my lonesome about my responsibilities. The caretaker said the office sergeant had the key, the sergeant said it was in the possession of the transport man and he in turn sent me to see the captain in the officer's quarters. The captain's wife said he might be around somewhere but, perhaps, he had gone into town for the day. So I did not get to see.

"And now I wend my lonely way to Greyfriars Abbey, sometimes called the French Church, to pay my respects to Niall O'Neill (1658—1690).

> 'At the battle of the Boyne he was placed with his dragoons at the ford of Rosnaree, a little below the bridge of Alane, which had been previously broken down, the object was to prevent Schomberg crossing and attacking the flank of James II's army. For some time O'Neill defended the ford with conspicuous bravery, more than once charging through the river and beating back Schomberg's troops. At length he was wounded and his troops gave way. He was carried from the battlefield to Budlin and thence to Waterford where he died. He was buried in the church of the Franciscan abbey at Waterford, where his tomb is still extant.'

"The inscription on the grave slab has been almost obliterated by time. The slab is now propped against the wall on the left side of the chancel. Restored it would read:

> *Here lyes the body of Sir Neal O'Neill, Baronet of Killeleagh in the county of Antrim, who dyed the 8th of July, in the year 1690, at the age of 32 years and six months. He married the second daughter of Lord Viscount Molyneux, of Sefton, in Lancashire, in England.*

1971. The Boyne Valley.

"The morning of the battle of the Boyne dawned bright and fair on the hostile camps. The Protestant army of William of Orange numbered at least 45,000 men, many of them veteran troops, while the Irish and French

"Catholic army of James came to at most 23,000 many armed only with pikes. The white uniforms of the regular French regiments were in striking contrast to the irregular dress of the native Irish soldiers. King James from the beginning of the action, appeared more concerned for his personal safety than for anything else and he had little inclination to take the offensive. This craven attitude on the part of their king doomed the Irish cause from the beginning. It was with great difficulty that he was finally convinced that he should take some serious precautions to protect the river passages. Only on the eve of the battle was he most reluctantly to send Sir Niall O'Neill with his regiment of horse to defend the ford of Rosnaree about four miles from the Irish camp at Slane. When the inevitable and overwhelming attack came in this quarter the Williamite cavalry forced the passage of the river which was most gallantly defended by O'Neill who was mortally wounded and who lost seventy of his men. Schomberg's troops now crossed the river not only at this vital point but also at Slane further up; this was about ten o'clock in the morning. The Irish and French at bay showed a grim and determined front fighting a continuous rear guard action until ten o'clock in the evening when the Williamite foe drew off and allowed the defeated Jacobite army to continue its retreat, a retreat that was to be maintained until the army took up its last defensive positions on the Shannon.

"No atavistic longing (an assumption) had brought me to the Boyne valley this sparkling summer's day in 1971.

"In fact, I had come for a reunion with Brian. Some considerable years gone by I had been employed by a government Board to direct a topographical survey of the twenty-six counties of our land and Brian was most capable and enthusiastic assistant.

"Since 1962, a programme of excavating and restoring Newgrange had been carried out under the supervision of Prof. Michael J. O'Kelly, Department of Archaeology, University College Cork, the spectacular end results of which are all to evident today.

"Brian, who has been excavating the place for the past ten years, took me through on an individual guided tour while a long line of visitors had to wait outside. Standing in the central chamber we held happy discourse on time, place and history. What, to me, was of greatest interest was the calculated orientation of the builders. Claire will not object to my quoting from her book regarding this most remarkable circumstance: 'A matter frequently raised in connection with prehistoric monuments and one that is increasingly studied at the present time is to what extent they were aligned so as to coincide with the rising and setting of the sun, moon, etc. The orientation of Stonehenge in the direction of the midsummer sunrise is one of the best known instances and probably accounts for the frequency with which visitors to Newgrange enquire if a similar phenomenon is to be witnessed there. Its orientation precluded this since it faces south-east but it was felt that observation of midwinter rather than midsummer sunrise might be rewarding.

"It was found that four minutes after local sunrise on December 21 the sun's rays shone in along the passage and reached across the chamber floor as far as the basin stone in the end-chamber. More surprising still was the fact that the light penetrated, not through the entrance proper, but through the slit or gap in the roof-box ...

"On-the-spot observations made by Professor O'Kelly on December 21, 1969 and again in 1970 were recorded by him as follows: 'At exactly 9:54 a.m. (BST) the top edge of the ball of the sun appeared above the local horizon and at 9:58 a.m. the first pencil of direct sunlight shone through the roof-box and right along the passage to reach across the tomb chamber floor as far as the front edge of the band and swung across the chamber floor, the tomb was dramatically illuminated and various details of the side-and-end-chambers as well as the corbelled roof could be clearly seen in the light reflected from the floor. At 10:04 a.m. the seventeen cm band of light began to narrow again and at exactly 10:15 a.m. minutes, therefore, at sunrise on the shortest day of the year, direct sunlight can enter Newgrange, not through the doorway, but the specially-contrived narrow slit which lies under the roof-box at the outer end of the passage roof.' The angular relationships involved are such that it seems unlikely that this is due to chance. Further observation has shown that direct sunlight penetrates to the chamber for about a week before and a week after the solstice but not as fully as on the few days centring on the 21st.

"Witnessing this phenomenon for myself has caused me to remember that I dismissed as an 'old wives' tale' a tradition current many years ago to the effect that at a certain time of the year the sun lit up the three-spiral figure in the end-chamber.

"I would have dearly like to spend a night alone sealed in the great tomb but I was afraid that such a suggestion might cause apprehension on the part of my dear friends. Brian drove me along by the Boyne to Drogheda. We passed close by the Ford of Rosscaree but we made no delay as I had to catch a train to Dublin.

Paddington – Fishguard – Rosslare – Comeragh Mts.

"The moment I arrived back Máire told me Bernie was dying. We drove to the next county to share his last moments. We had not met for forty-nine years but he seemed to be expecting me. When we were alone together he spoke of the sad results of our youthful activities.

Mt Melleray Abbey

"As we waited in the monastery garden for the guest brother to call us to Vespers my companion sought to enlighten me on 'the troubles' in the north. The solution was really quite simple he explained. Fifty thousand of the leading Protestant families should be provided with compensation or 'quit rent' and moved to England or preferably Scotland, where they originally came from, then all the rest of the Protestants would be glad to come in with the Catholic south. Catholicism had a special position in Ireland and Protestants would have to learn the fact. But suppose, I asked, the over a million Catholic emigrants in England were returned to Ireland, what then? He said this would be just fine as the republic could create new industries to employ them all. Religious wars are particularly horrible and they all tend to end in a blood bath. I think it was that wise man Leonard Woolf who said that the whole of history shows that the savage xenophobia of human beings is so great that the introduction into any populated country of a large racial, economic, religious or cultural minority always leads to hatred, violence, and political and social disaster and therefore until the human race becomes more civilised everything should be done to prevent the creation of new centres of conflict between minorities and majorities.

"Up to the suppression of the monasteries in the early sixteenth century there appears to have been no less than forty Cistercian abbeys in Ireland of which Mellifont was the motherhouse. It was not until 1832 that the Cistercians again became established in the country here at Melleray, at that time called Scrahan. 'Scrahan' means coarse or mountain land covered with a thin surface of peat or 'scraws'. Due to the dedicated labours of the monks over the years, this desert has been made to bloom. Here I would like to quote from the excellent little history I purchased at the monastery:

> 'On the next day the Prior again interviewed Sir Richard Keane at Cappoquin, and, on the suggestion of the baronet, both of them rode out together to Scrahan where they dismounted and strolled leisurely over the property. Arriving at the place where the present porter's Lodge of Mount Melleray Abbey stands, Sir Richard abruptly halted and addressing his companion, said: 'Here now is Scrahan; take it or leave it. I seek no pecuniary advantage from you or your community, yet I believe my property will be improved by your establishment, because my waste land, and the morals of the people will be improved, if a place of worship is erected here.' Fr Vincent, feeling, as he later related, an extraordinary and unaccountable conviction that this was the place the Lord had chosen, unhesitatingly replied: 'I am satisfied; that the Abbey should be built on the spot where the agreement had been made, and having duly marked the place with a stone, the landlord and his tenant went back to Cappoquin.'

"Thomas Merton says that the monastic vocation tends to present itself to the modern world as a problem and a scandal but in a basically religious culture like that of India or Japan the monk is more or less taken for granted. In this quest for a true reality, eastern and western monks seek the same thing. There would appear to be an essential difference in as much as in the Christian case the approach is dualistic, whereas the Buddhist acceptance is quite the opposite. One says God is above, the other, God resides everywhere and in everything. One prays 'Show me Thy fact', the other asks 'Where is my original face?' Both agree, 'Be still, and know that I am God.'

"In comparing the Trappist monk with the Zen monastic we find both similarities and differences in living, in method and in technique. Both are generally silent ('Be still'). Both are abstemious and vegetarian in diet. Both chant. Both are completely immersed in and dedicated in their work. Both are detached enclaves in a turbulent world. Both are cenobites. Trappist monks pray, Zen monastics meditate. The Trappist monk is pietistic; the Zen monk is (but seemingly) sacrilegious. The Trappist is mentally quiet, the Zen applicant is engaged in a 'ferocious' and continuous struggle for mental mastery. Trappists are celibate, Zen monastics (men and women) generally are, but not always so as they are not obsessionally hung up on the life instinct.

"In a Zen Centre both sexes meditate and work together: children may be found in such a place; perhaps an unmarried mother and her child arrives and they are enfolded into the community; such a situation would, of course, cause consternation in a Christian monastery.

Christianity is a religion.

Zen is a religion only in the sense that it is the religion of no religion.

Christianity can be put into words – theology.

Theology is anathema to
Zen: He who knows does not
speak He who speaks does
not know.

"Zen is not of words or of explanation but is direct experience and this is to be arrived at by Awareness, Awareness, and again Awareness.

"The equivalent of the Christian retreat is the Zen sesshin. The former is, comparatively speaking, painless, while the latter is most fearfully exacting and involves long hours of almost continuous sitting in intense concentration. Zen sitting in an immovable position can be most physically painful and the concentration demanded of the student can be a form of mental torture, at any rate, for the beginner. It has been said that it may take fifteen years for a Zen student to learn to sit properly and twenty years to attain enlightenment.

"People in ordinary life, that is in the outside world, find it hard to understand why other mortals should submit themselves to such exacting and demanding disciplines. What they do not understand, having never experienced it, is that monastics are upheld by a feeling of supernatural gladness and at times joy. Ordinary folk have but little comprehension of the very close bond of affection that sustains an advanced community where the worst suffering of all, alienation, can be quite absent. Perhaps it should not be referred to, or even hinted at, but – if one spends a really dedicated period in such a community one has an experience – vulgarily described as a heightening of consciousness – perhaps a very minor one, but after which there is little desire to become ever again completely absorbed in a world of just three dimensions.

Liverpool – Brockwood Park – Winchester – Waterloo

"London is one of the few places I feel safe in. Growing more and more timid with the years I never feel really secure unless there is a bobby within call. My bobby said the Tate Gallery was in Millbank, quite a distance from Tottenham Court Road. He suggested a bus, but I chose to walk. Niall O'Neill was awaiting my inspection almost just inside the front door. The original portrait came up to my expectations.

September 27, 1971.

"The sun has again come out today, as of yesterday, and may continue to shine on our departure tomorrow (it has been a wonderful summer.) I find some changes after the passing of the years. Innovations have come to the monastery and they may be all to the good. Amenities have been installed in the guest house and I have been glad to avail of such comforts as I am coming near the end of my journey and I am beginning to feel tired. This itinerary was undertaken to rid myself of an image but, alas, that egotistical mirage has not as yet been altogether quite dispelled:

"As day began to break they became closer together on the great rock or their Gethsemane. Two hundred and fourteen human souls, men and women. As tokens of their love and esteem they pressed pathetic little gifts on each other and exchanged the last kiss of peace. Calling aside the seventeen perfecti the bishop spoke to them of their long years of renunciation and gladly accepted suffering. He spoke also or the evils of the flesh that dragged down the spiritual yearning of the soul. They were the pure ones, the undefiled, and as such they would step into the flames. As he turned to succour the credentes seven stepped forward to receive the consolamentum at his hands. After this had been most solemnly administered he spoke to all the others a the man temptations and defilements a their past life now coming to a close. In the life to come they would be incarnated in a body better suited to their future spiritual welfare but they would et have man temptations to test them before coming to that state of pure being sought for b true Gnostics.

"Families now embraced each other for the last time and all moved out through the sun gate to be manacled. Men-at-arms immediately seized on the heretics an dragged them falling and stumbling down the west side of the mountain.

313

"Meanwhile other men-at-arms from the camp below had been erecting a huge pyre at the base of the mountain to consume the people. Trees and large branches had been cut down to provide a foundation and over this was piled a great mass of straw and faggots with pitch to provide ready combustion. A palisade of stakes and gales was built all around as there was not time to provide individual stakes.

"First the wounded and the sick were thrown on the faggots, then the others were forced in and the palisade was secured and fired at the four quarters. Before being thrust in, they were called on for the last time to recant; a score did so and one hundred and ninety-four were given to the flames. As the fire took a fierce hold the air was rent with screams of pain and agony which gradually died down and the ghastly odour of burnt flesh spread down the valley.

"He watched as a novice came out and one by one put out the candles on the side altar and the church sank into darkness.

"Darkening clouds now shrouded him about. He was walking amongst a great multitude of people across a vast plain. Gloomy mountains were far off and far behind. The were all moving form Nowhere to Nowhere across the plain and a dark cloud hung above them. As they marched the people sang a dolorous song to the measure of which the dragged their tired feet.

"Now his course was deflected from the others and he entered a most gloomy defile through which he forced his weary limbs. Forbidding cliffs reared their threatening heads on either side of his path which was strewn with rough unhewn boulders and craggy flinty stones. He continued on and on, on a pilgrimage that seemed to have no end when at last there appeared a faint light looming afar off.

"Suddenly he awoke to find himself back in the Glen and his dog was coming towards him, barking and making wild ecstatic jumps. Kathleen and the constabulary sergeant were some way off beckoning him on. Leaving her companion she came to meet him and this time he did not repulse her. Kathleen no longer looked sad and they smiled happily at each other. The three of them walked hand in hand towards the source of the mountain stream. As they walked along the little stream gurgled and sang. The mountain was a mass of yellow gorse that gave off a faint and pleasant perfume.

"Slán"

George's wanderings next brought him to Kilmacthomas, obliging him to hire an expensive taxi. Until March 1967, it would have been possible for him to catch a train from Waterford city. In that month however, CIE carried out a decision to end passenger services on the Waterford to Mallow line. All services between Dungarvan and Mallow were ended and farmers and bulldozers went to work on obliterating all traces of any railway line there. The line between Waterford and Dungarvan was granted a new lease of life in 1970 with the establishment of the Quigley magnesite plant at Ballinacourty and freight trains continued to operate along the line between a quarry at Bennettsbridge in Kilkenny and the extension built to Ballinacourty. Although several level crossings continued to operate, the railway stations at Kilmeaden, Kilmacthomas and Durrow were left silent and derelict.

"The taxi left me off in the middle of the village as I wanted to say goodbye to Mother Kent. Mother Kent [Kate Cullinane] has brought a golden brood of children into the world and she is now counsellor and general helpmate and advisor to all the country around. When we first met (half a century ago) she was a young nurse just back from England. It was many years since we had last seen each other."

'You just missed Lena [Keating],' she remarked as I came in the door.

'Oh, I'm sorry about that, I'm very fond of Lena,' said I.

'And she of you too, there was always a thing between you.' We sat down and looked each other over.

'So we lost the poor doctor,' said she.

'Poor Joe [Walsh],' said I.

'The poor doctors last wish was to be buried with the lads in the republican plot.' 'I know.'

'Pat [Keating] was the first to go into the plot and the poor doctor was almost the last – almost.' Here she gave me a most meaningful look.

'I don't intend to be buried in any plot, I'm going to the crematorium.' Nothing ever startled her but this did.

'Cremated. What would you be doing a thing like that for and all the lads waiting for you up in Kilrossanty graveyard?'

Great dark wings seemed to be rustling about us.

'Listen Kate, I can't stay to lunch today but I will be back as soon as I can.' 'Tomorrow evening then, Father Jack, Ned's son will be here.' 'Poor Ned.' We both nodded over this memory.

'When Ned was dying he begged the poor doctor to come back to the church but the doctor said he would have to think twice about that – well, they have both gone to their eternal reward now.'

One of the consoling things about Ireland is that everybody apparently goes to Heaven, including atheists.

'I'll have the lads take a fish from the river for you and Lena will come with the car for you tomorrow.' 'It will be great to see Lena again.'

'Of course it will, why do you think I am sending her?'

We parted most amiably and after walking along for over a mile I rested on a ditch to survey the beautiful country, a place I was now reluctant to leave. Both Kate and I knew that time could not be far off. All the people we most loved were gone away and were now most anxiously awaiting us to join them.

Life, Death, - why swellest thou?
One short sleep past we wake eternally
And death shall be no more ...

A car drew up.

'Why, Lena.'

'Kate thought you might get tired from the long walk back.' I sat in and we drove off together.

The night shades are falling and it is time for me to make my exit. My friends across the sea await me and I must be walking on.

'Drive your horse and your plough over the bones of the dead',

A wise man has said But now the time has come and we must go away – I to die and you to live. Which is better is known to the gods alone.

Epilogue

George Lennon had another twenty years of life left to him. He returned to Rochester in early 1972, his wife remaining in Ireland for a few more months. It was at this time that Lennon worked to complete his memoirs, *Trauma in Time*.

Hugh Curran recalled:

"In 1972 we [the Currans] moved to a farm fifteen miles away from Rochester. I had begun a separation from PK, no longer feeling any real empathy with him, a necessary condition if one wanted a good teacher student relationship. For two more years we continued to see George and on a couple of occasions I brought my father to visit him. They reminisced about the old IRA and the people they knew in common. My father had a prodigious memory for names and was a fluent speaker of the Irish language, and having spent sixteen years in both the Irish army and the Garda Síochána, he seemed to know everyone who had been involved in the Irish independence movement. As a result the conversations between George and my father began with 'And so did you know...' and of course they did know.

"With our young son Oisín we travelled to Donegal for several months, and after returning, moved to Vermont and a couple of years later to Maine where we joined Moonspring Hermitage (now known as Morgan Bay Zendo). During those times we still managed to keep up contact with George by phone calls and letters."

In 1976, George and May Lennon returned to Ireland for the last time and they resided at Palmerston Park in the leafy Dublin suburb of Rathgar, where their son Ivan, his wife Susan and grandchildren Kristin and Colin visited them that summer. George and May left for Rochester later that year. They never saw Ireland again.

Many of the old West Waterford column were still alive in 1980, when they were interviewed by local historians Seán and Síle Murphy for their history of the time, *The Comeraghs; Refuge of Rebels*. Indeed, Mick Mansfield, Pax Whelan and George Lennon all lived into their early nineties.

After May's death from cancer in 1983, George lived alone until 1987, when in declining health and suffering from the lingering effects of tuberculosis, he entered Beechwood Nursing Home.

In 1987, the city of Rochester was twinned with the city of Waterford. In that year, a delegation from the American city visited its Irish 'Sister City,' and included Ivan Lennon and wife. Recent years had been hard ones for Waterford, with factories closing with resultant high levels of emigration and unemployment. Even the 'troubles' in Northern Ireland came this far south of the border; in the summer of 1979 PIRA paramilitaries carrying out a bank robbery in Tramore shot dead a local man in front of his four year old son.

In 1982, the magnesite plant in Ballinacourty closed for business, and the Waterford–Dungarvan railway, so heavily fought over during the War of Independence, finally fell silent. The railway tracks remained in place until the year 2000 (some of the sleepers still bearing the legend 'GS&WR [Great Southern and Western Railway] 1924'), after which they were removed, with the exception of a tourist railway between Kilmeaden and Waterford city. Today the route of the old railway forms a very successful Greenway between Waterford and Dungarvan.

George Lennon died in 1991, in his 91st year. In accordance with his wishes, his remains were cremated. Hugh Curran remembered:

"After George died we were given his ashes and took them back to Downeast Maine and placed them at the foot of a tree behind our owner-built home. Keeping George's tree area cleared of weeds and long grass was a task I gladly took on to honour his memory. Eventually some of the ashes were sent back to Ivan in Rochester with the understanding that some of them would be placed in the Rochester Zen Center retreat area where Philip Kapleau had been buried."

Appendix One

Summary Of IRA Service

I left school Easter Week 1916, to take part in the rebellion and was constantly engaged in army activities during the whole period to August 1922. I did not work at our family business or any other occupation during this time. Most of the period from 1916 to 1919 was spent in organizing, training and securing arms. I was almost constantly on the run up to the end of hostilities. The early part of 1920 I spent operating in the areas of West Limerick, East Clare and East Limerick. At the request of Liam Lynch I also went to Cork 2 area to help organise the first column to operate there. Having the necessary active experience I returned home and organised the West Waterford flying column which I commanded up to the Truce. I took part in a total of seventeen engagements with British forces. During the Truce period I took over Waterford city from the evacuating British military and commanded the garrison there until driven out by the Free State army in July 1922. Owing to a difference of opinion with the HQ of the 1st Southern Division as to the stand to be taken and the tactics to be employed in the Civil War I resigned to Liam Deasy on or about the 1st of August 1922. I went into civil life and got my first job in Feb 1923. I was then 23 years old.

(Statement made by George Lennon to Military Service Pensions Board, dated 2 January 1935)

Appendix Two

RIC Barracks In Co. Waterford

1918

Waterford City

Lady Lane   Mary Street
Mahon Street   Peter's Lane
Ferrybank

Waterford County

Dungarvan Castle
Tramore   Dunmore East
Passage East   Butlerstown
Ballyduff   Ballymacarbery
Killeenagh   Lismore
Cappoquin   Tallow
Ballinamult   Villierstown
Abbeyside   Portlaw
Ardmore   Annestown
Cappagh   Bunmahon
Clashmore   Clonea
Colligan   Kill
Kielys Cross   Kilmacthomas
Lemybrien   Kilmeaden
Ring   Stradbally
Rathgormack   Callaghane

RIC Barracks in Waterford Brigades area, 11 July 1921

Waterford City

Lady Lane   Mary Street
Mahon Street   Peter's Lane

Waterford County

Tramore   Dunmore (East)
Passage (East)   Portlaw
Dungarvan   Cappoquin

(Source: NLI MS 31,213 – Flor O'Donoghue papers)

Appendix Three

Portrait Of A Black And Tan

Victor Lewis Cady was born in Suffolk in January 1902. After the outbreak of World War One, Cady misrepresented his age by giving a false date of birth (19 December 1898) and enlisted in the Royal Naval Reserve (RNR) as a Boy Cook. In December 1916 (the date of his presumed majority but in fact just short of his fifteenth birthday) he became a "Trimmer Cook" – a trimmer being the RNR term for a coal stoker, an unpleasant and dangerous but vital role on the steam-powered vessels of the time. Combining this role with cooking might not have appeared to be a hygienic option but Cady served on a number of small vessels such as armed trawlers, where crewmen were required to be versatile. After the close of hostilities, Cady was demobilised in February 1919 and was awarded the British War Medal, the Victory Medal and the 1914-15 Star. He was hardly seventeen years old.

On 7 March 1921, Cady applied to join the Royal Irish Constabulary (RIC) at a recruiting office in Ipswich and was accepted for service a week later, being given the rank of Temporary Constable and the service number RN 79696. The holders of this rank were better known in Ireland as "Black and Tans." Due to a catastrophic level of resignations from the RIC as a result of the Irish War of Independence, the British Administration resorted to recruiting large numbers of former servicemen in Britain, who were initially kitted out in a mixture of RIC and British Army uniform. These individuals often proved unsuitable for service and tended to greatly escalate hostilities wherever they were deployed.

Cady was a case in point; only a fortnight after his enlistment and with no training, he was deployed to Dungarvan on the first of April 1921. Although local RIC commander District Inspector Timothy Powell Sheehan had kept an unusually tight leash on his local Black and Tans until now, tensions were running high due to the deaths of RIC Sergeant Michael Hickey and Temporary Constable Sidney Redman in the recent Burgery Ambush. Two days after his arrival in Dungarvan, Cady was involved when Black and Tans raided the public house of ******* in Abbeyside; the owner was interned at this time and his wife was running the business and caring for their child. During this raid, "looting and overtures and acts of indecency" occurred according to Jeremiah MacVeagh MP who later raised the matter in the House of Commons. Less euphemistically, the local IRA identified a Black and Tan as "concerned in rape case - Mrs ******* Abbeyside Dungarvan." ******* and her barmaid Bridget O'Neill made an official complaint to the local RIC and identified Temporary Constable Cady as one of the men responsible. Cady had a distinctive 'bracelet' tattoo on his left arm which might have led to him being recognised.

On the night of 13 April 1921, *******'s public house was set on fire and ******* escaped with her six year old child over a high wall before the building and a neighbouring shop were gutted. The nearby Strand Hotel and a neighbouring house were also destroyed by fire, the female owner barely escaping with her life. Later that night an elderly shoemaker named William Moran was taken from his home in Davis Street and was shot dead.

Although Cady was fined five shillings on 17 May for a minor offence, he was not charged with the attack on ******* until late

June. Mrs ******* unsurprisingly declined to give evidence at his trial and Cady was acquitted on 1 July. He however resigned from the RIC on 4 August 1921 for reasons 'not given.'

Sources: UK Census 1911 RG 14, UKNA BT/377/7; Hansard 16 June 1921 Vol 143 cc 583-4; NLI FOD MS 21,204; *The Black and Tans,* DM Leeson (Oxford University Press) 2011 p219-220; *Waterford News and Star* 15 Apr 1921; *Skibbereen Eagle* 16 Apr 1921

Appendix Four

British Army Intelligence File

The British Army intelligence file on George Lennon during the Truce period and updated during the Civil War. Not all information is accurate.

NAME & ADDRESS: LENNON. G. Capt. Devonshire Arms Hotel, Dungarvan

INFORMATION AVAILABLE: Of Dungarvan.
V/Comdt, 2nd West Waterford Brigade.
Was Quartermaster, Dungarvan Battalion,
and afterwards Brigade Adjutant.
Delegate at Convention. (Mulcahy's docs).
Paid organiser.
At one time got two months for illegal drilling.
Suspected of shooting Head Constable
RUDDOCK at Youghal.
Attended a meeting at Dungarvan to consider
Lloyd George's offer.
Led raid on Sir Richard Musgrave's house at
Cappoquin.
Responsible for attack on Kill Police Bks.
Reported to have been in charge of a party
who fired on Police Tender 12-10-20.
One of the men who shot Constable QUIRK
On 27-11-20.
Gas Fitter. Age 22. Thin and delicate looking.
Stoops when walking. Sallow complexion.

Has now resigned from Irregulars & left Dungarvan.
(Ref. *'Irish Independent'* dated 31.7.22.)

Source: UK National Archives WO 35/207

Terence O'Reilly

Terence O'Reilly is a former member of the Defence Forces who completed several tours of duty with the United Nations peacekeeping force in Lebanon. He has a keen interest in Irish military history and has written extensively on the subject.

Terence would like to extend his grateful thanks to all those who assisted me in the writing of this biography:

Ivan Lennon for providing vital information and family documents; the Irish Military Archives for providing a full set of the Bureau of Military History Witness Statements at a very opportune time; the Irish National Archives; the UK National Archives in Kew; the local history department of Waterford City Library; Police Historian Anthony Rae; Mercier Press for first putting this story into print; and to William Whelan and the Waterford County Museum for their invaluable help with research and for giving this book a new lease of life.

About Waterford County Museum

Waterford County Museum is a volunteer run museum dedicated to preserving the history of County Waterford, Ireland. Based in the town of Dungarvan, the museum is open to the public throughout the year, admission is free of charge. The museum operates a very active volunteer community archaeology group. A number of lectures, educational events and exhibitions are run by us during the year. We also publish books and e-books relating to County Waterford history. You can keep up to date with museum news and happenings at:

Email: history@waterfordmuseum.ie

Web: www.waterfordmuseum.ie

Twitter: @waterfordmuseum

Facebook: @waterfordcountymuseum

Other Books in the Series

This book is part of a series of Waterford history books that the museum is republishing as Ebooks or making available to print on demand on the Amazon web site. For a complete list of our books search for "Waterford County Museum" on Amazon. Other books in the series include:

The Comeraghs, Gunfire and Civil War

by Seán and Síle Murphy

The story of the War of Independence and Civil War in Dungarvan and West Waterford in the words of the veterans. This important work was originally published in 1980 as *The Comeraghs, Refuge of Rebels*. In 2003 a revised and expanded version was published under the title *The Comeraghs, Gunfire and Civil War*. The 2020 edition has been further updated with additional content including notes from the original interviews and 31 photographs. The book's importance derives from it being compiled using the first-hand accounts of the Co. Waterford veterans who participated in the struggle for Irish independence. The republication of this seminal history of the Déise Brigade IRA from 1914 to 1924 is a collaboration between the authors, Seán and Síle Murphy, Waterford County Museum and the Commemorations Committee of Waterford Council.

Desperate Haven: The Poor Law, Famine, & Aftermath in Dungarvan Union

by William Fraher, Bernadette Sheridan, Seosaimh O'Loinsigh, & William Whelan

Originally published in 1996, this book is the definitive study to date of the Great Famine (or Irish Potato Famine) and its effects in the towns and villages of West Waterford, Ireland. This long out of print and much sought-after volume was the product of more than 5 years of research by Dungarvan Museum Society (now Waterford County Museum). It provides a fascinating insight into the lives of the poor in mid-19th century Ireland, the response of the authorities to the unfolding tragedy and the conditions which saw many Irish people create new lives for themselves in America, England, Canada, Australia and elsewhere. Tracing the development of the Dungarvan Poor Law Union from its establishment in 1839 to its abolition in 1920, the workhouse figures prominently in the story. The chapters covering the Famine period are based on the minute books of the Dungarvan Board of Guardians, the Famine Relief Papers in the National Archive, and contemporary newspapers. The book examines in detail the lives of the workhouse inmates, with sections on diet, education, work, the workhouse farm, religion, the treatment of women and children. There are also chapters on the effect of the Famine on the fishing industry, and on emigration from West Waterford during and after the Famine. At the height of the Famine 4,000 men, women and children from all over West Waterford were housed within the workhouse and auxiliary workhouses of Dungarvan. Thousands more were dependent on soup kitchens and 'outdoor relief' to prevent themselves starving. For specialist historians and genealogists, it is hoped that the book will be of assistance in prompting further research. For the general reader, and particularly for those whose origins are in the locality, it is hoped that it will provide insights into a tragedy which even yet marks the area after the passage of over a century and a half.

A History of Dungarvan in 33 Illustrations: The Grattan Square Heritage Plaque Project

by William Whelan & Rachael Power

A handy introduction to major events, people and industries from Dungarvan's past. This 'Greatest Hits' of Dungarvan history had an unusual genesis. It started life as a project to lay commemorative plaques in Grattan Square, Dungarvan. The story behind each plaque was originally told in a series of articles written for the local newspapers. These articles by Willie Whelan, have now been compiled into this booklet. We have included the original illustration for each plaque drawn by Rachael Power.

Illustrated History of Dungarvan

by Edmond Keohan

Originally published in 1924, this first Dungarvan history book set the standard for future local historians. It is an important eyewitness account of the town's Victorian, Edwardian & revolutionary periods. Keohan used all his journalistic skill to provide an entertaining and very readable eyewitness account of the Dungarvan from over a hundred years ago. This new much expanded edition published by Waterford County Museum includes an author biography by William Fraher, photos from Keohan's photographic career, a tourist guide to Dungarvan from 1917 and a history of Abbeyside Castle published in 1916.

This volume also contains annotations to the original work by Cian Flaherty and William Whelan. These annotations provide definitions for terms no longer in common use and notes occasions when Keohan may have been incorrect in his historical suppositions. This is no fault of the author as he was working with the material available at that time.

The real strengths of the book are the chapters covering the 19th and early 20th centuries when Keohan provides us with an eyewitness account of events that shaped the town and country to this day.

Ardmore: Memory and Story: The history, traditions and stories of an Irish village.

by Siobhán Lincoln

Stories of growing up in an Irish village told with a "blend of history, tradition and humour". Siobhán Lincoln records the social history of Ardmore village in County Waterford, tales of school days, dances, fishing, work, language and tradition. This book will be of interest to anyone who wants a picture of life in rural Ireland from the late 19th century to the dawning of the Millennium.

From the foreword by Fergal Keane: "The past slips away from us quietly. We are too consumed with the drama of the present to notice the departure of old ways and traditions. In an age of economic growth without parallel in the history of the state, we are all urged to speed into a bright new future. The places we came from, the landscape of our past recedes and is in danger of being lost. And so when a remarkable book appears like that now offered by Siobhán Lincoln it is important that we pay it proper attention. It is said that every village in Ireland has a historian: I can't vouch for that but know that Ardmore is blessed to have a woman like Siobhán who is so passionate in the cause of saving memory for the coming generations."

Rebel Heart: George Lennon: Flying Column Commander

By Terry O'Reilly

At the age of 20, George Lennon became the youngest commander of a flying column during the Irish War of Independence, leading the West Waterford column in ambushes and actions in the face of heavy odds against British forces across the county. When Civil War followed the War of Independence Lennon chose to oppose the pro-Treaty government and fought in the battle for Waterford city. However, he laid down his arms when it became clear that the anti-Treaty cause was lost and that continuing the fight would lead to further suffering amongst the civilian population. In 1927, Lennon emigrated to America, returning to Ireland ten years later where he made earnest attempts to develop the national economy of the new state through the Irish Tourist Board and the National Planning Conference. However, he became disillusioned with these efforts and returned to the United States in 1946, later becoming a dedicated pacifist and even a practitioner of Zen Buddhism. Lennon is a figure who deserves to be remembered. In this new and revealing biography, Terence O'Reilly brings to life the story of an intriguing and talented man using previously unpublished memoirs, Lennon's own letters and statements, and the recollections and statements of his family and comrades.